The Bodies Untamed.

Fine Art Nude Photography

By

Christopher John Ball

Britannia Street Theatre and Arts Publishing

'*The Bodies Untamed - Fine Art Nude Photography*' was first published, in the United Kingdom, in 2022 as an original Paperback by

Britannia Street Theatre and Arts Publishing
3/50 Britannia Street,
London,
WC1X 9JH
United Kingdom

Email: britanniastreetartspublishing@gmail.com

ISBN No: 978-0-9926899-1-9

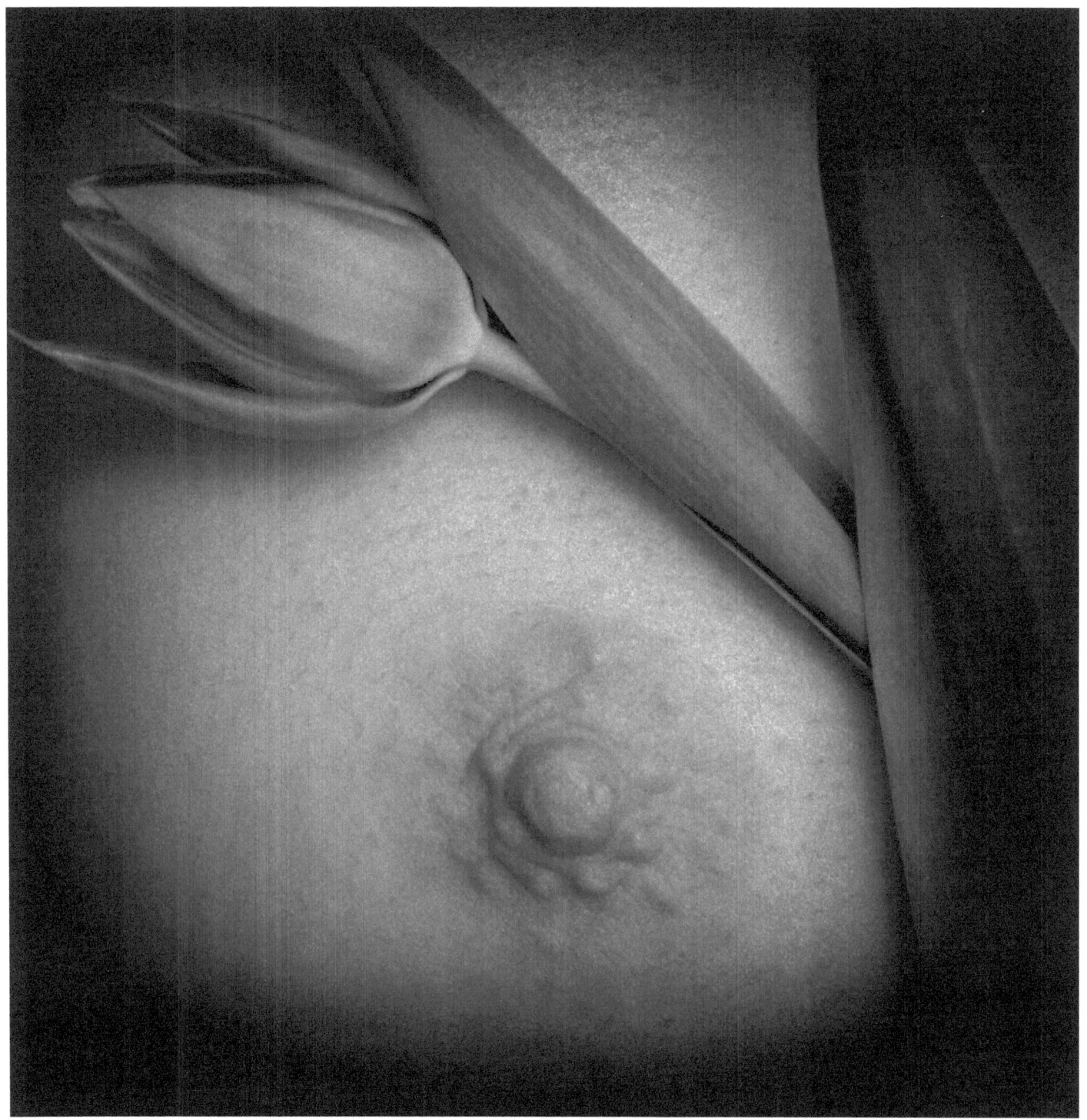

Introduction

"Beauty is unbearable, drives us to despair, offering us for a minute the glimpse of an eternity that we should like to stretch out over the whole of time." Albert Camus

Drawing inspiration from philosophy, film, music and disability politics; Christopher John Ball believes that how we see ourselves, alongside our objectification by the camera, society and the state, takes the form of an existential challenge and his work is an exploration of this rationale. Whilst his work covers both social documentary and fine art, his methodology is consistent throughout.

His images explore and play with the 'sense of distance', 'lack of access', and the 'mundane banality of modern life'. The themes of a 'sense of distance' and 'lack of access' have become increasingly important to Christopher as his disability deteriorates. The reaction of 'others' to a visible impairment can often be hostile leaving one feeling as an 'outsider', 'looking in' and 'kept out'.

Given that he is also a writer, and because he sees in photography a strong link to literature, it should come as no surprise to find that his photographs are often made to work in series, rather than individual images, so as to create a visual narrative.

Rarely working from studios; the choice of everyday locations for his fine art nude imagery is a deliberate intent to emphasise a mundane theatricality. Once at the location, and the frame composed, Christopher directs the model to interpret the space within the frame: to become as one with the landscape and mimic the branches and trees, to create rhythmic patterns and sculptural forms, but also to project their own personalities towards the camera. The body drives the narrative, carrying it forward directly towards the viewer. He is not after perfection but rather simple humanity; a reflection of us all.

The photographs within this monograph were made between 1996 and 2014 in the location of Trent Park near Cockfosters, London. This was once a very safe and quiet area to use as a location but, given the extensive building work that has taken place in this area, and with the model's safety being paramount, it has become increasingly difficult to use this location now. There are far too many dog walkers and children playing for Trent park to be safely used. In addition, Christopher's deteriorating disability has made it even harder to gain access. So, unless he can find a safe and accessible location, he fears that these may well be the last images he makes 'in the wild'.

Whilst having embraced the digital world, Christopher much prefers the organic qualities offered by film and the aesthetics of the square format. He used a variety of equipment, including TLR, pin-hole, Holga, Diana and various vintage cameras, to create the images within this monograph. He is also drawn to the use of alternative photographic processes, such as the Cyanotype, and he will often scratch and bleach negatives to create a distressed aesthetic.

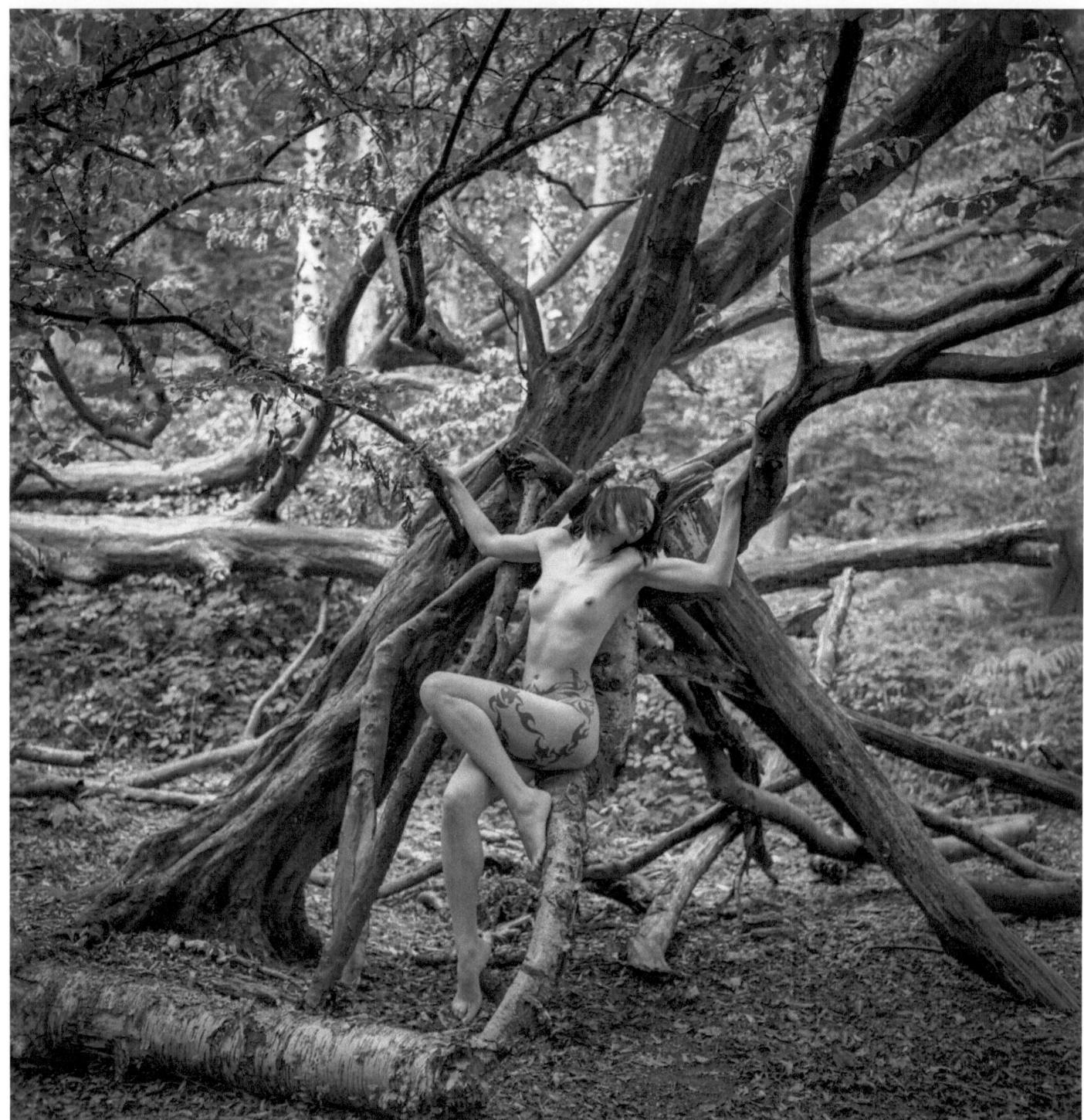

6

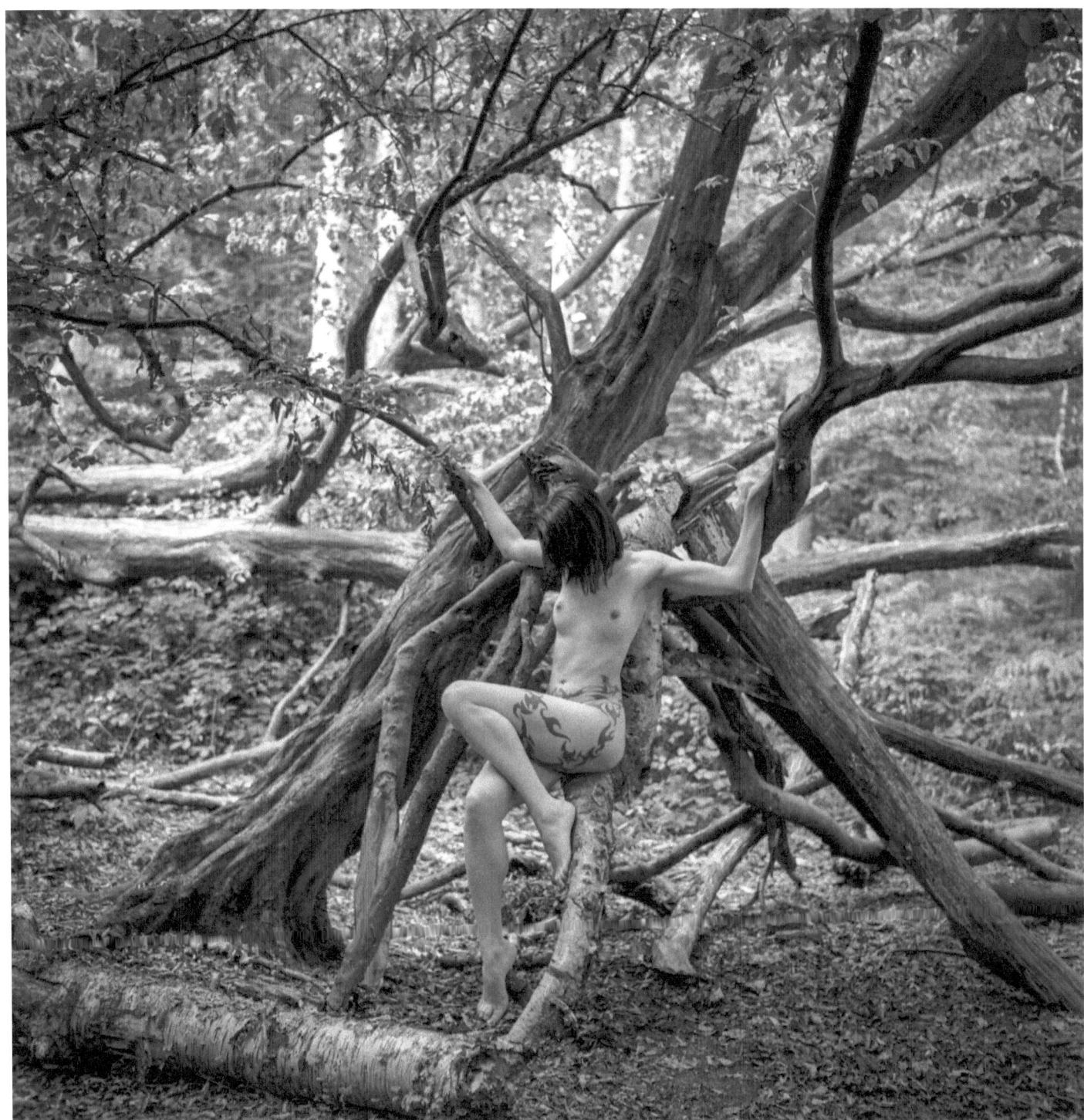

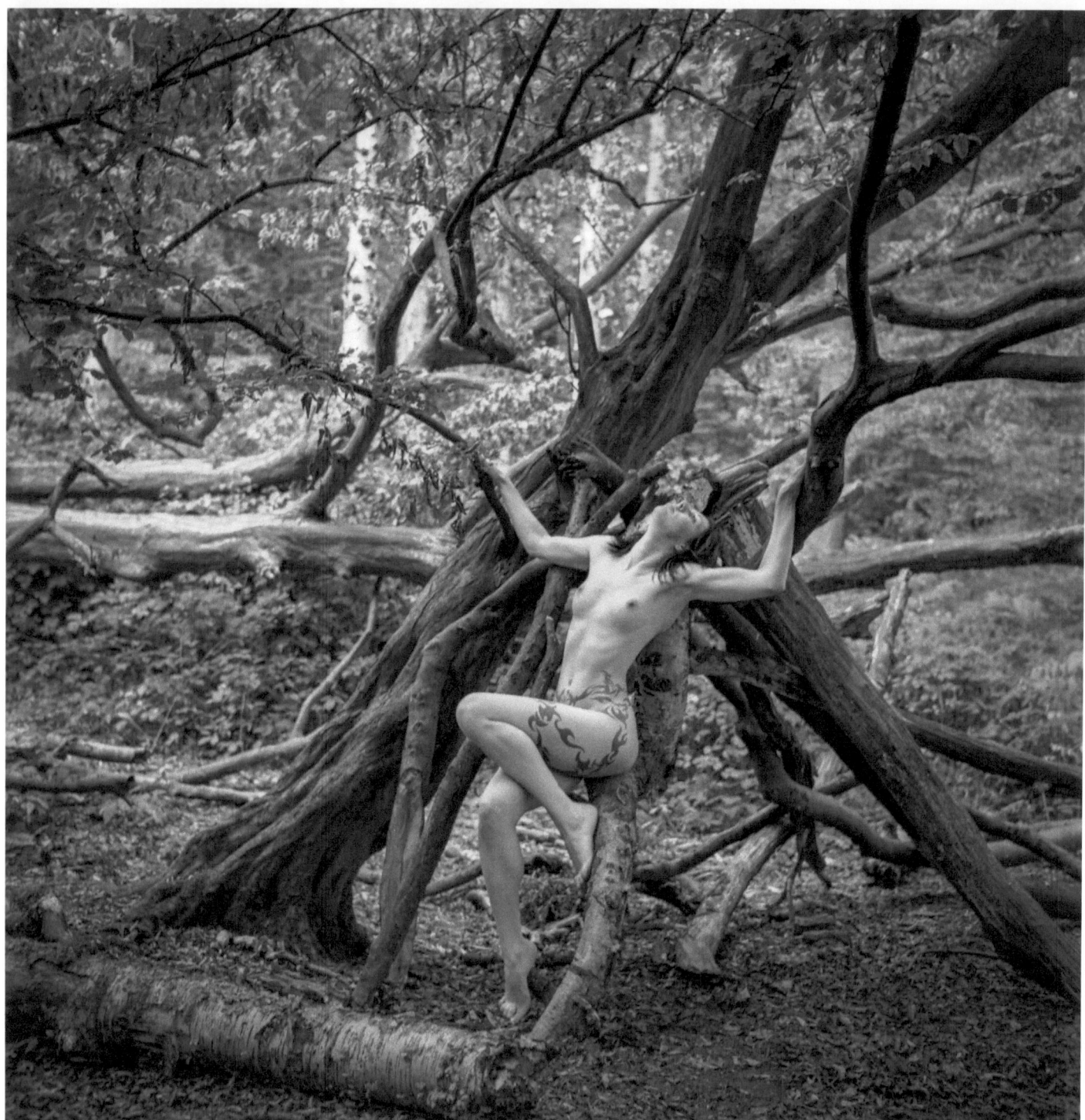

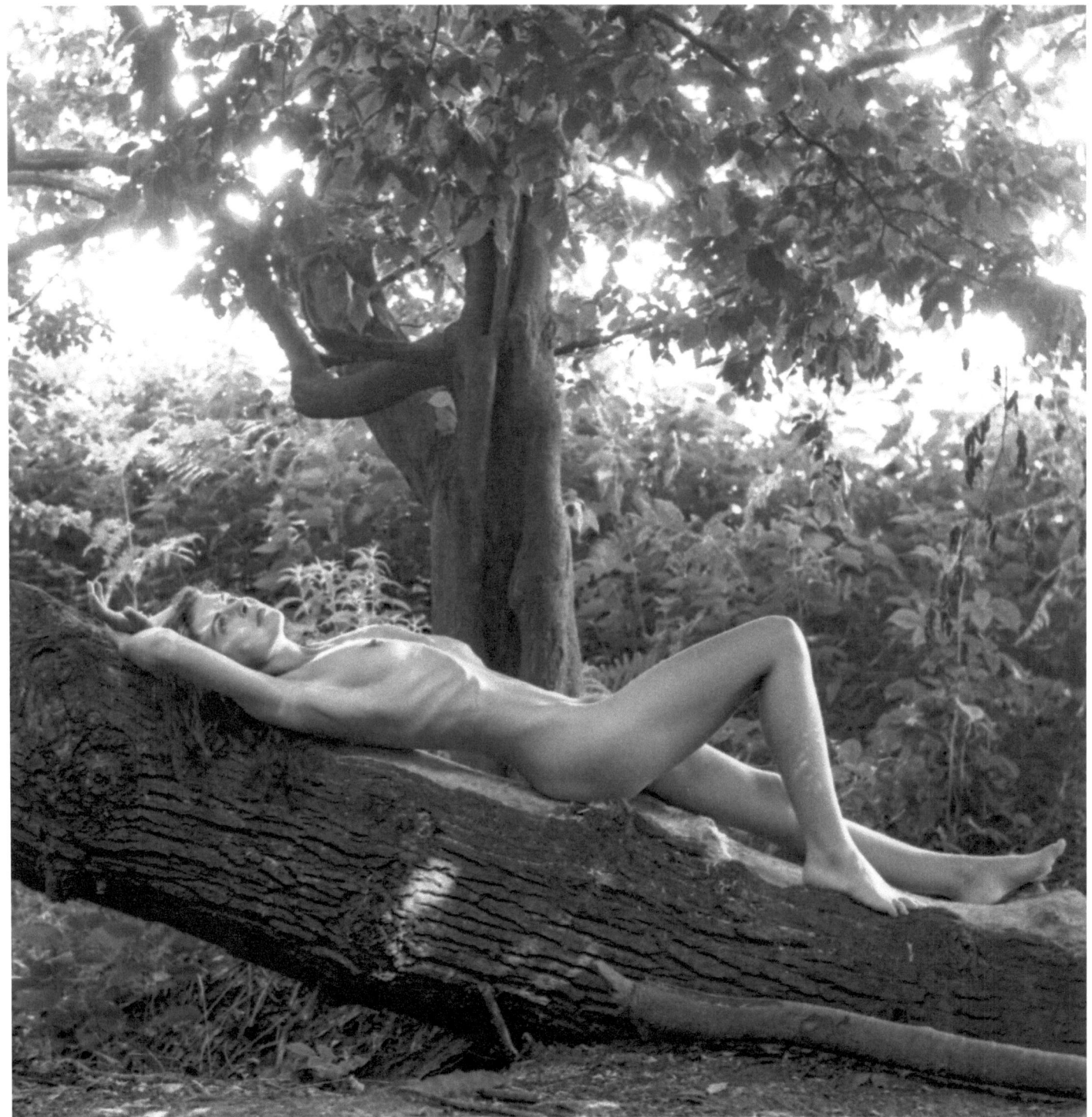

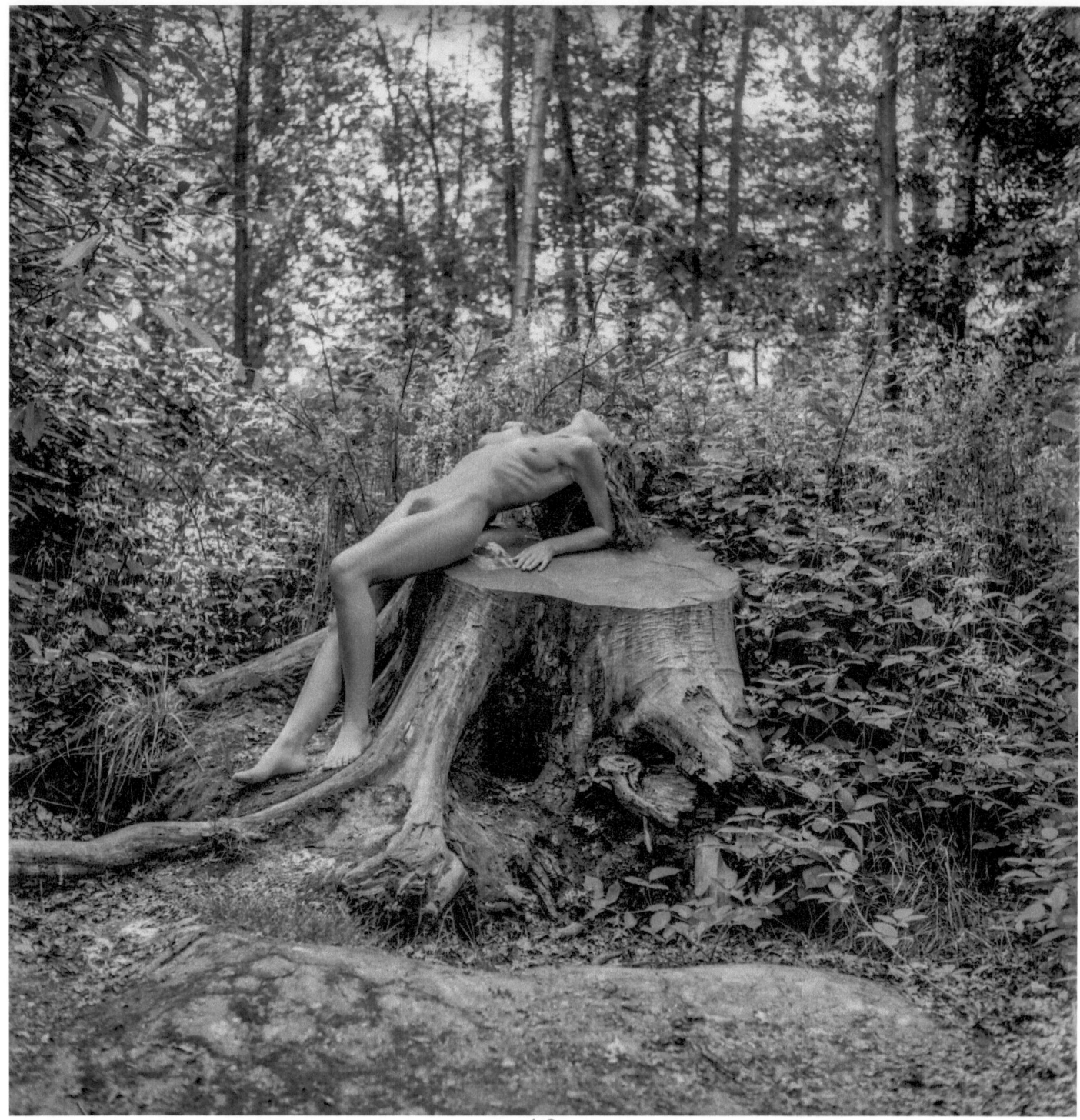

10

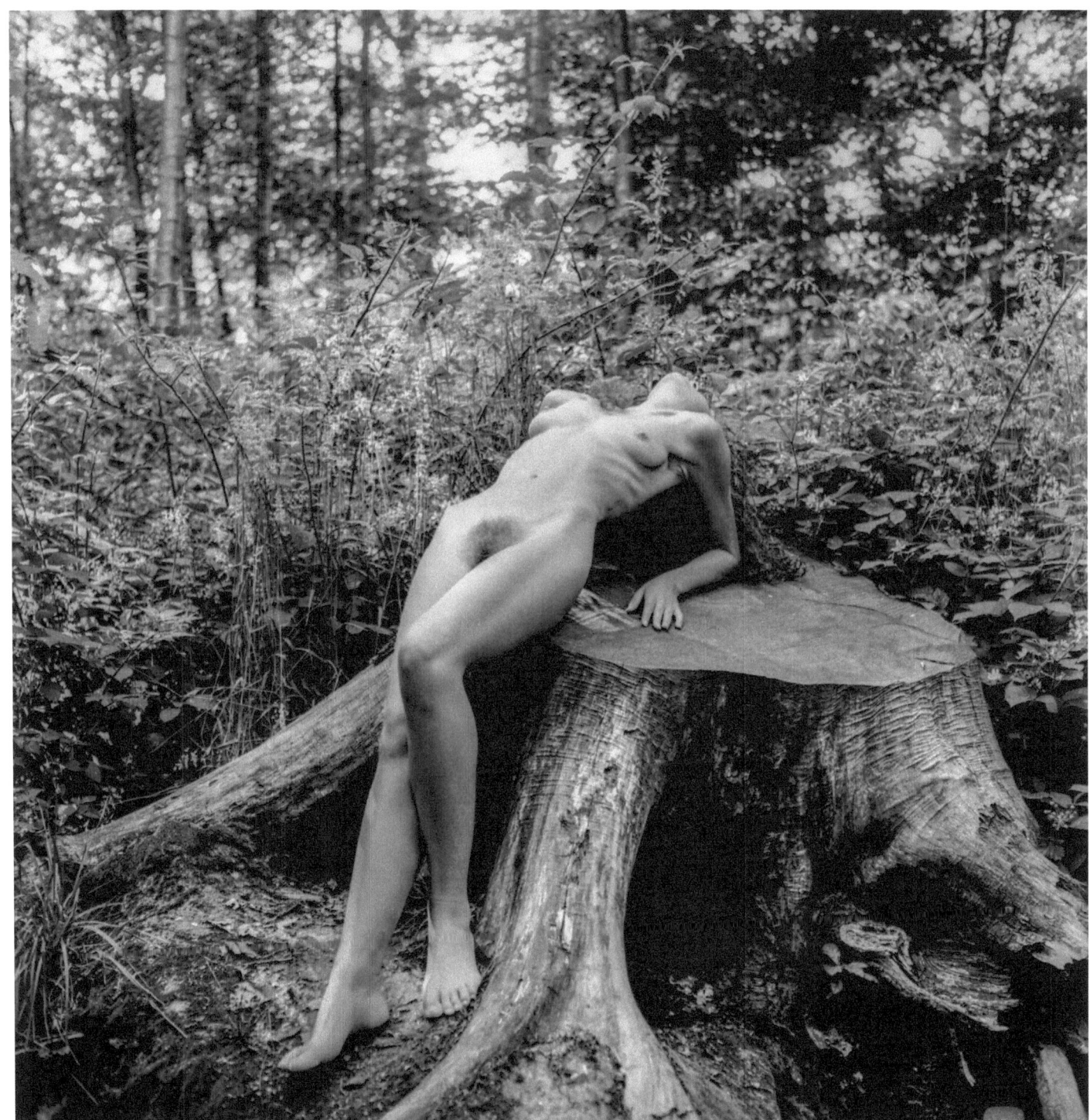

11

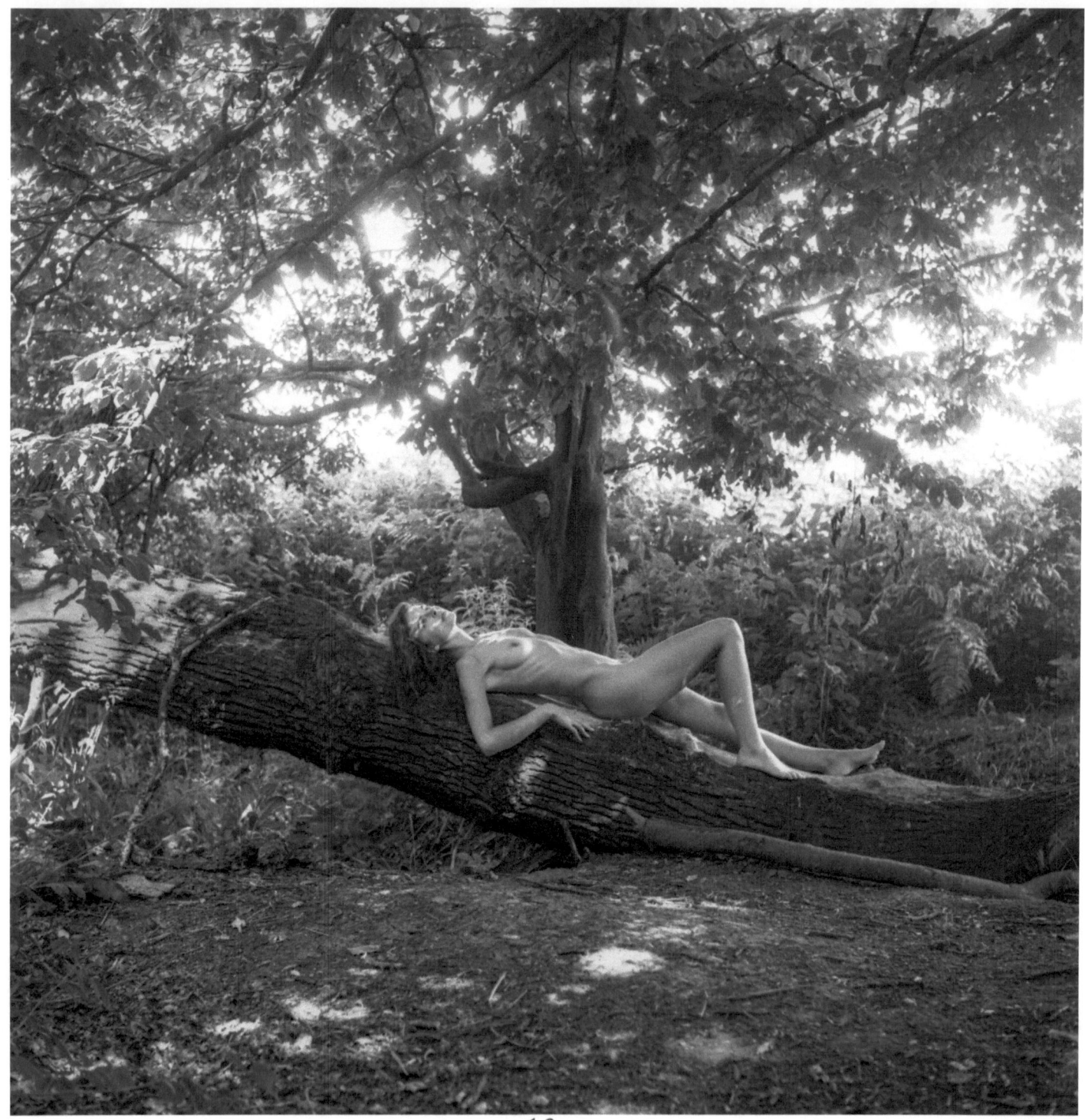

12

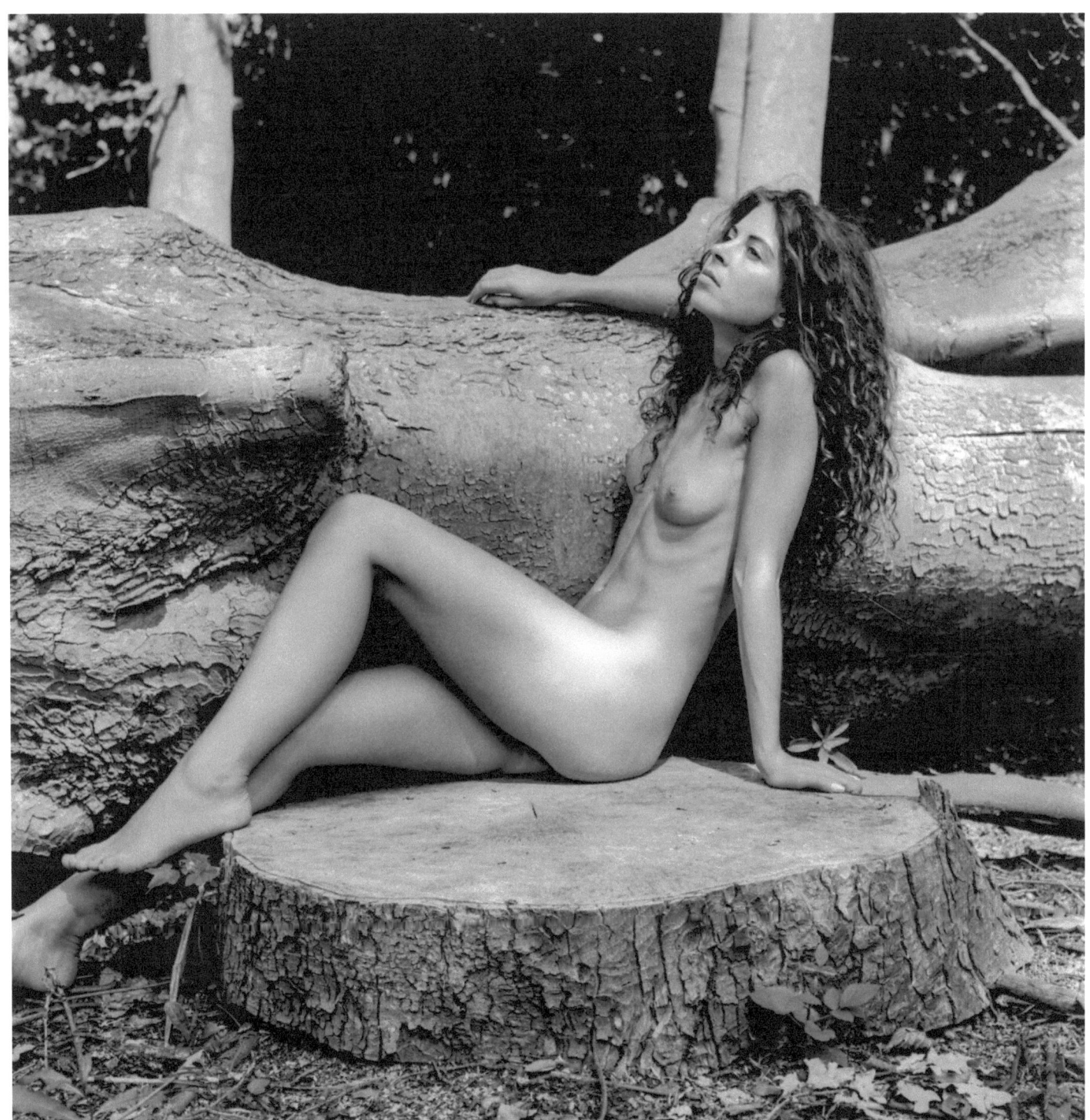

13

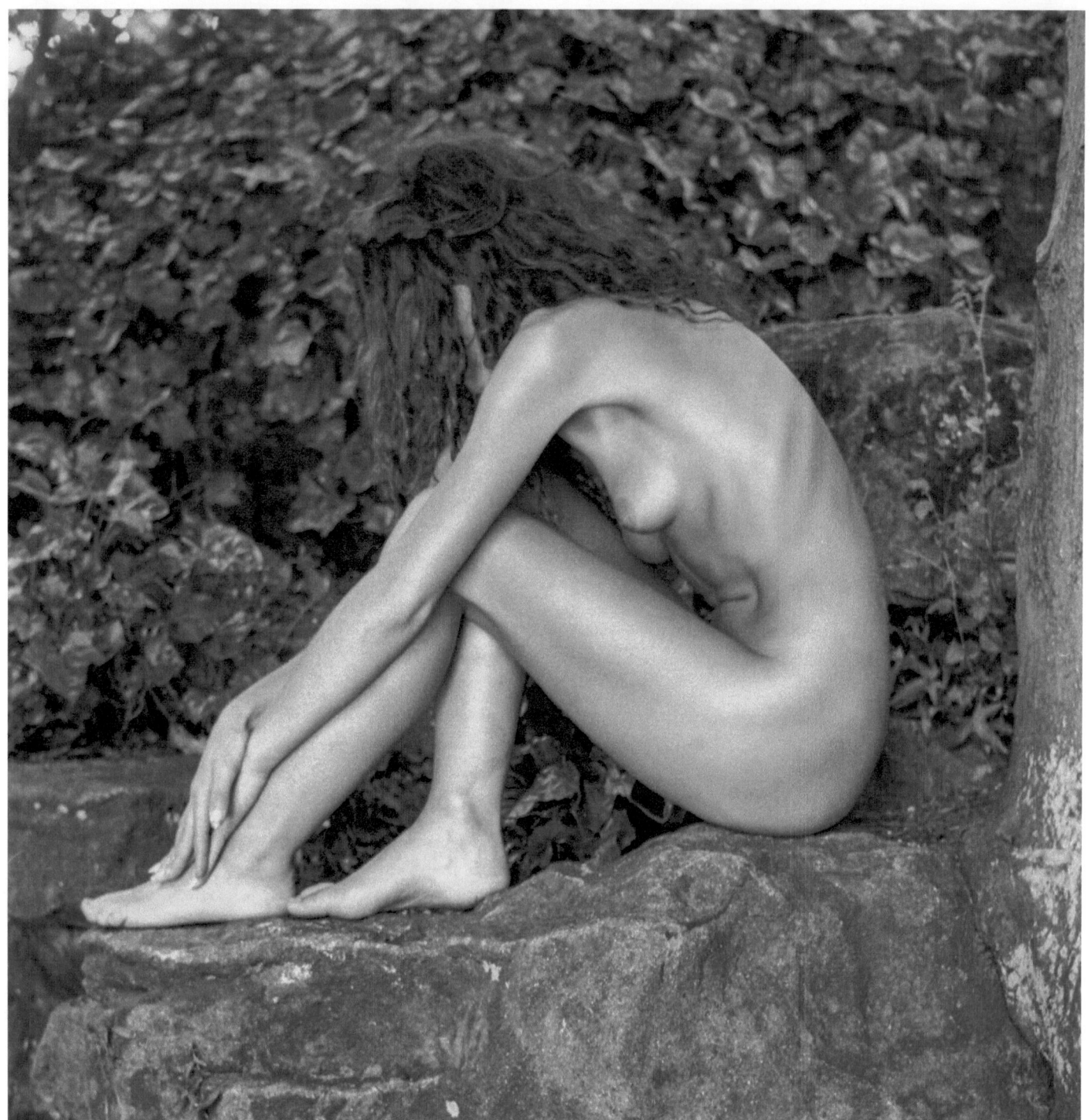

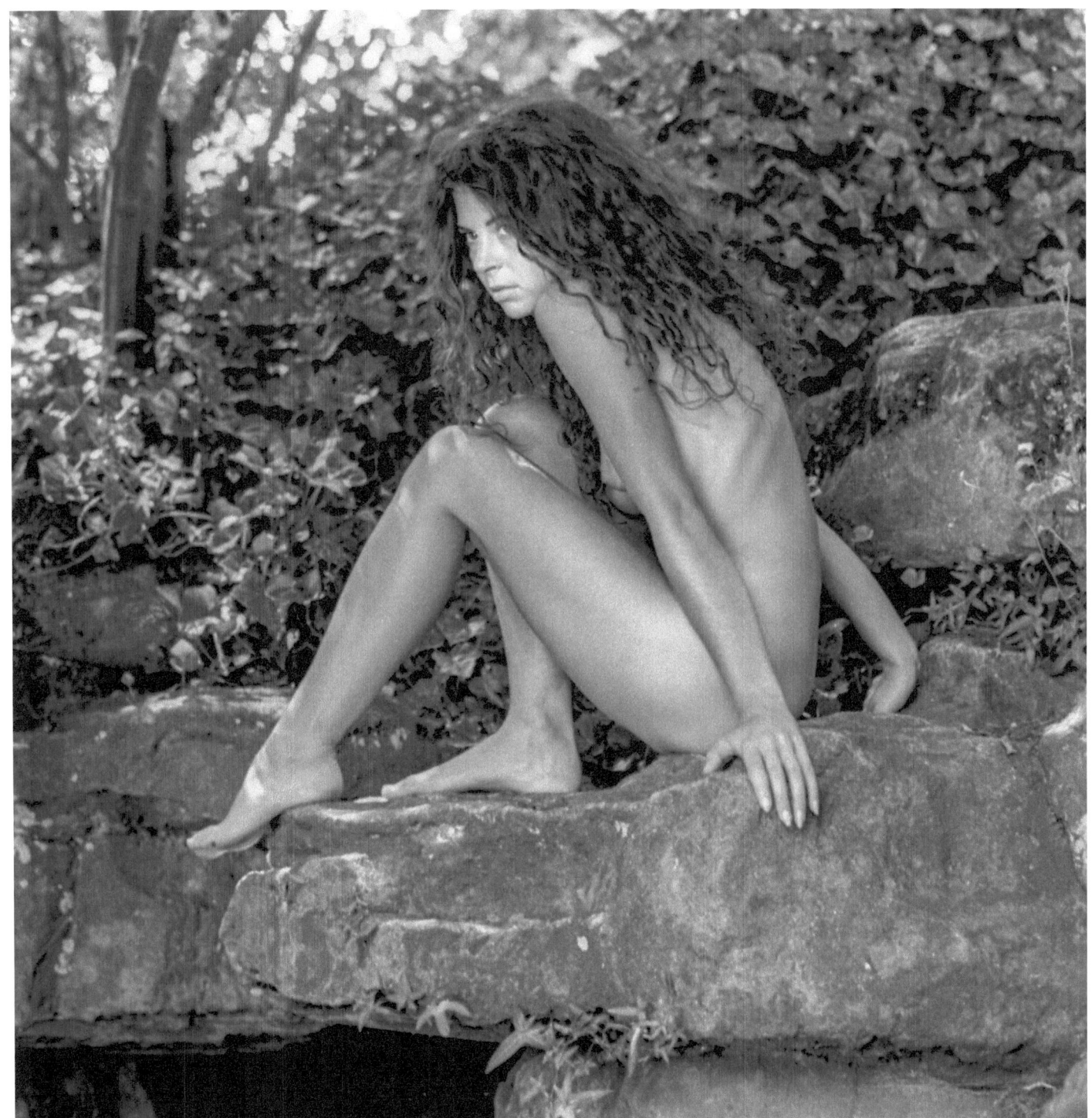

15

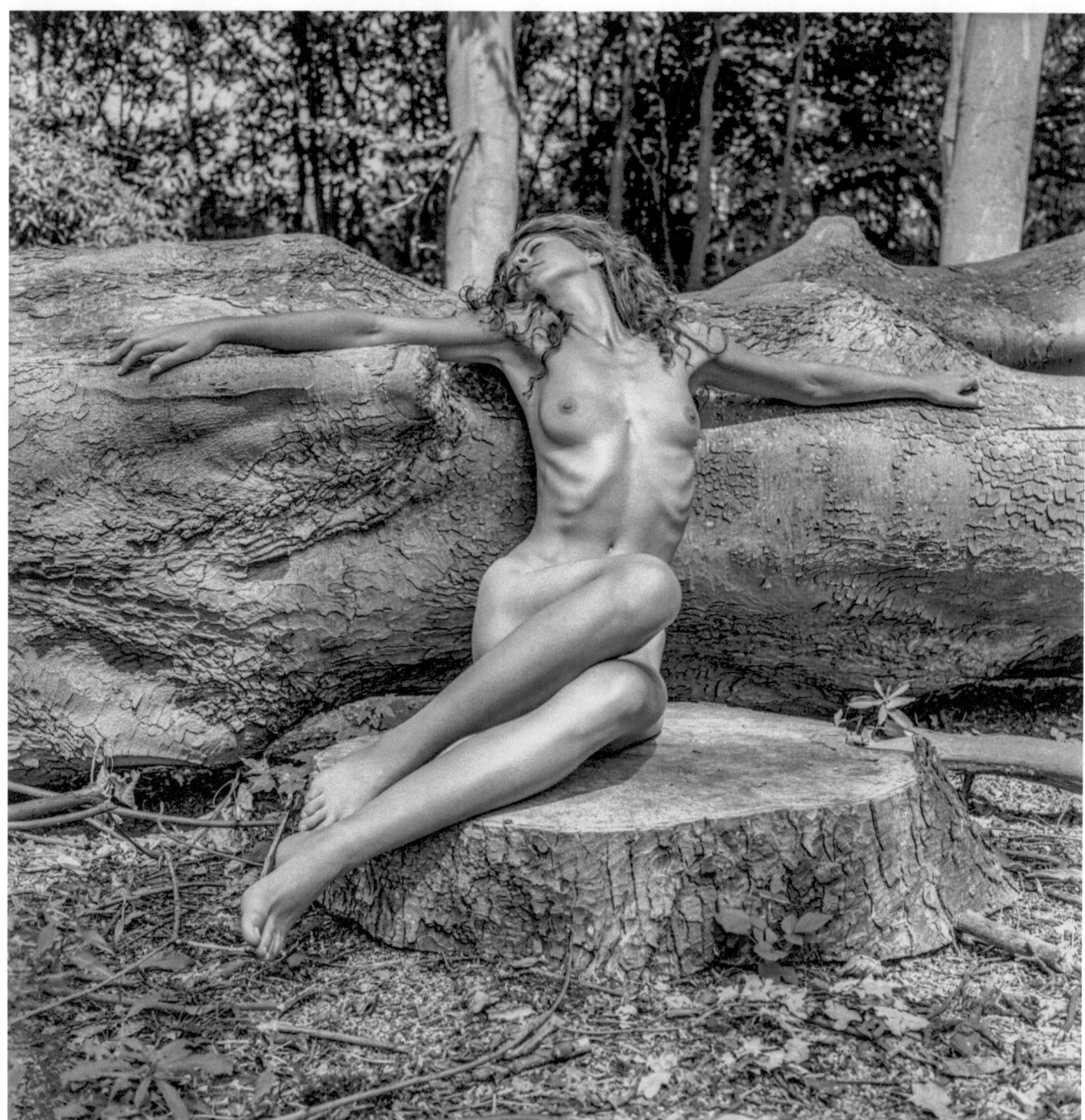

16

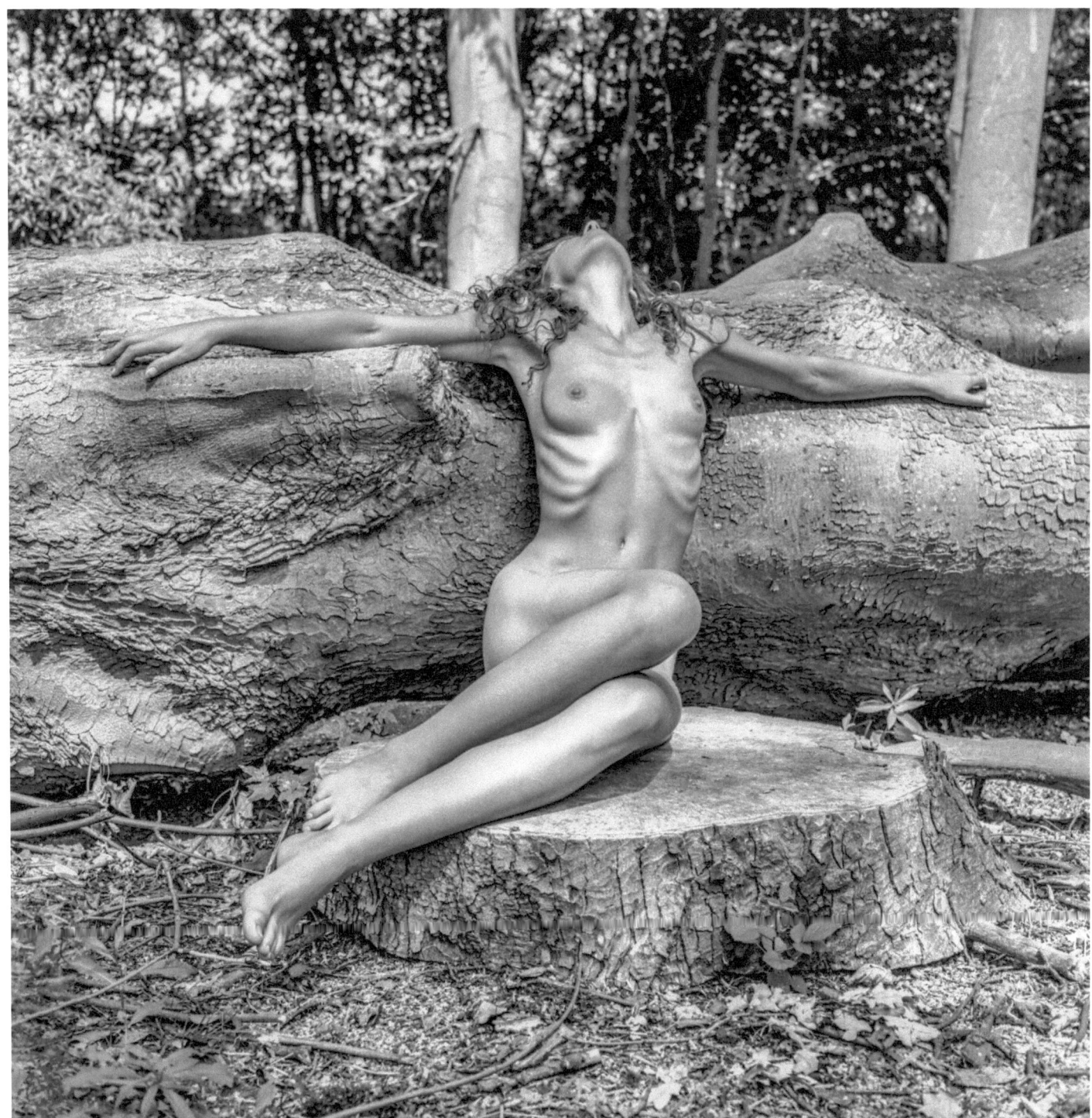

17

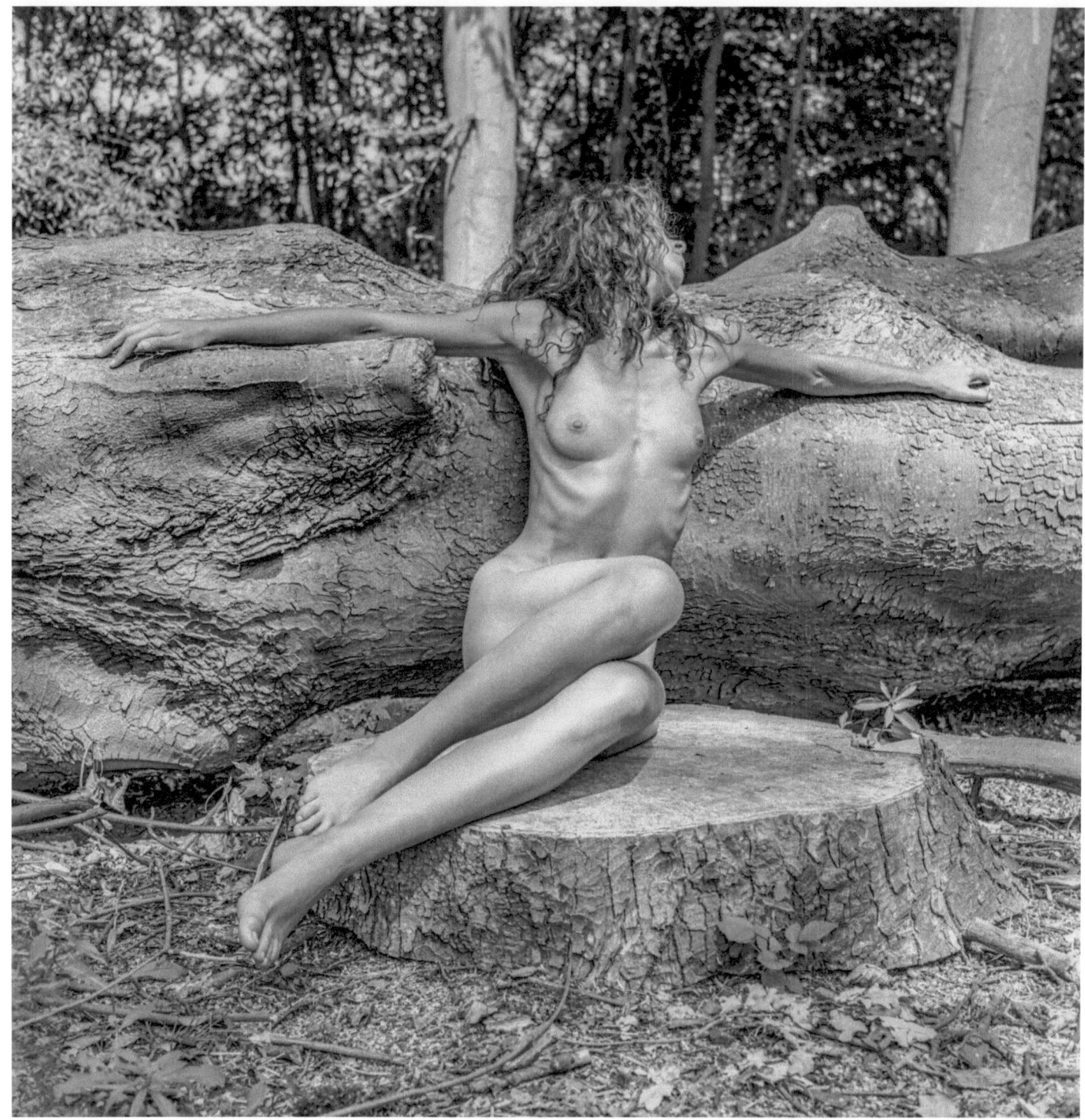

18

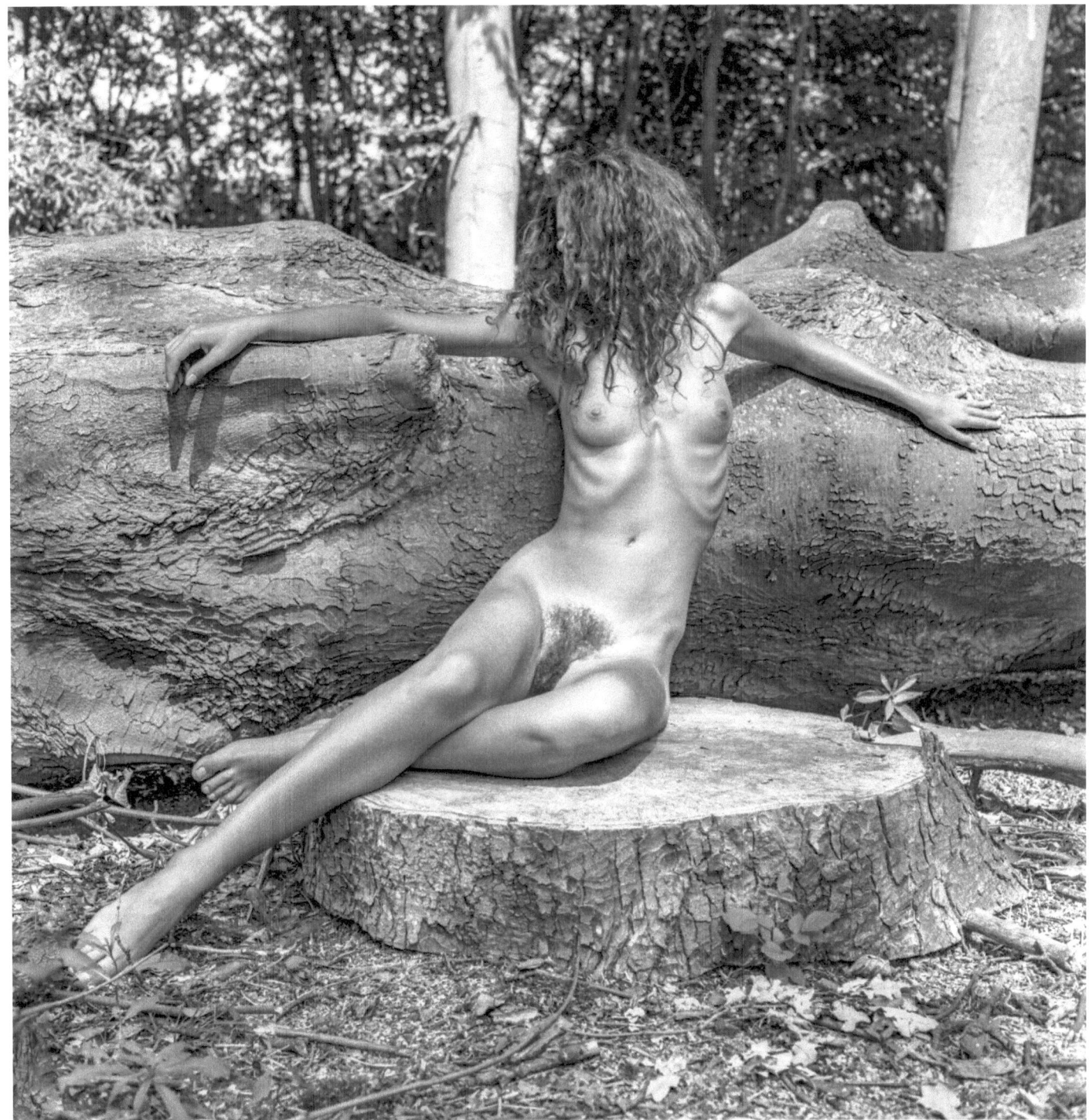

19

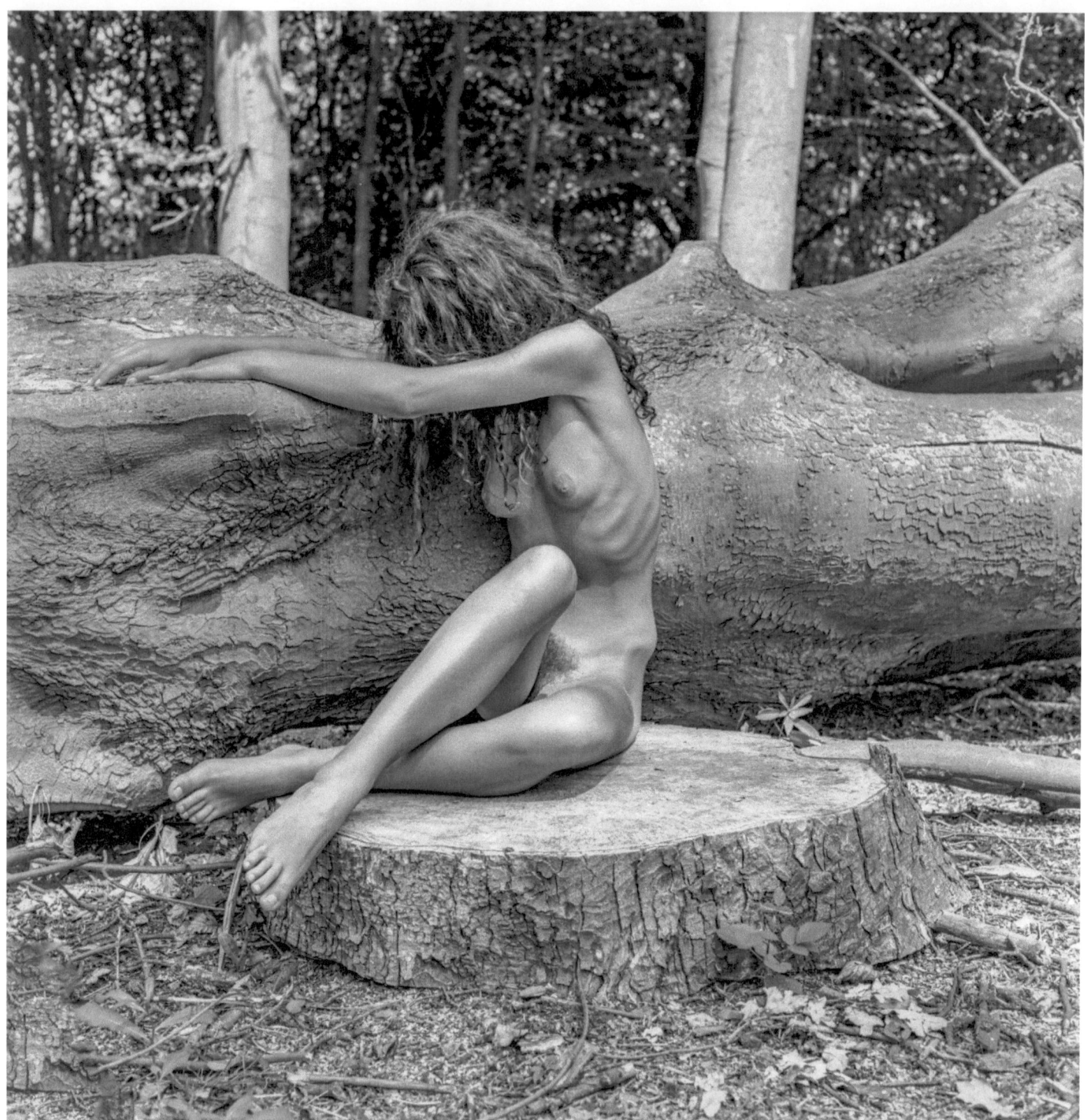

20

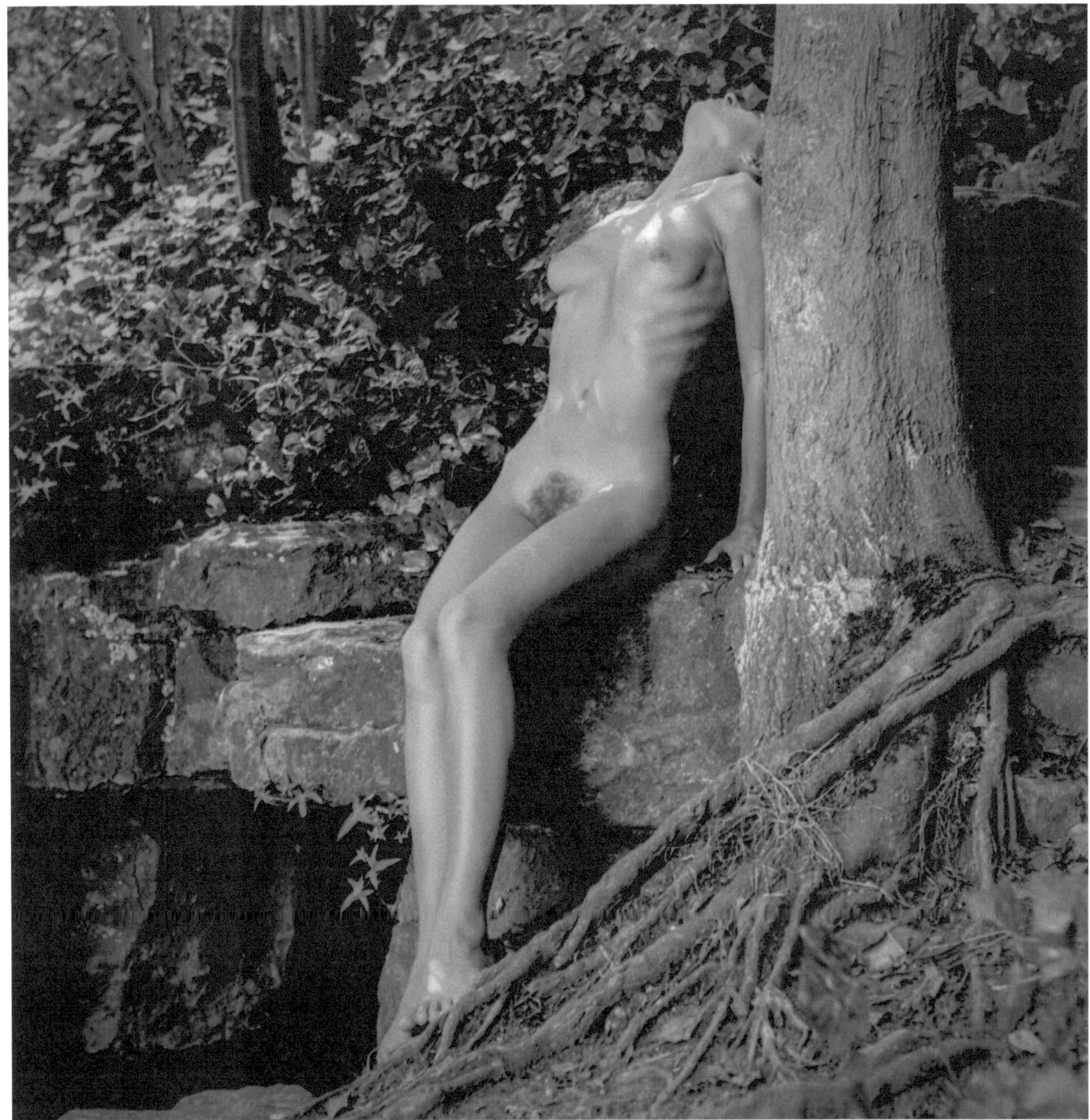

21

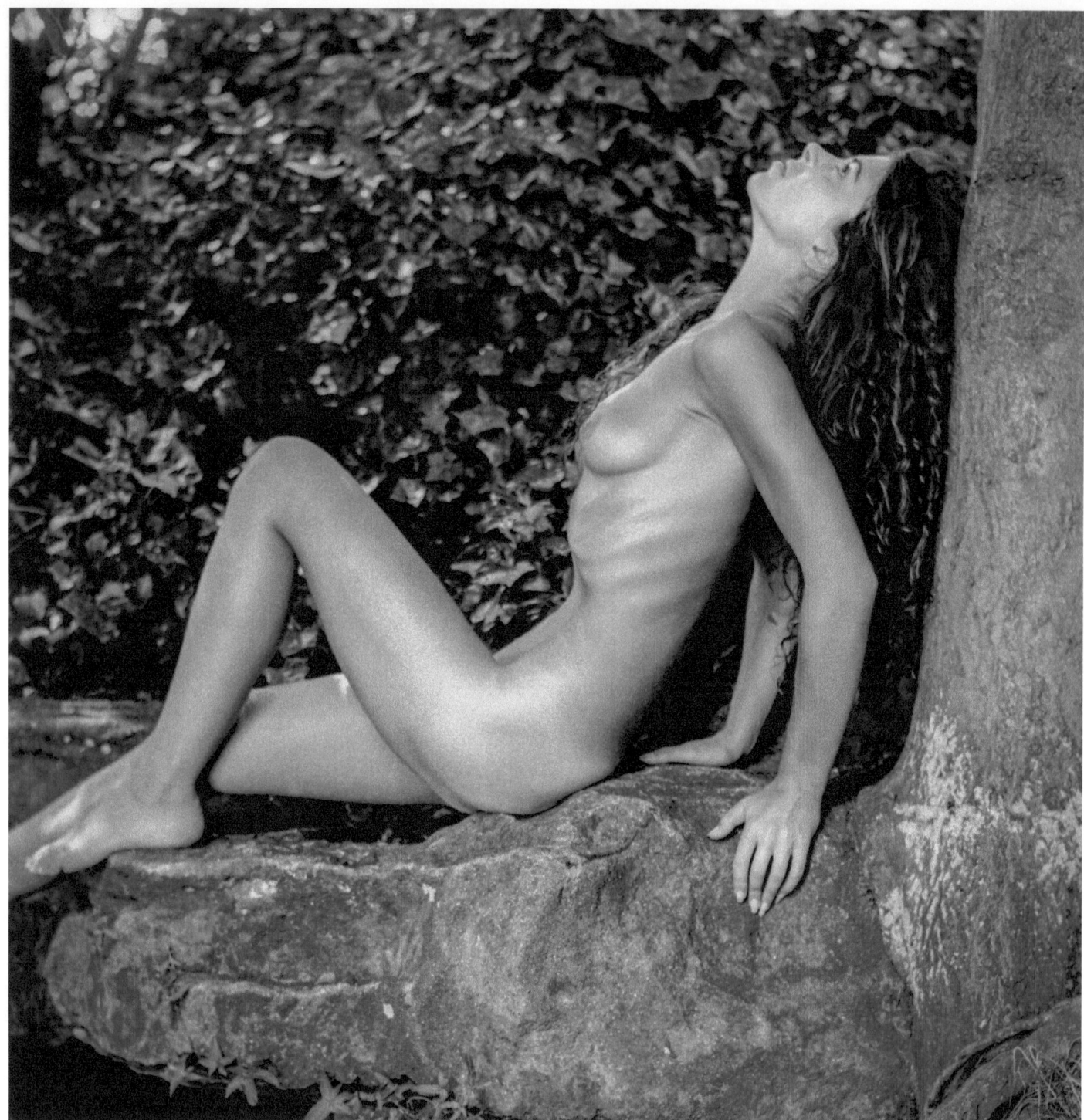

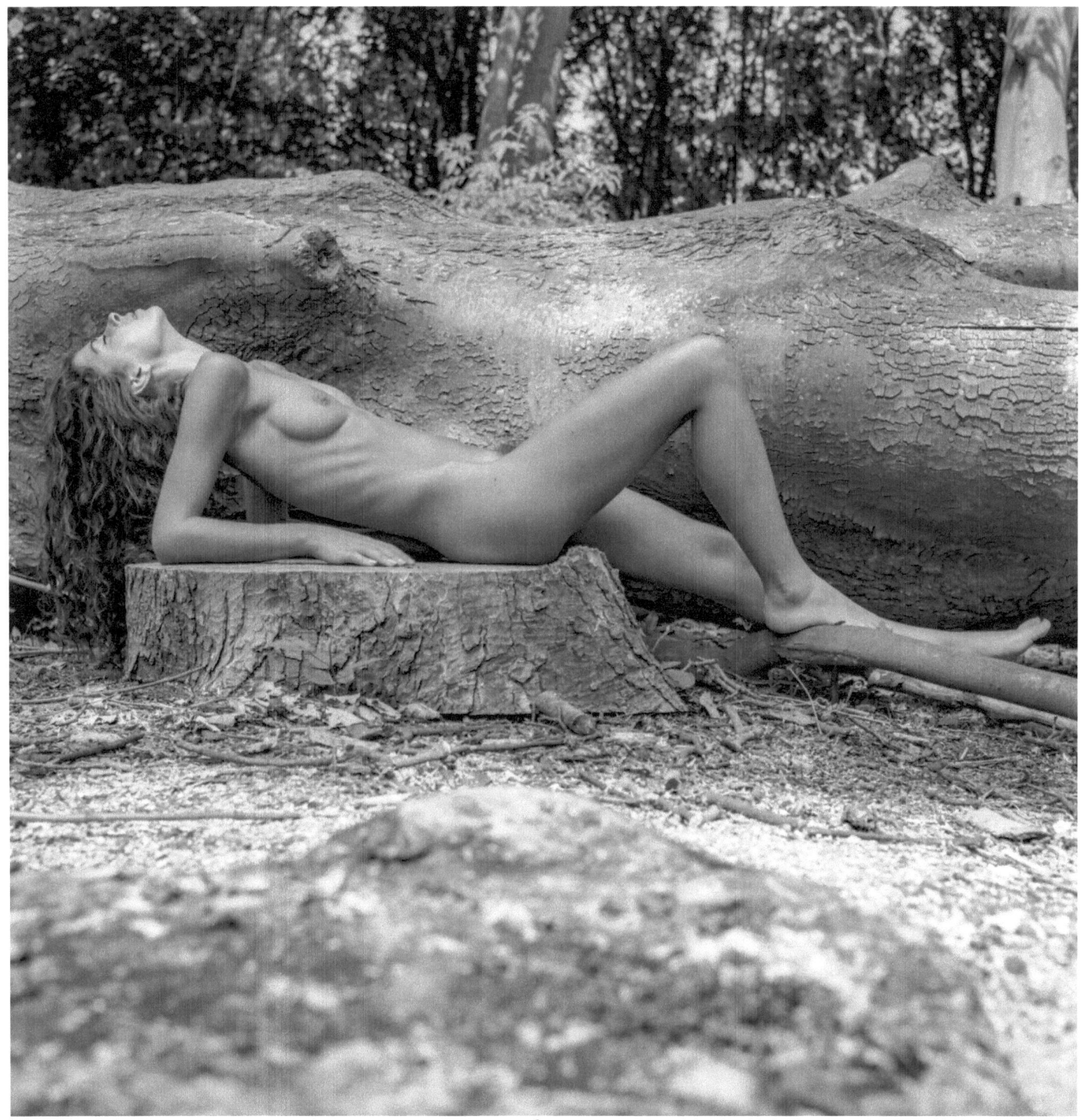

23

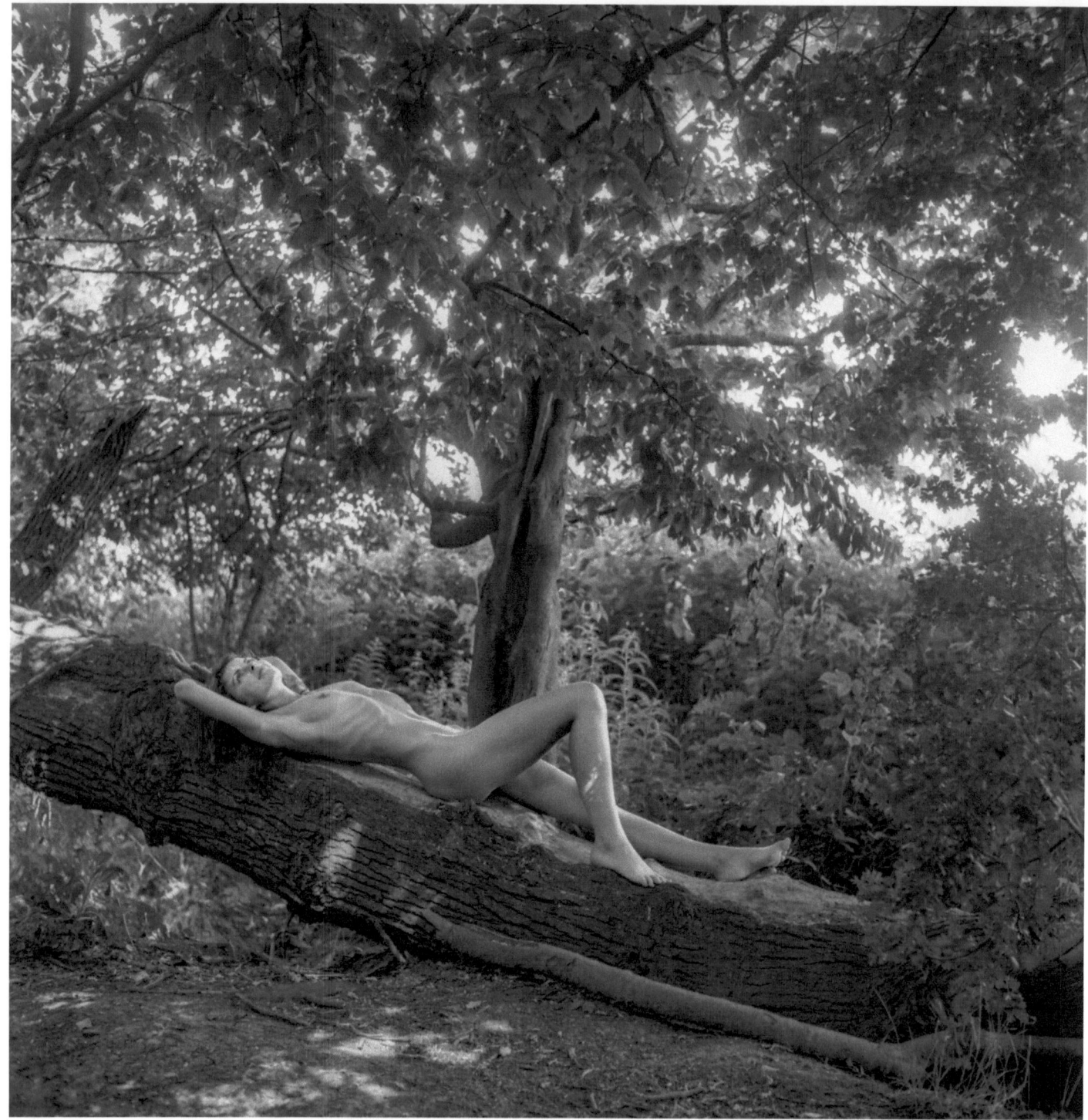

24

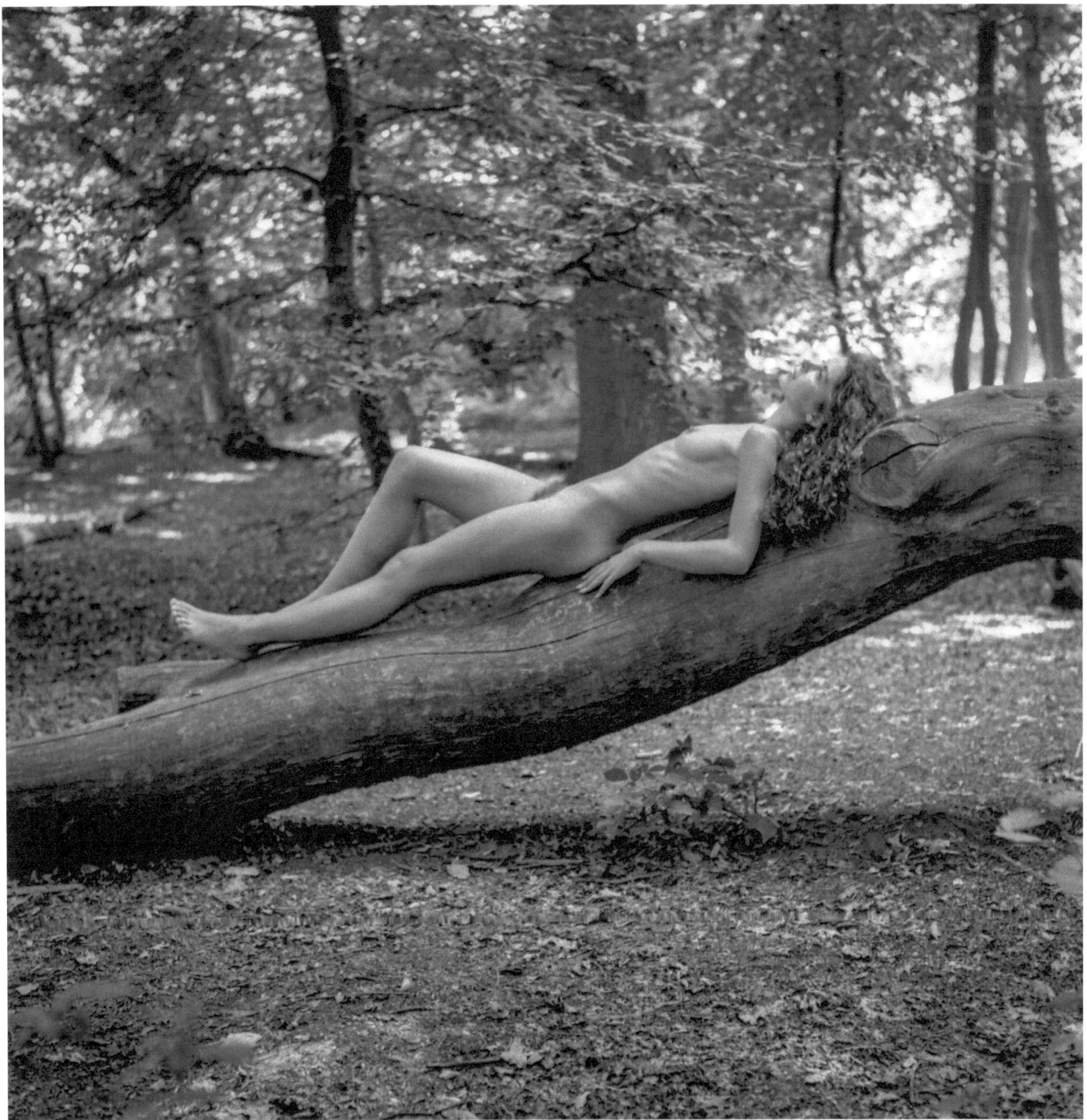

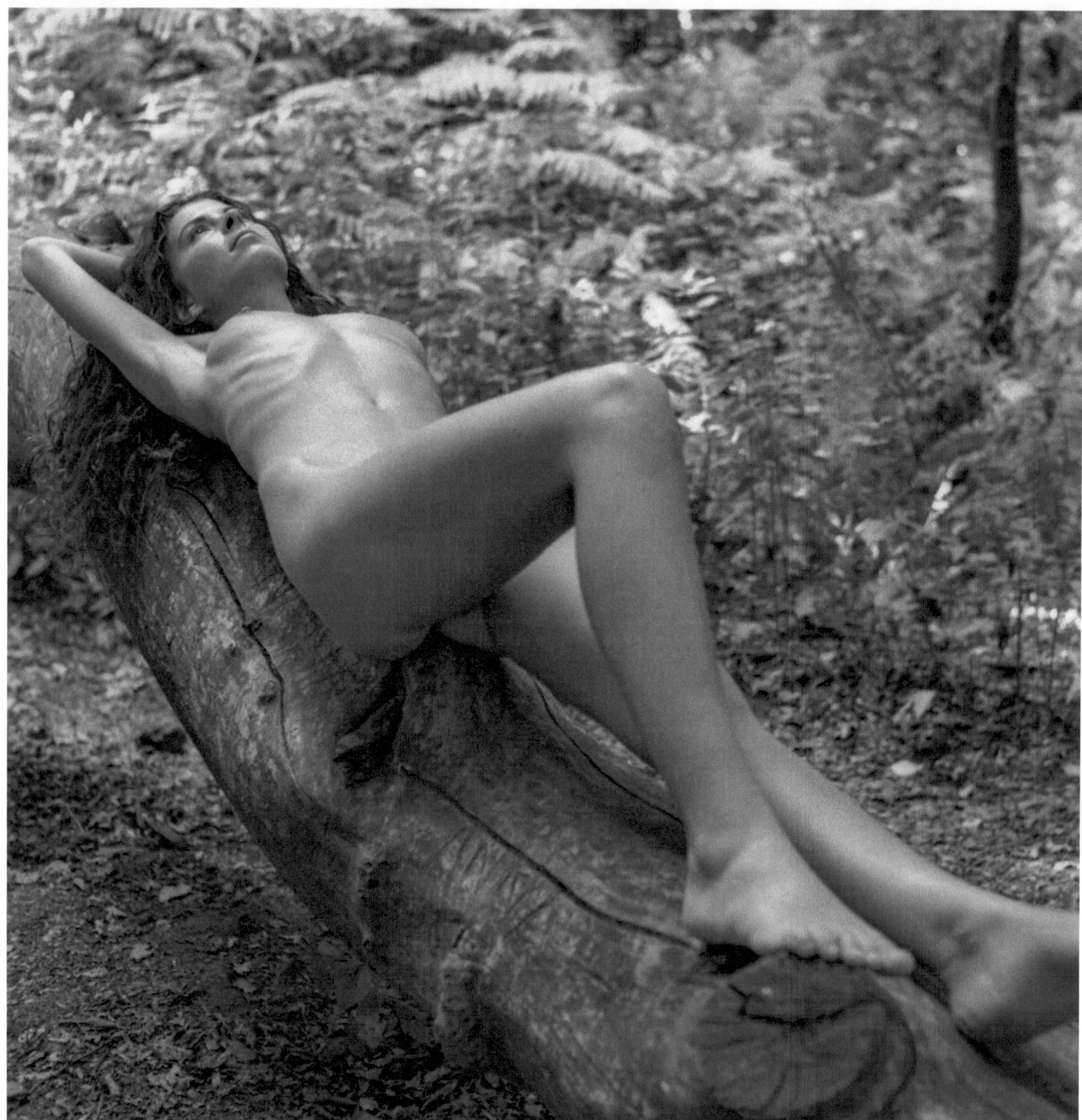

26

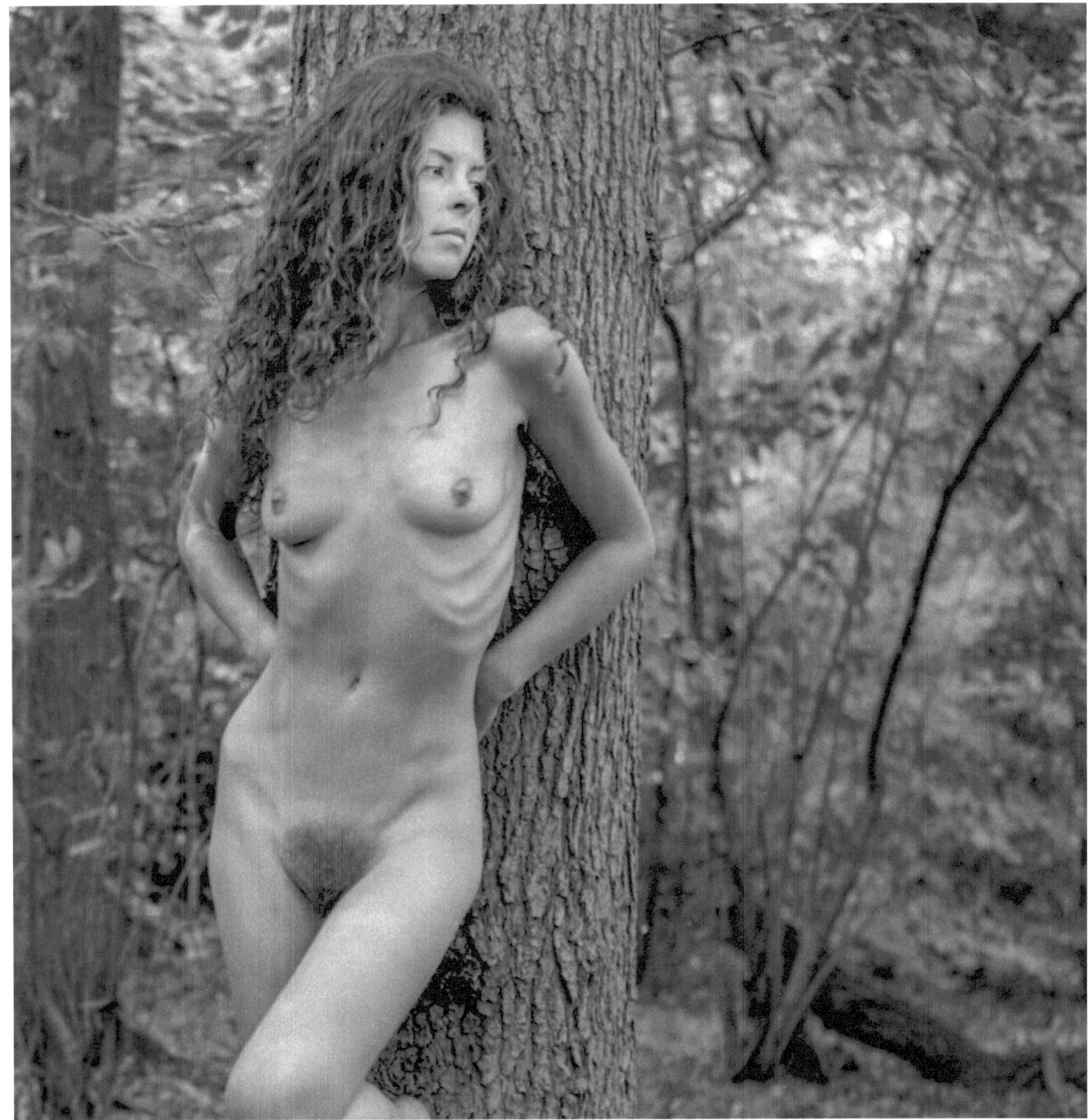

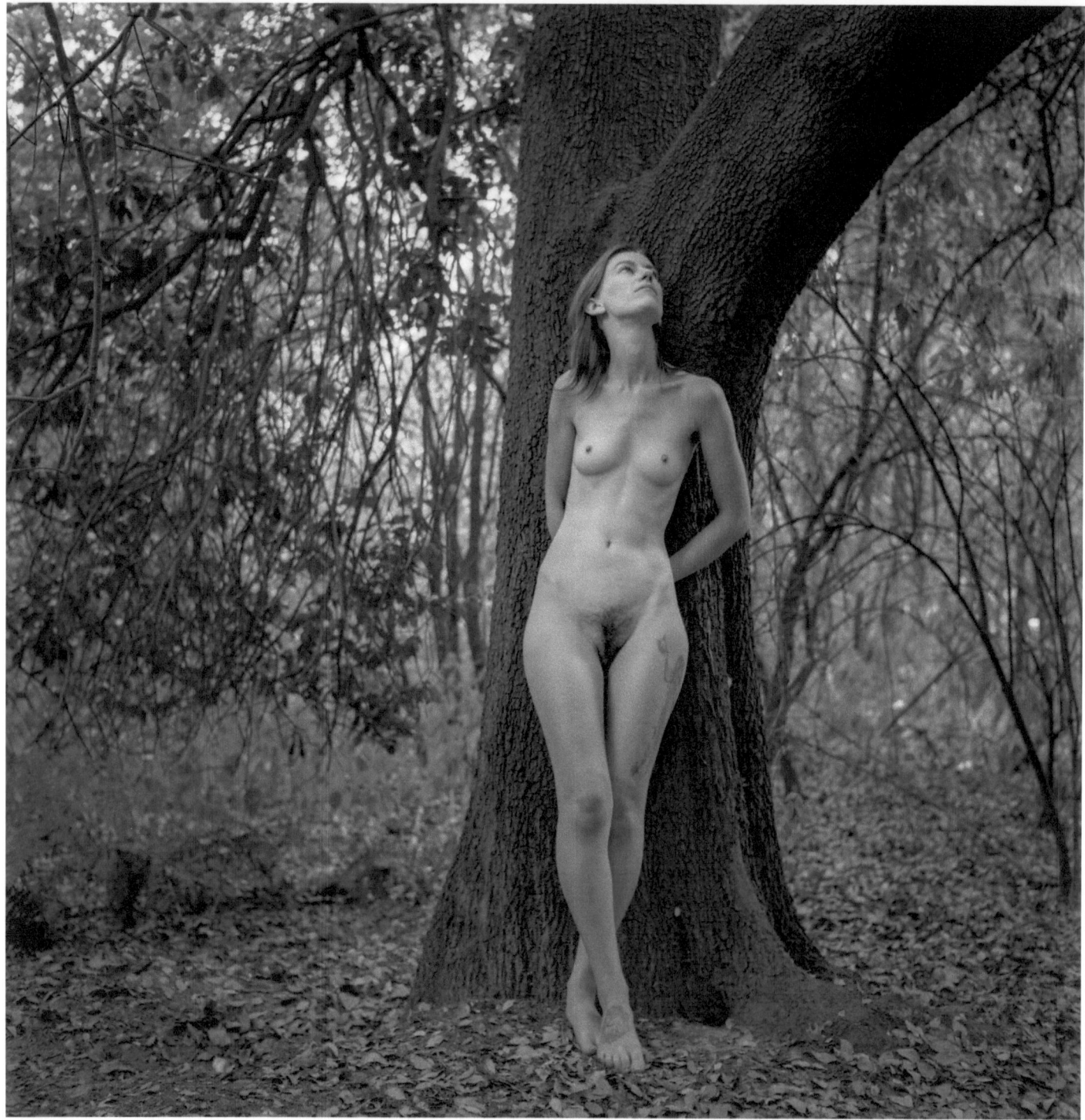

28

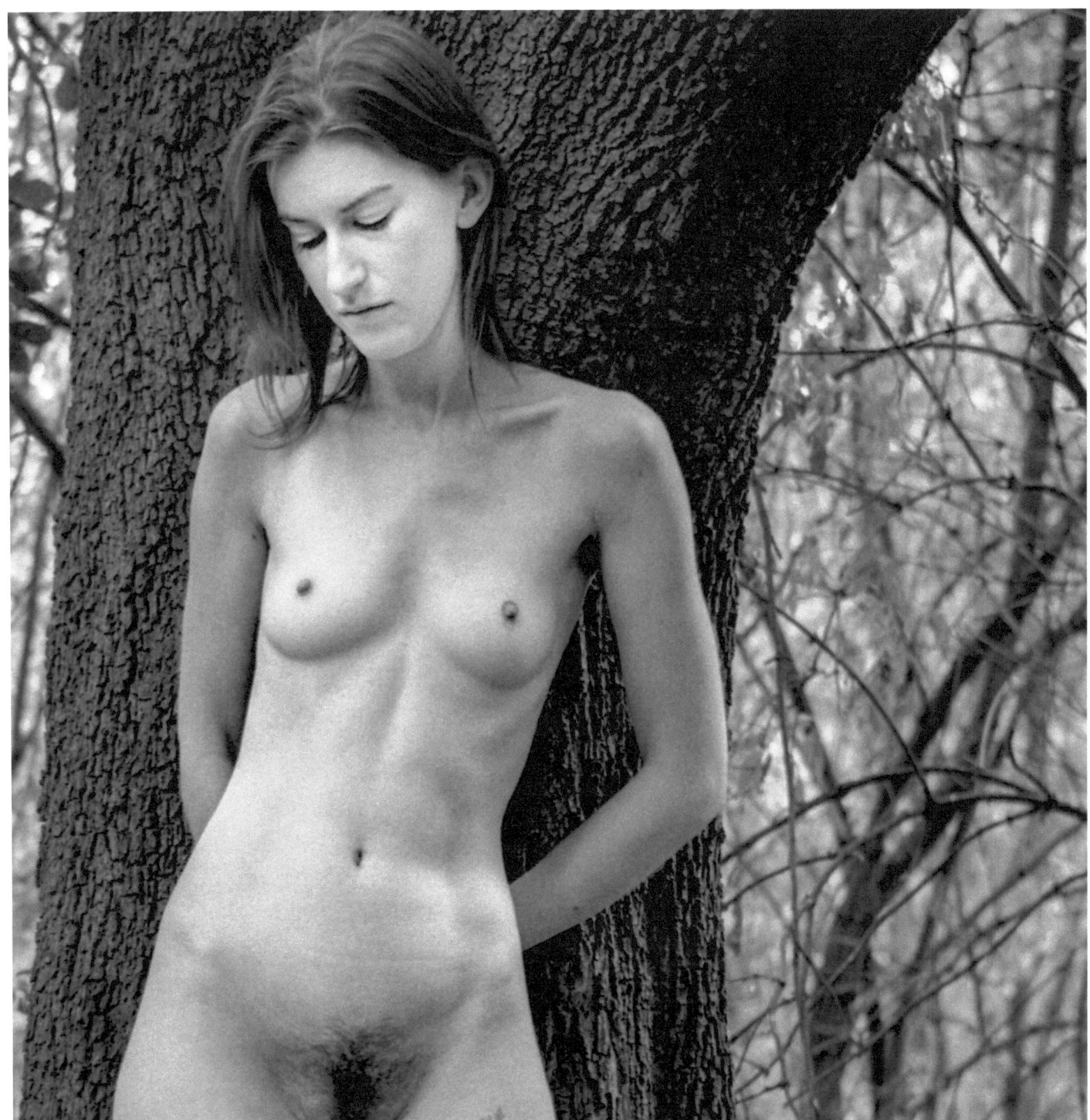

29

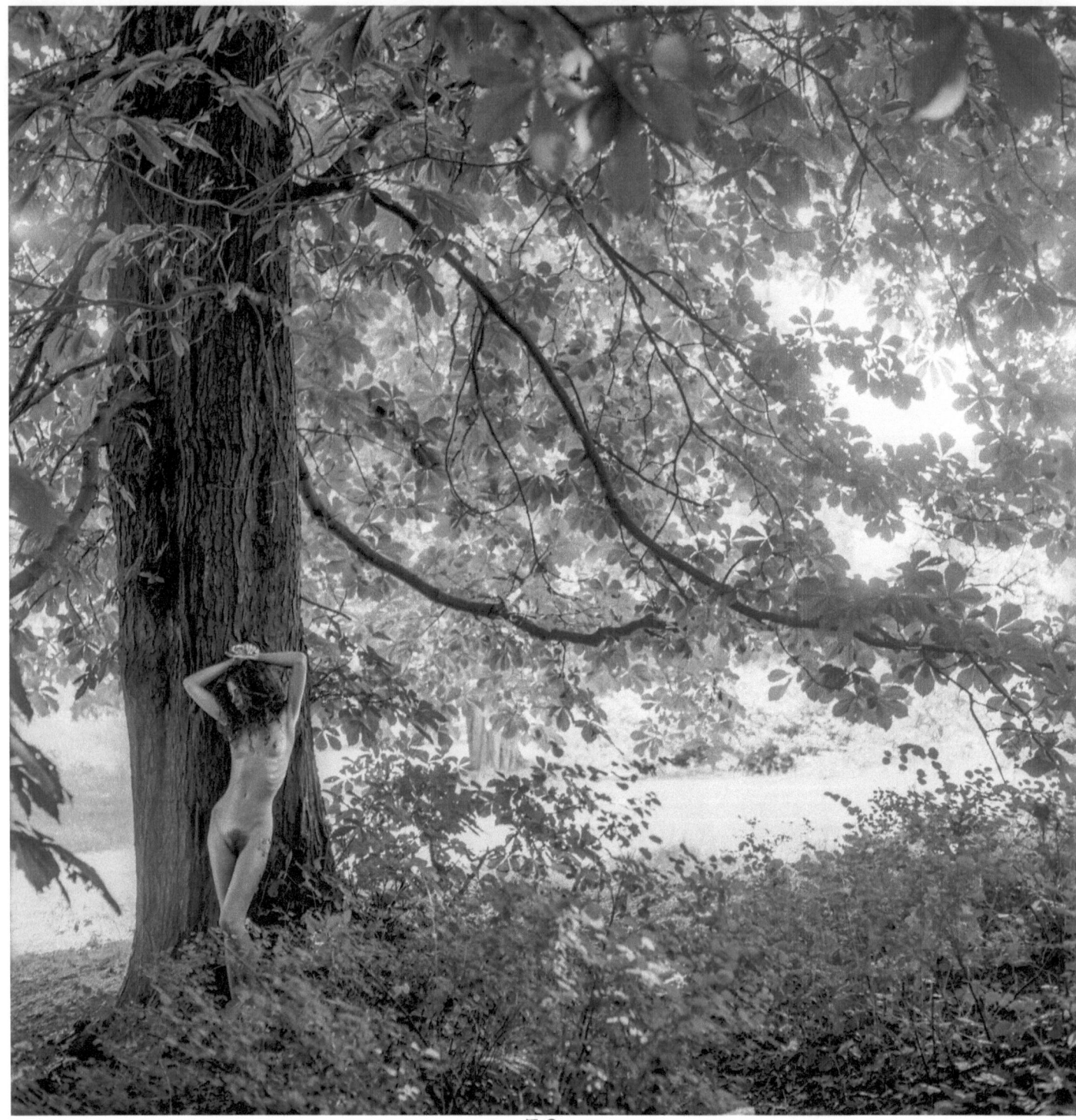

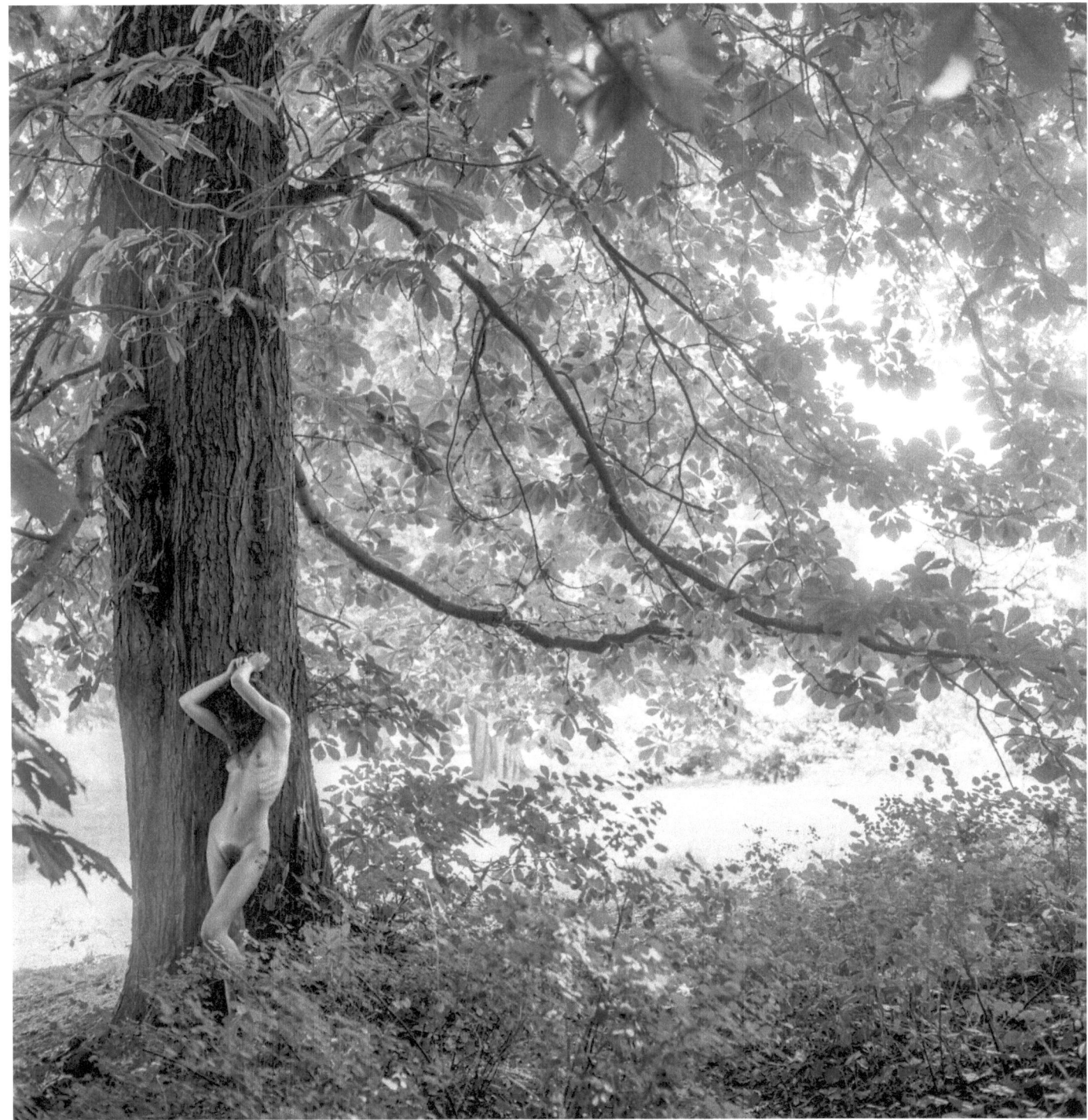

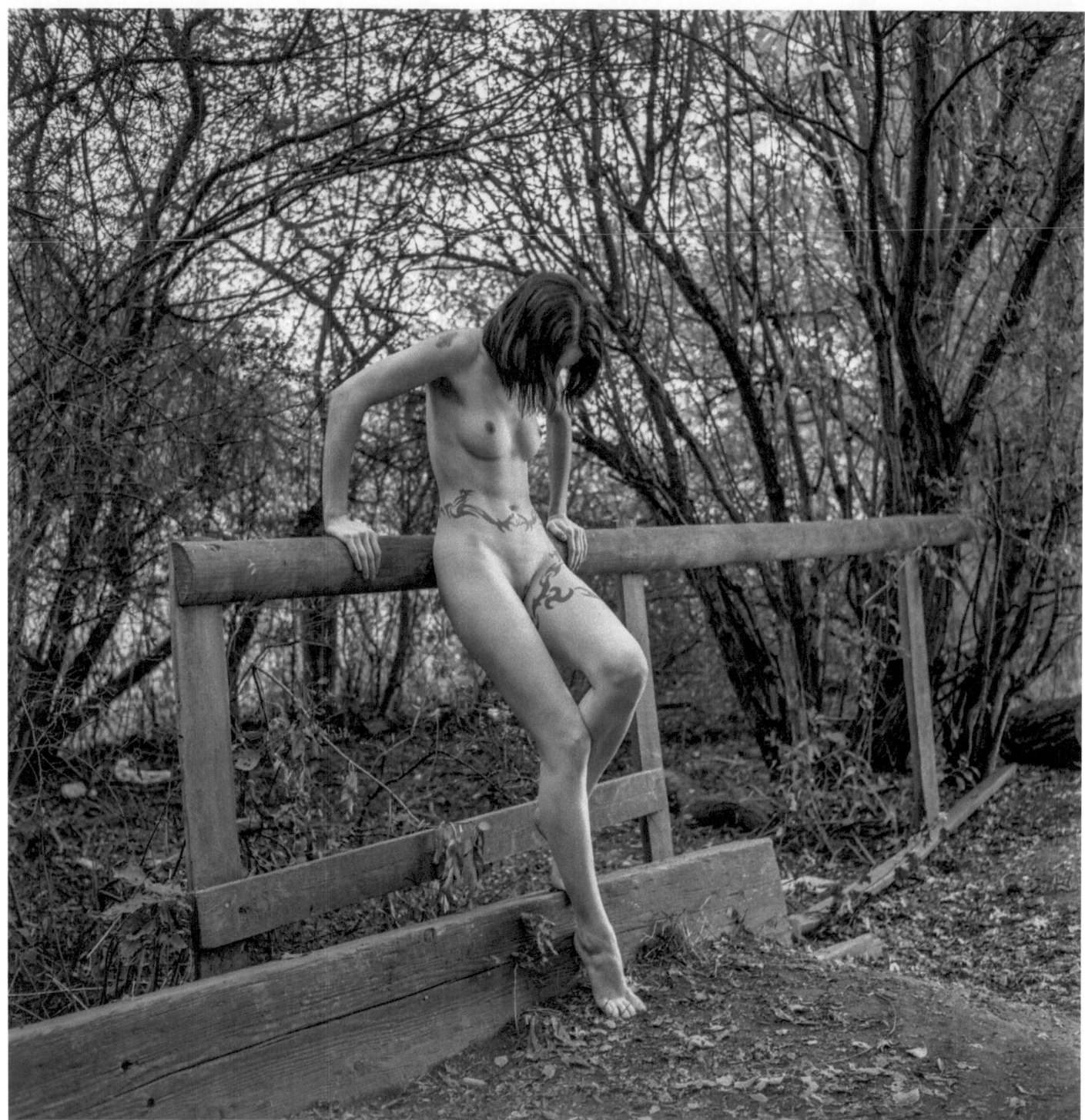

32

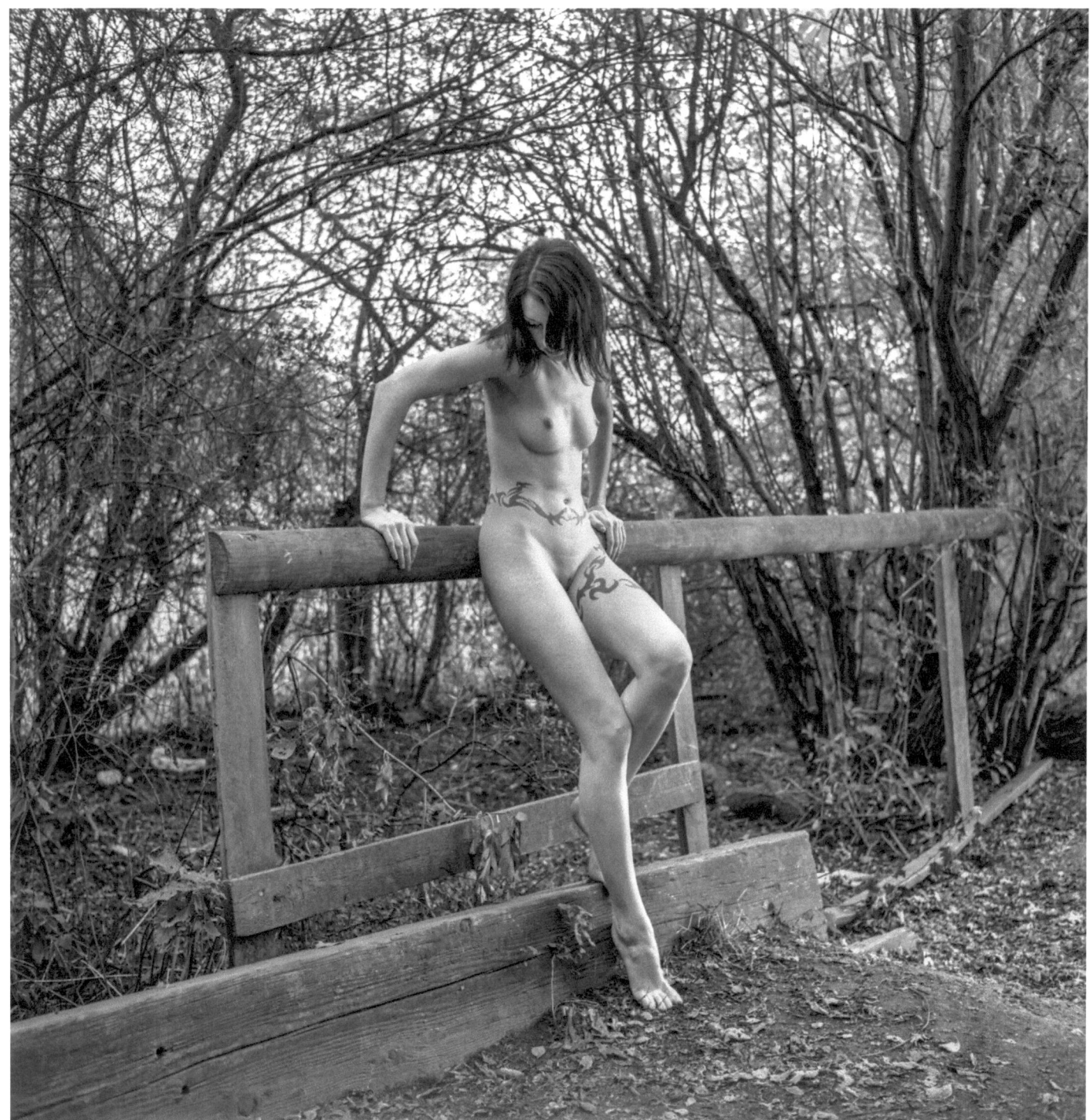

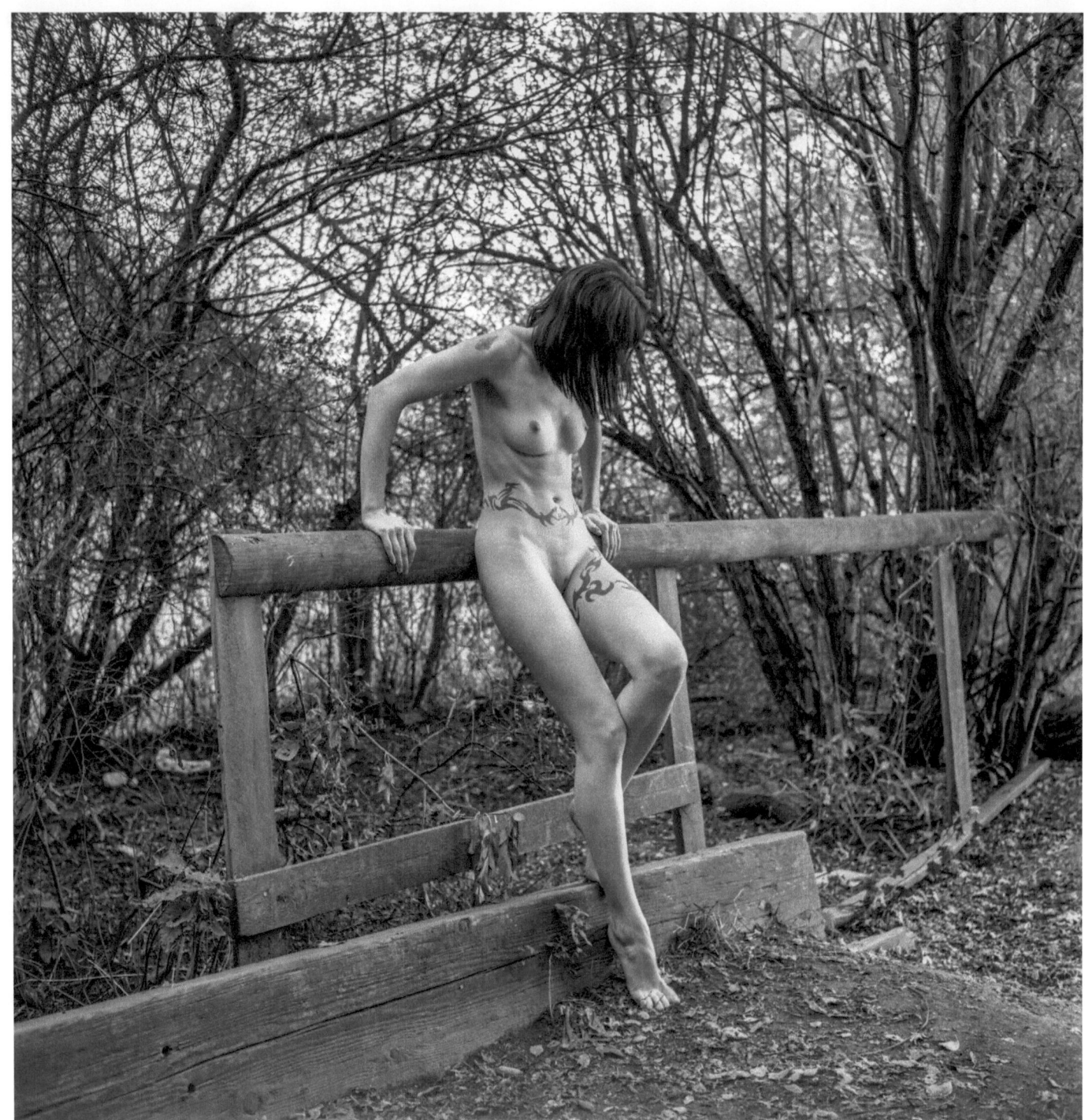

34

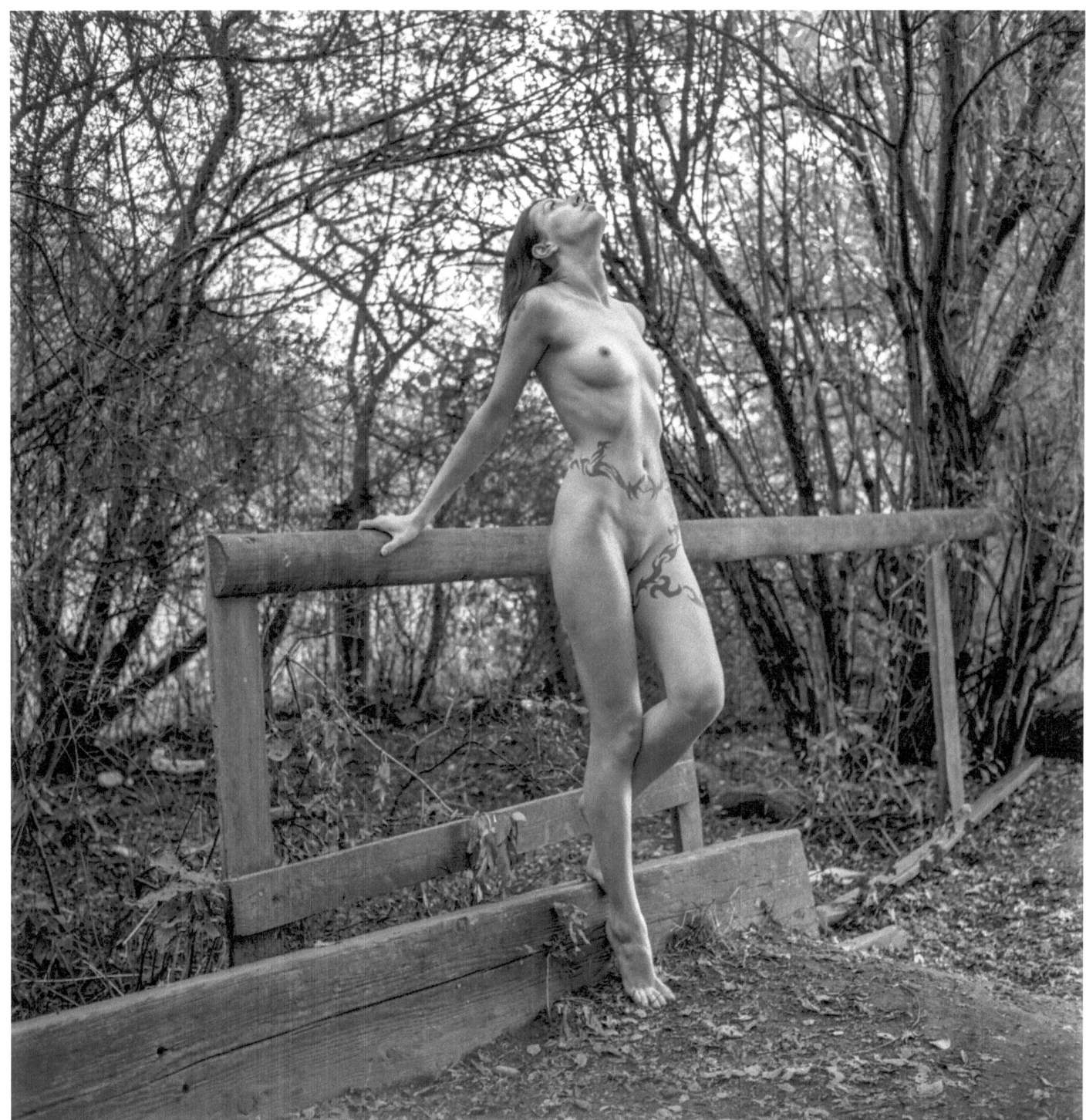

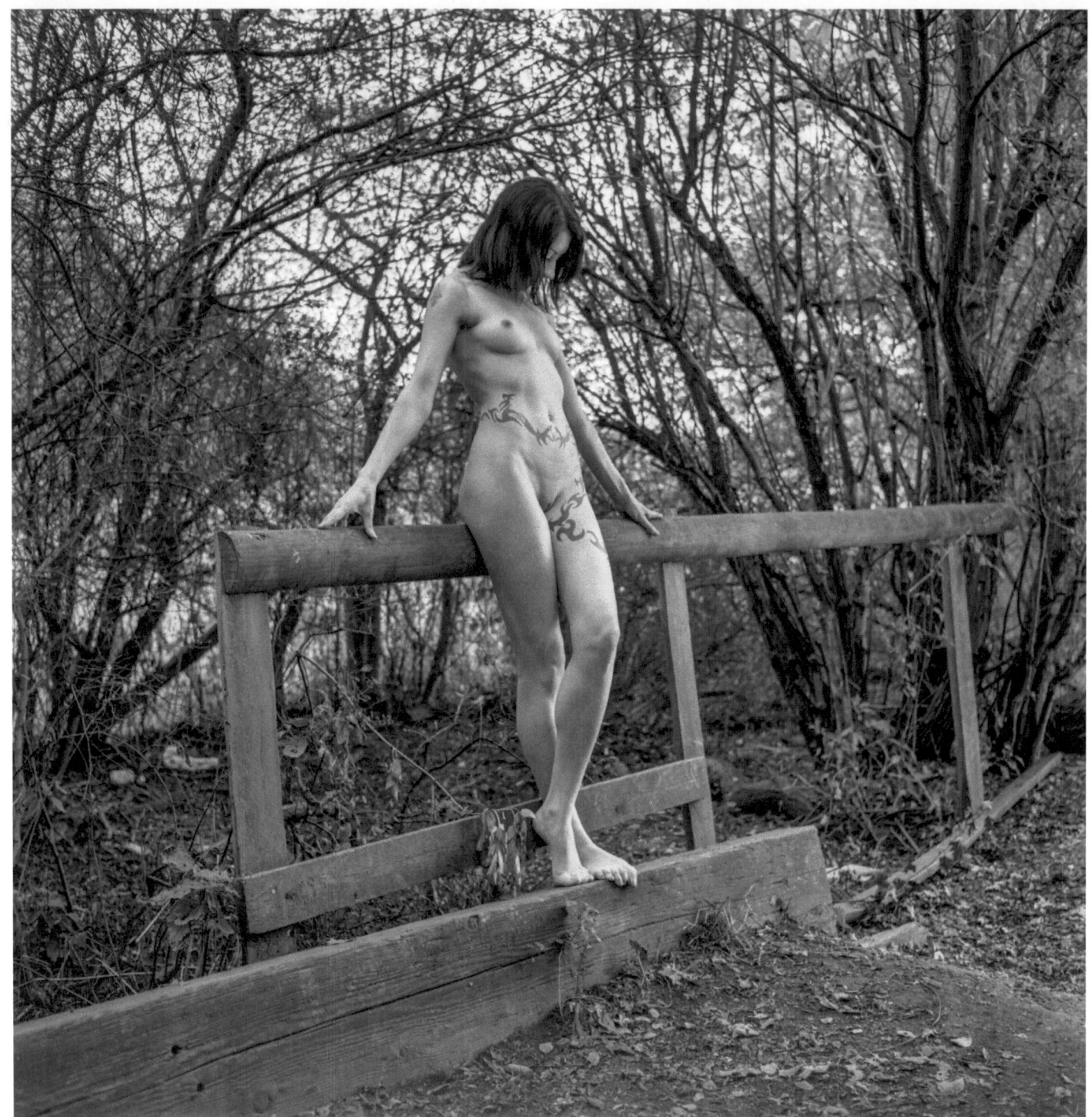

36

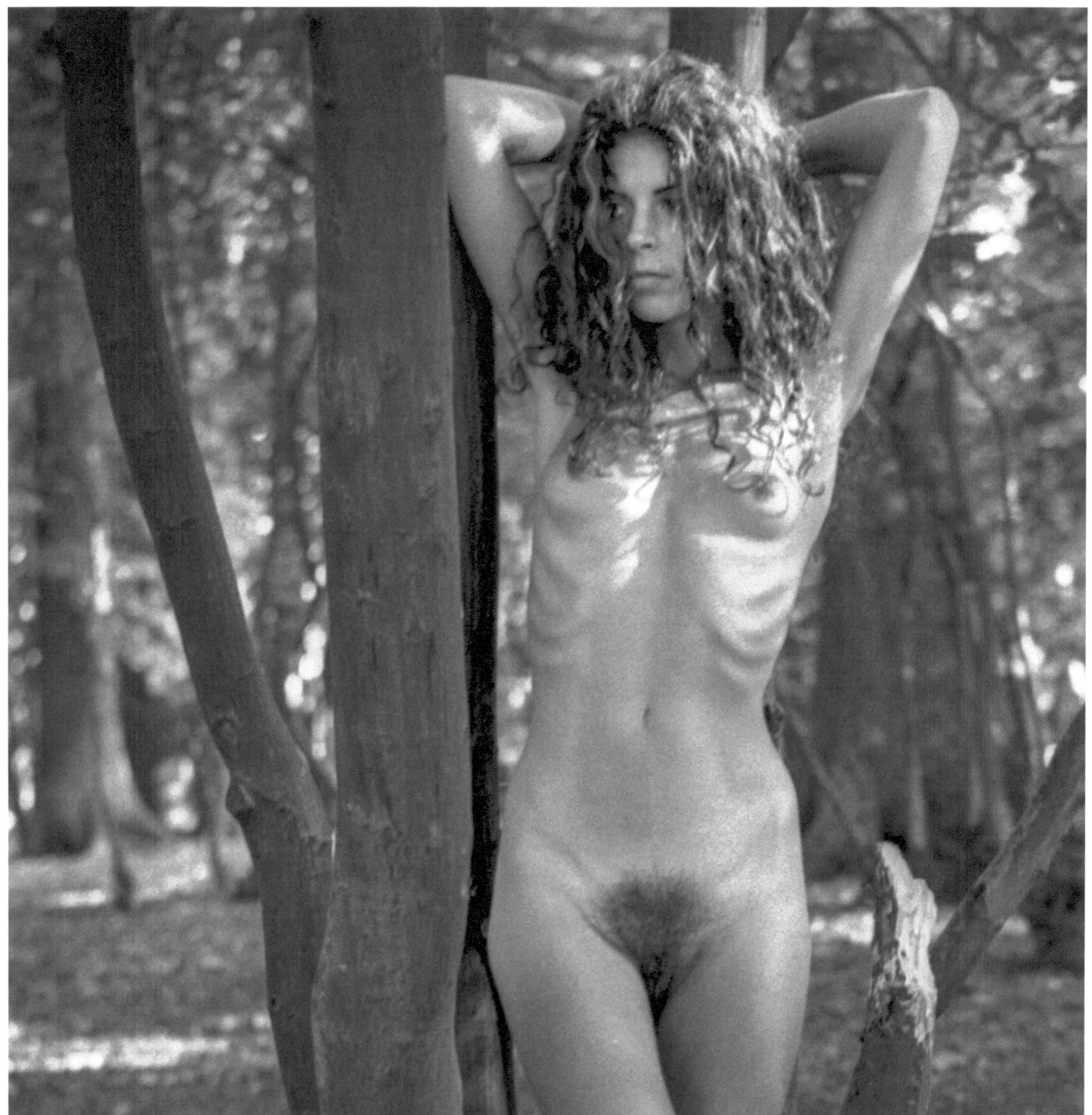

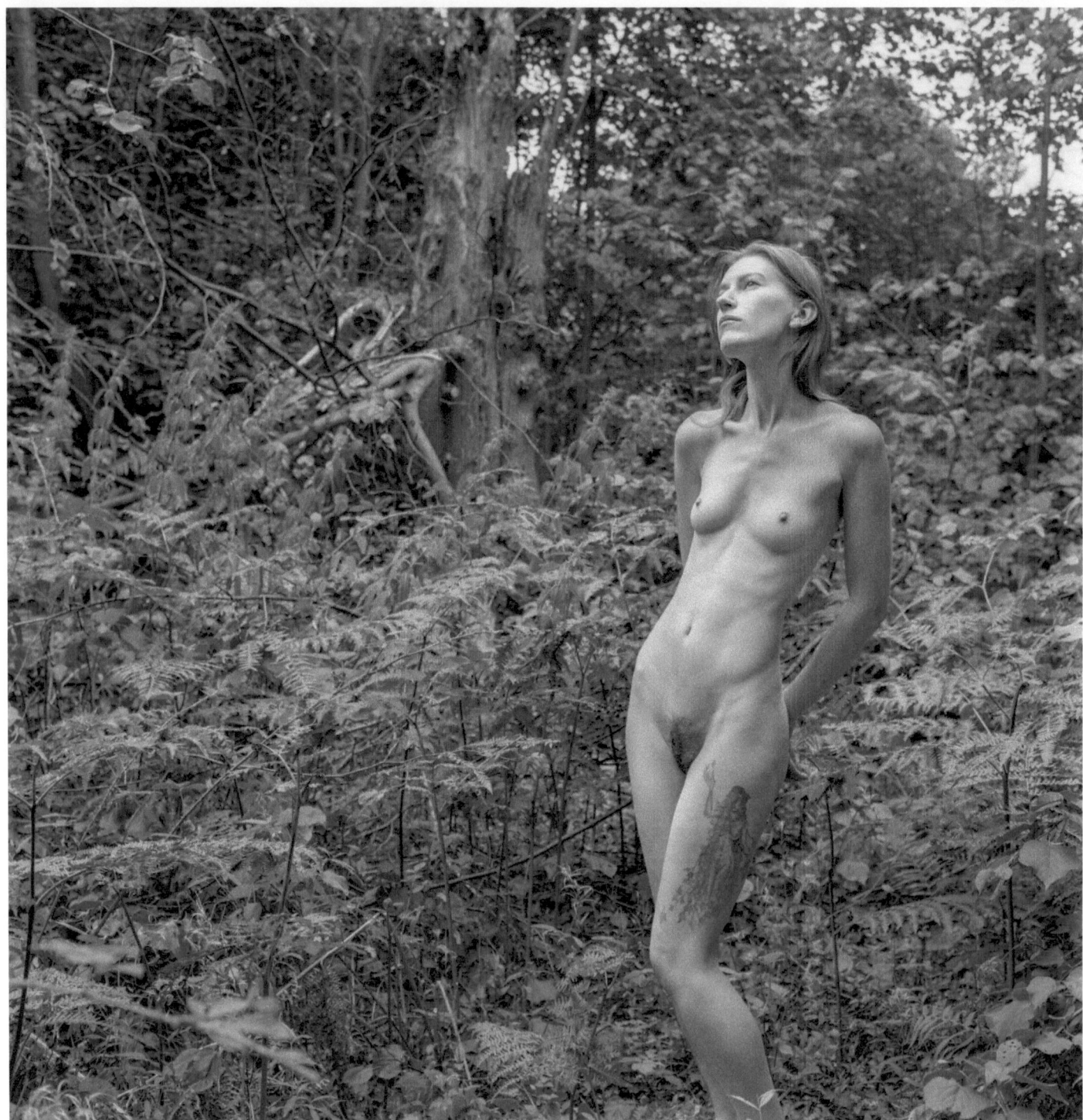

38

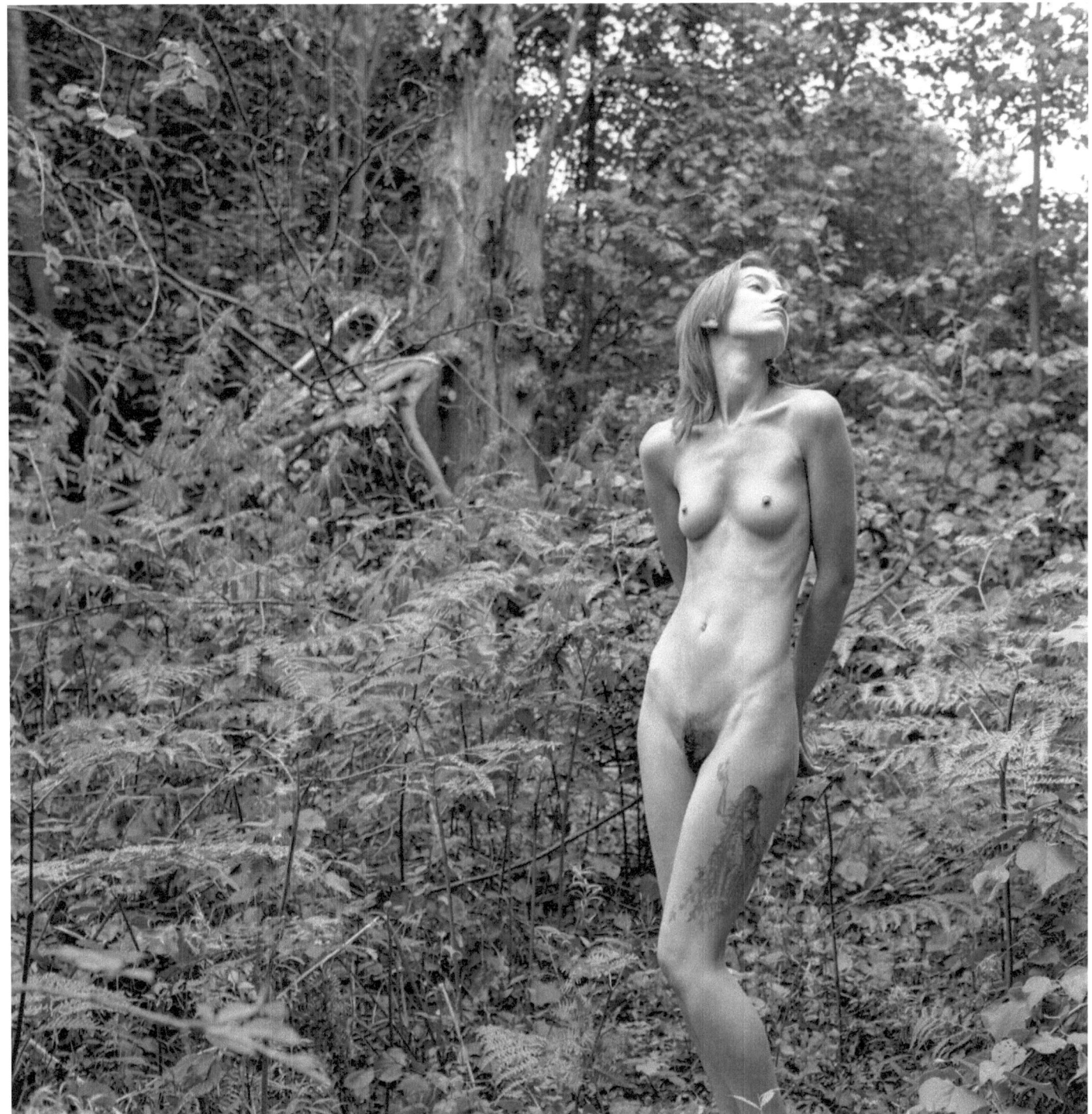

39

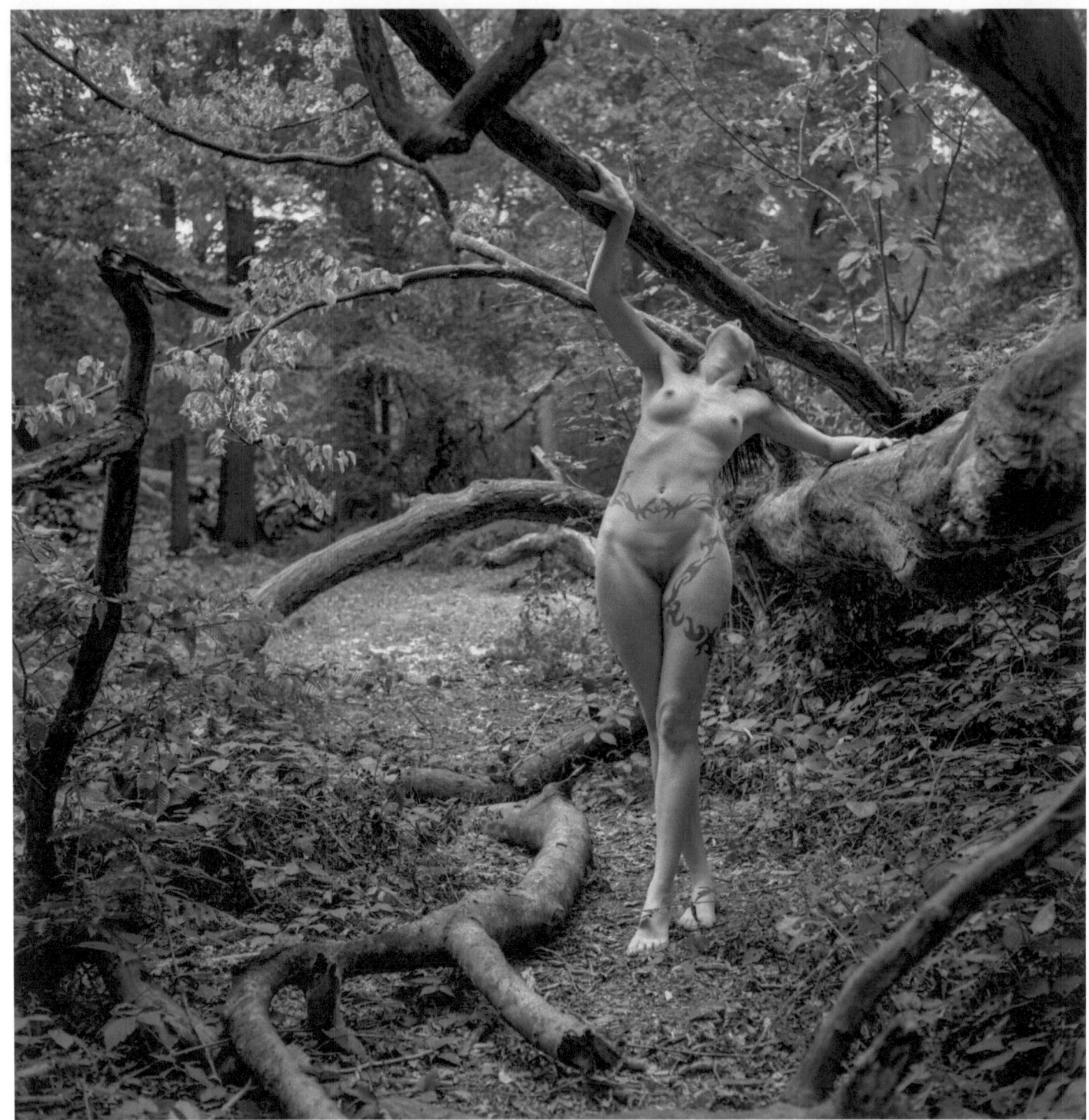

40

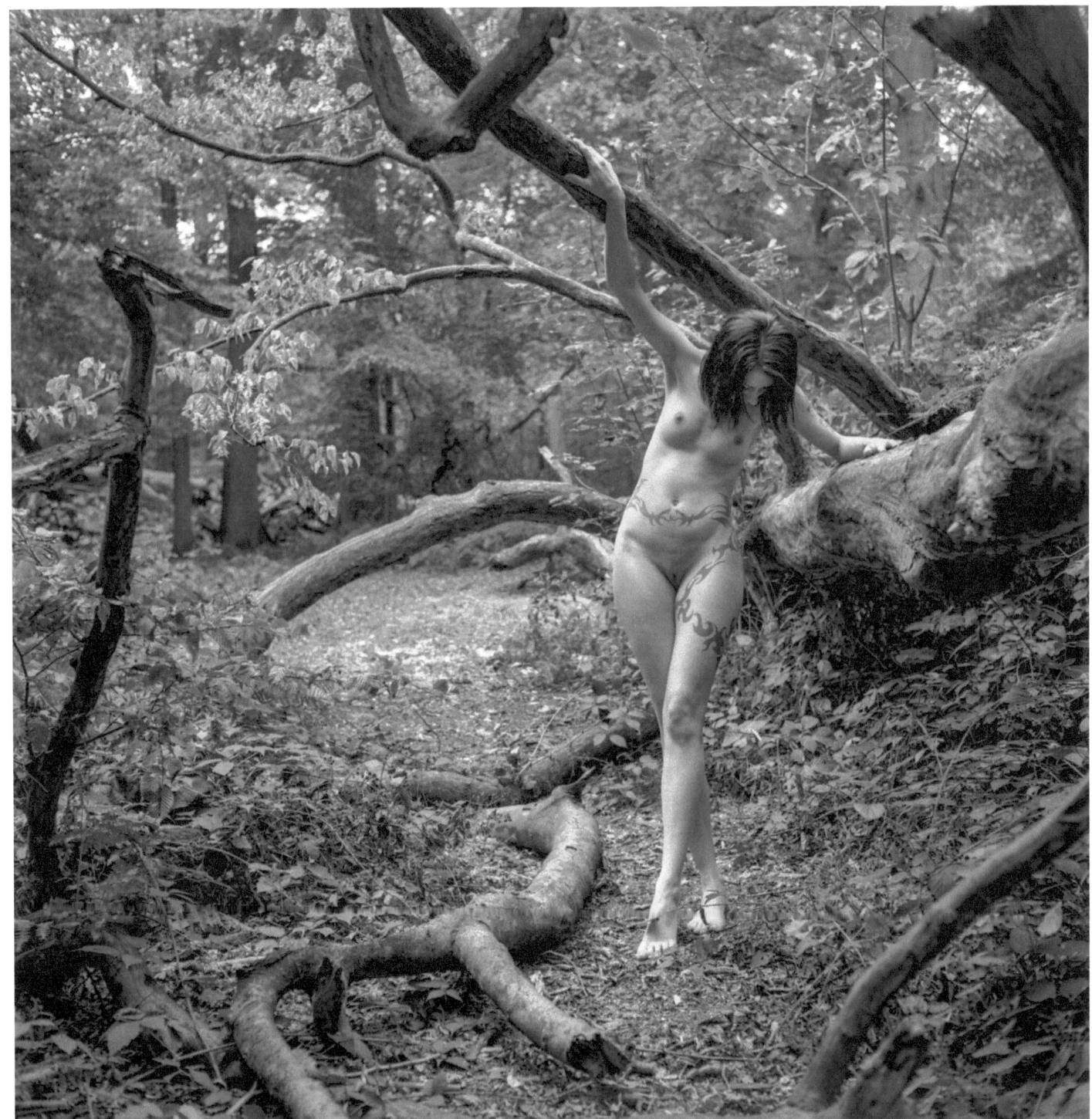

41

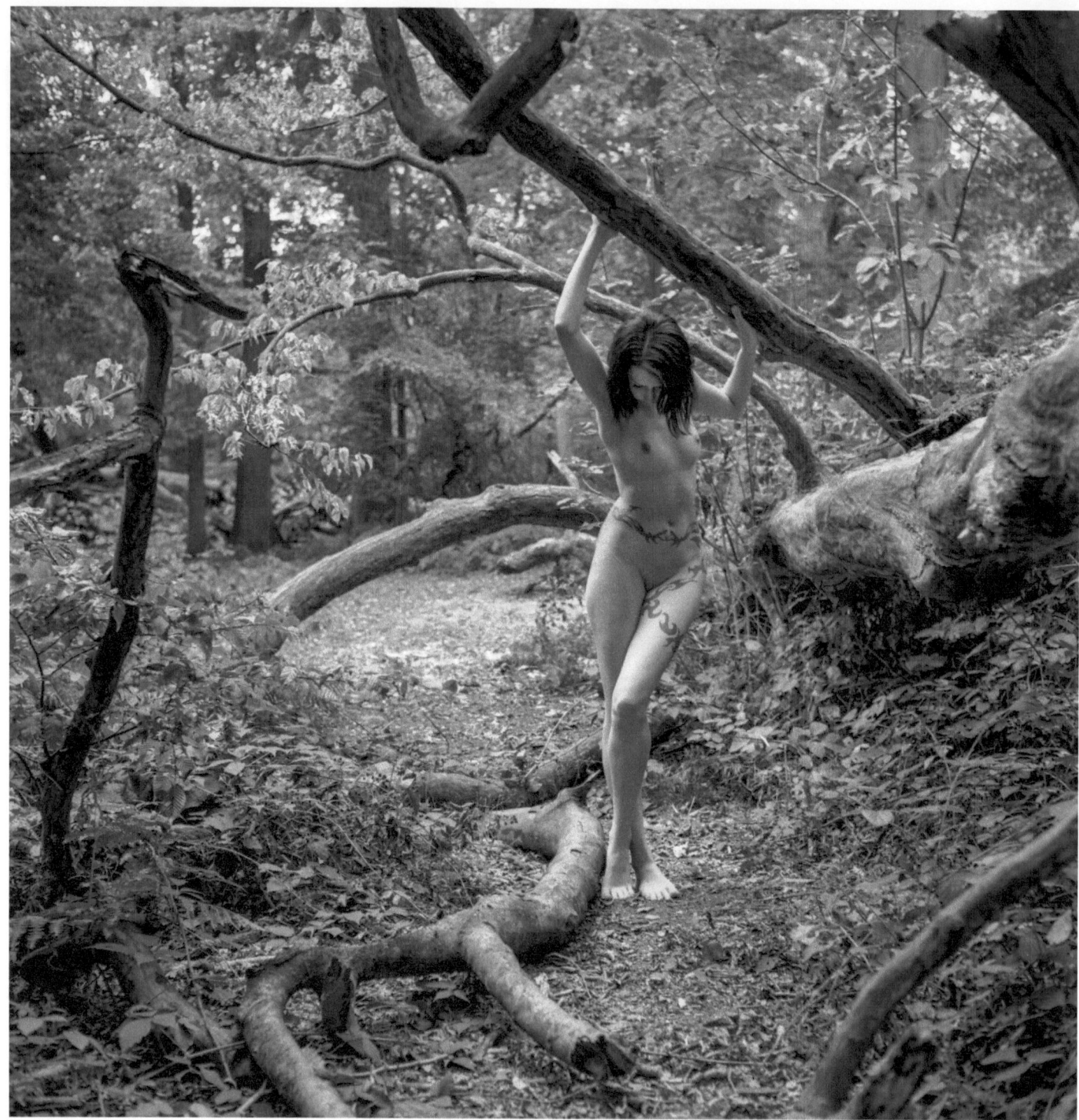

42

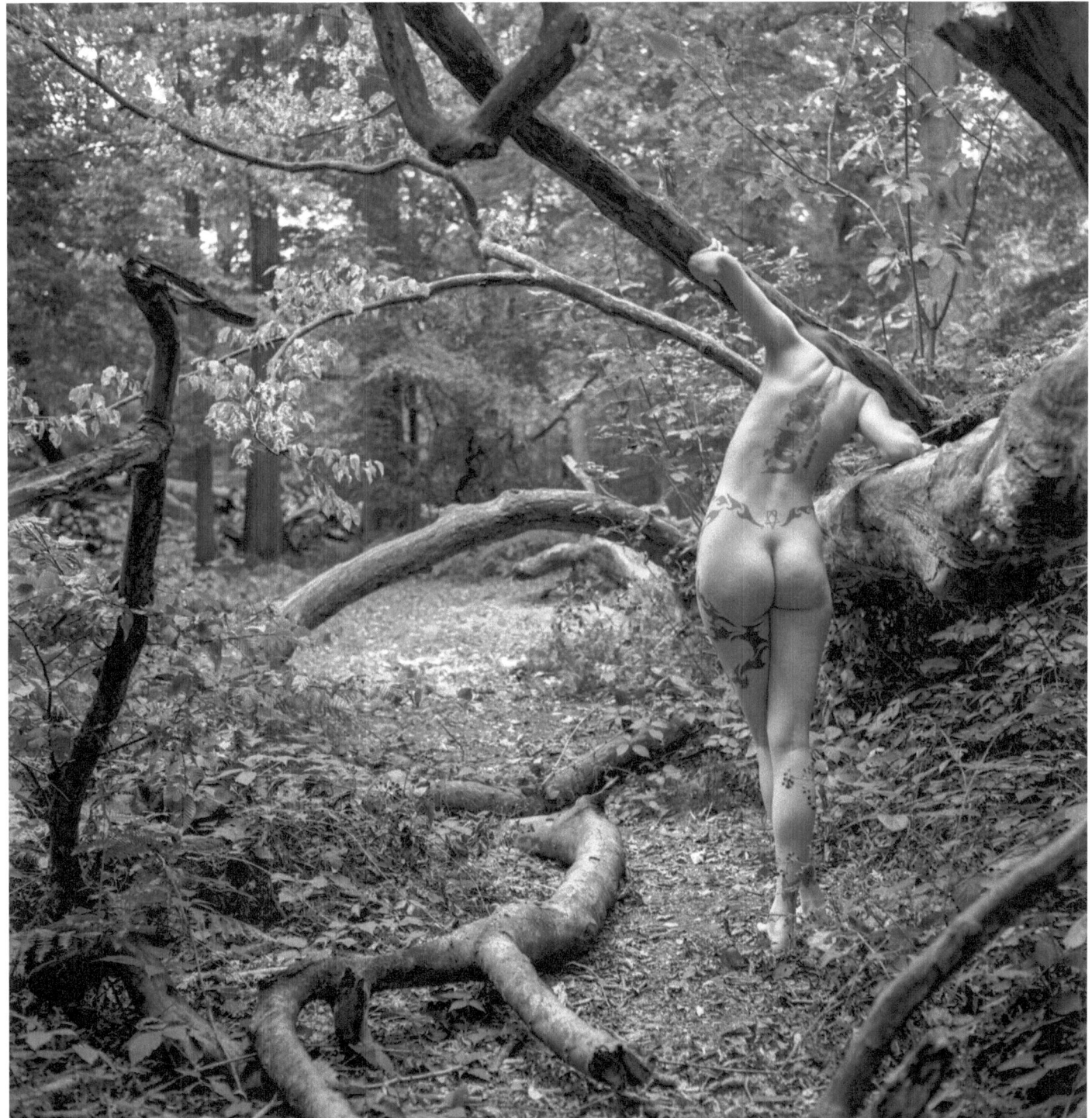

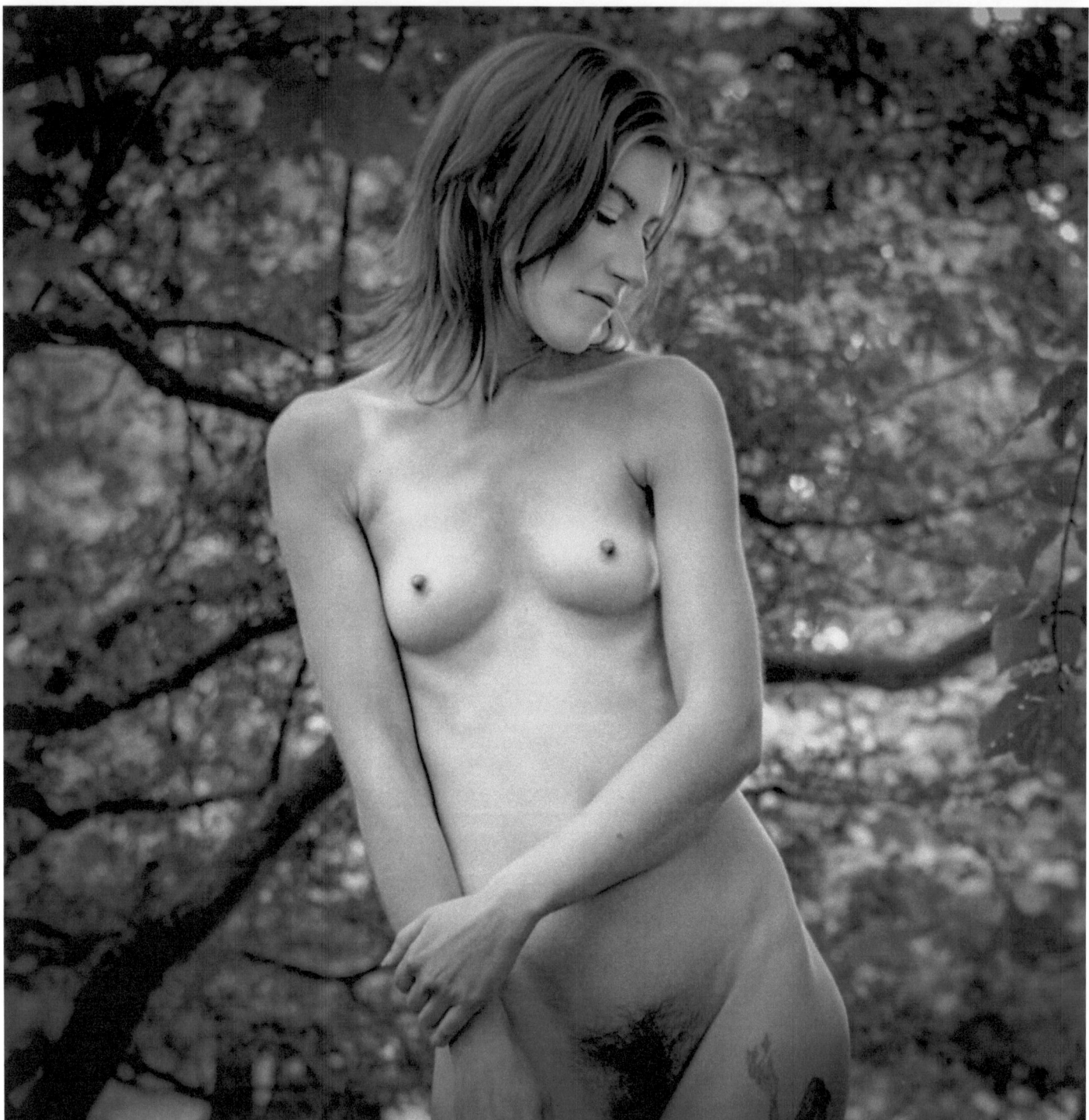

44

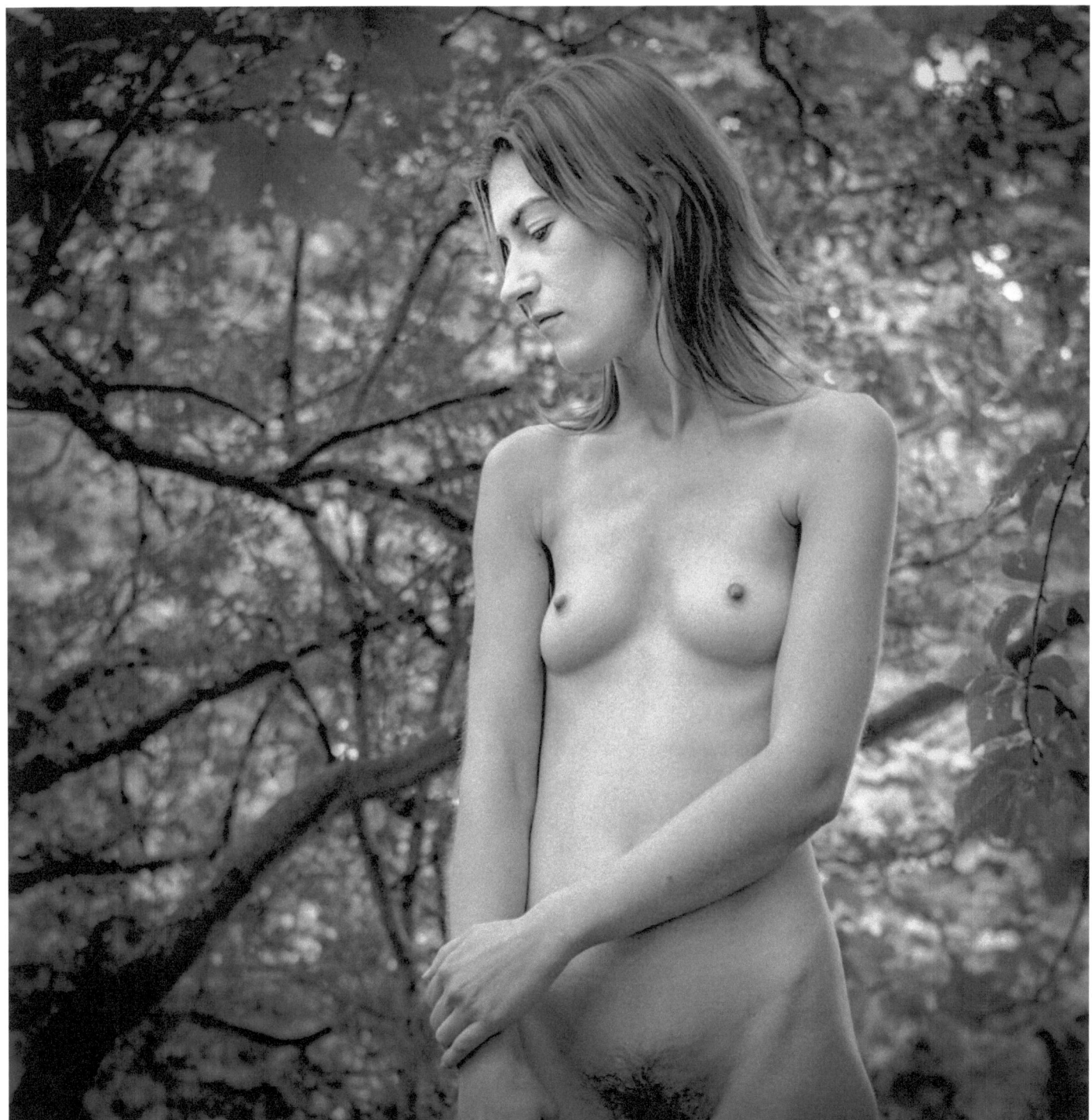

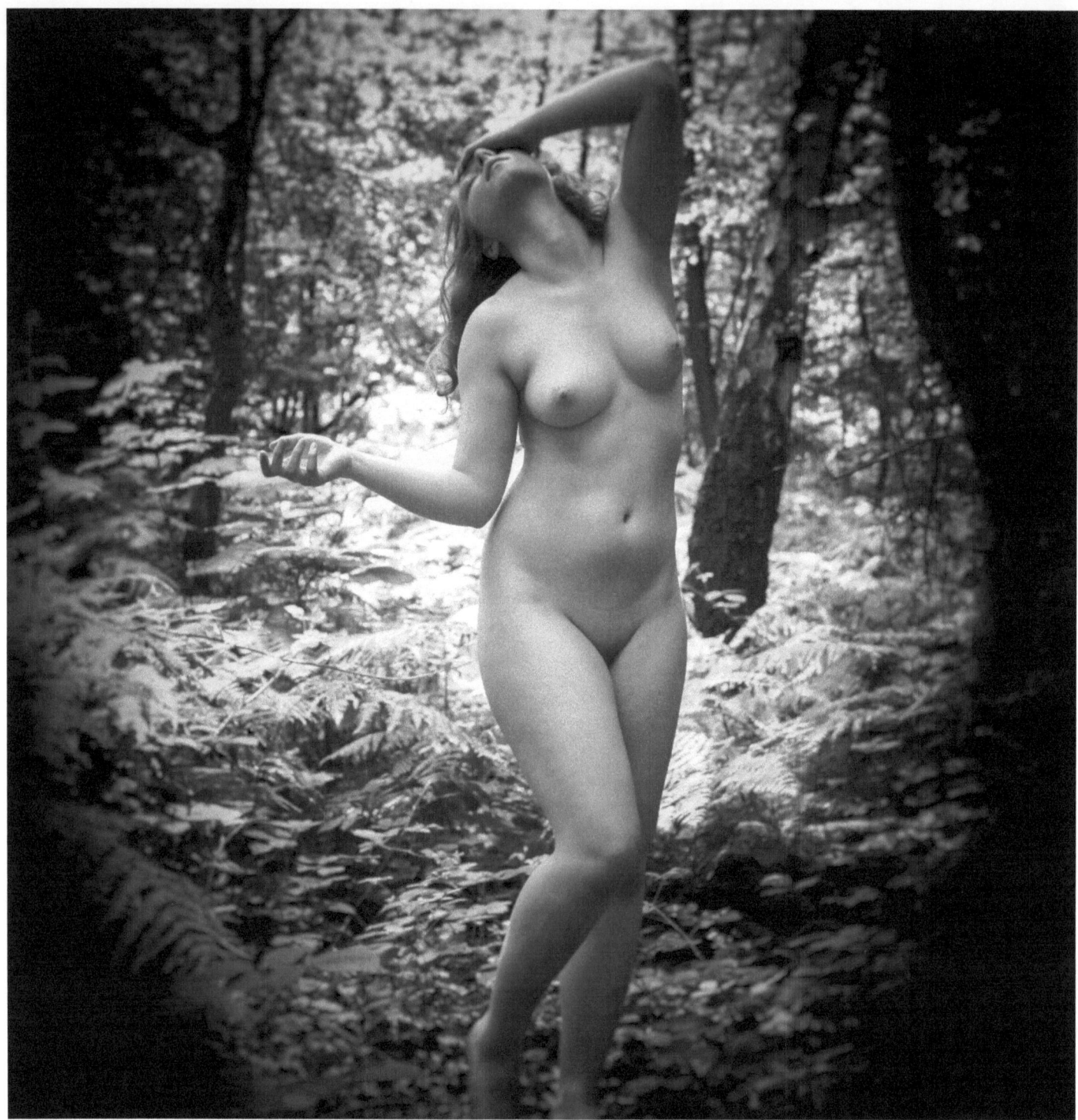

46

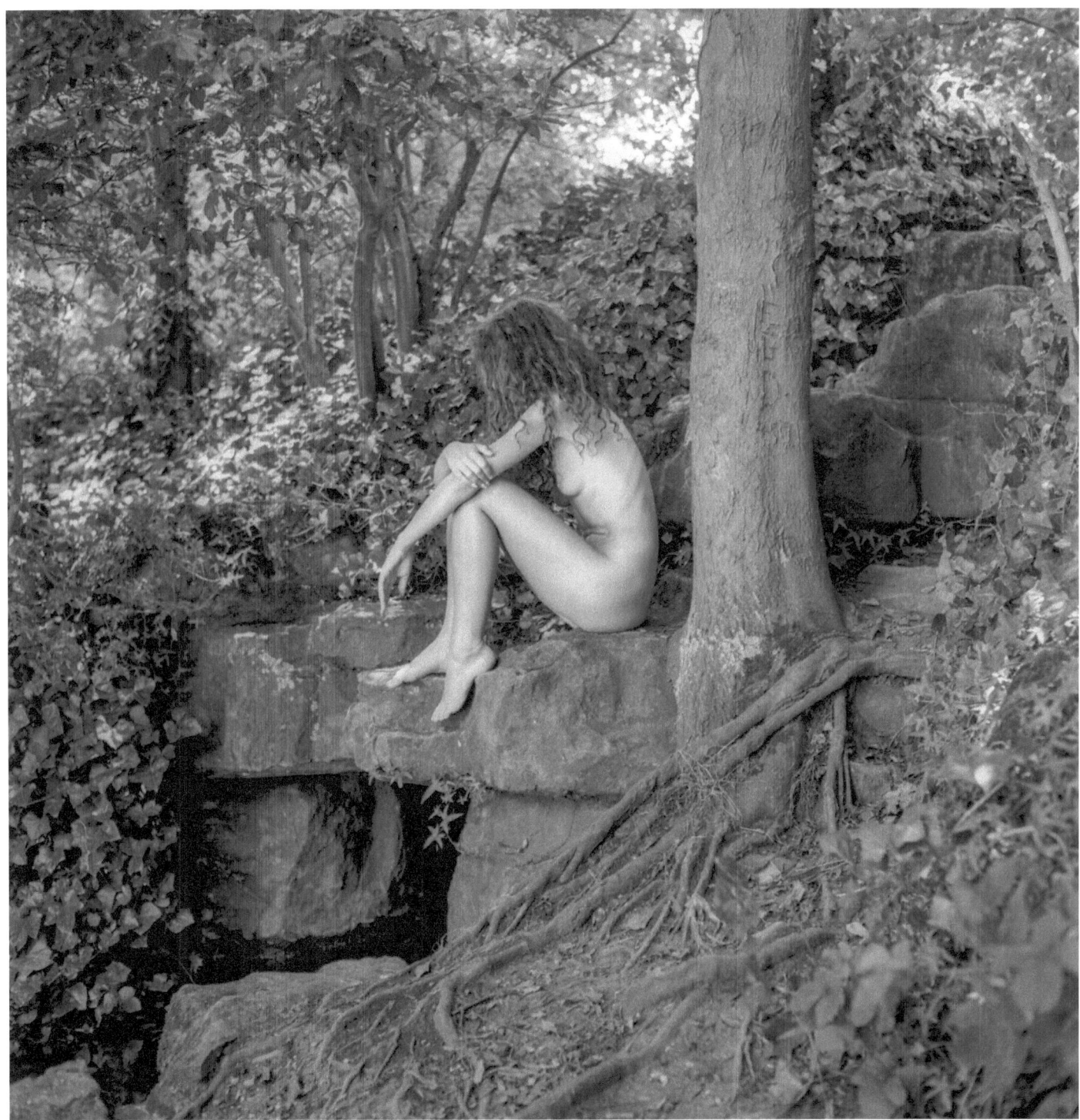

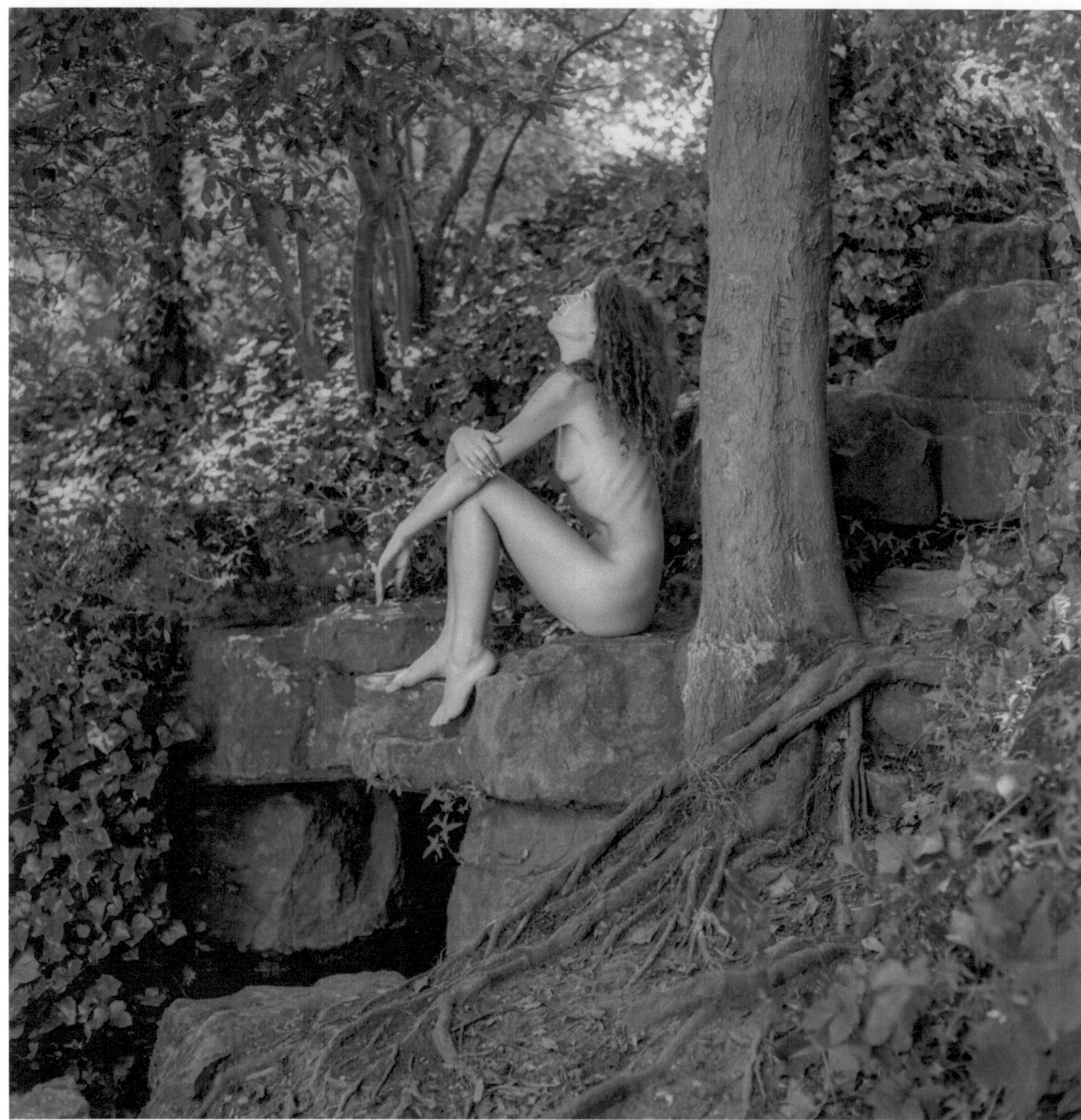

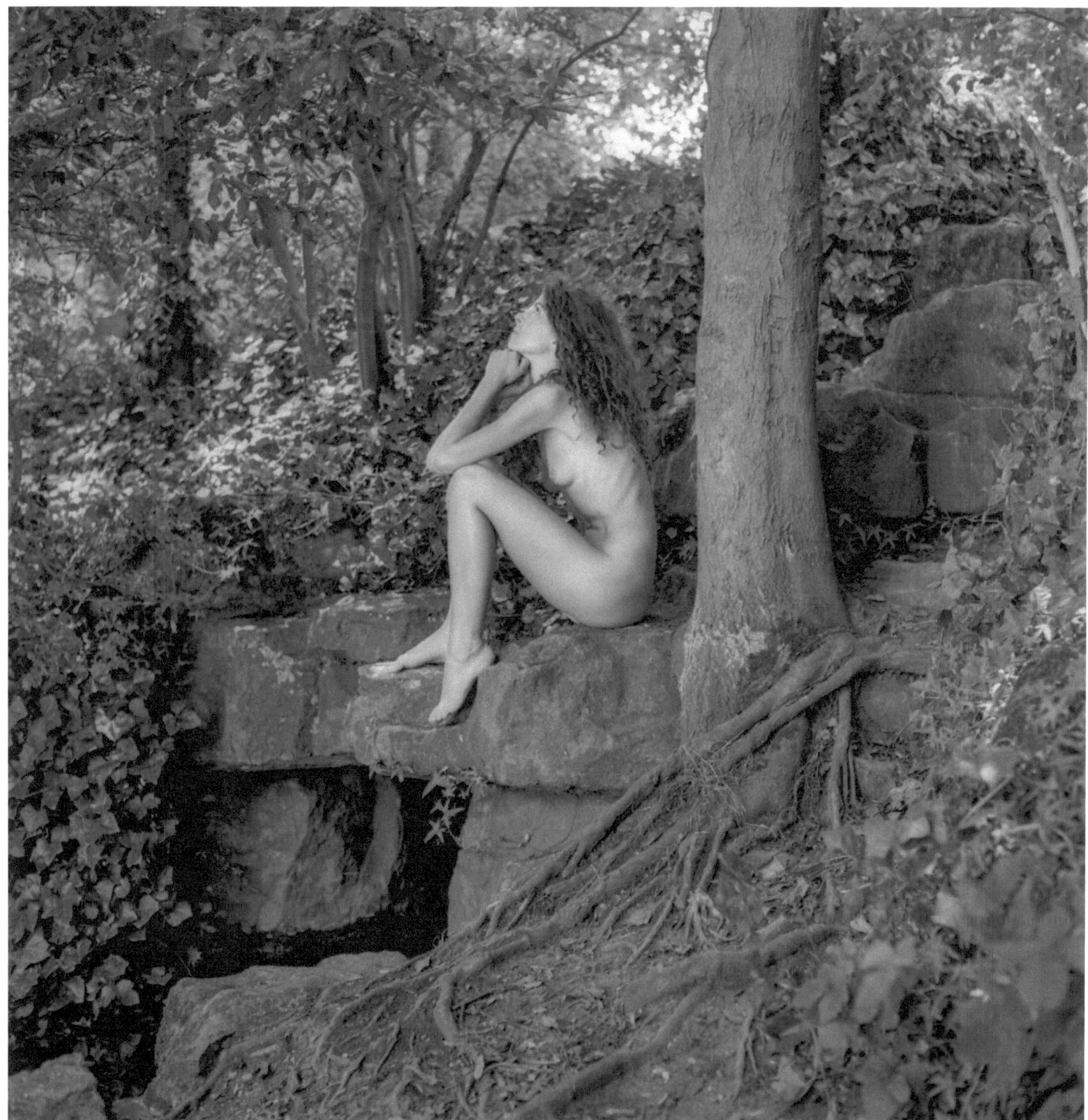

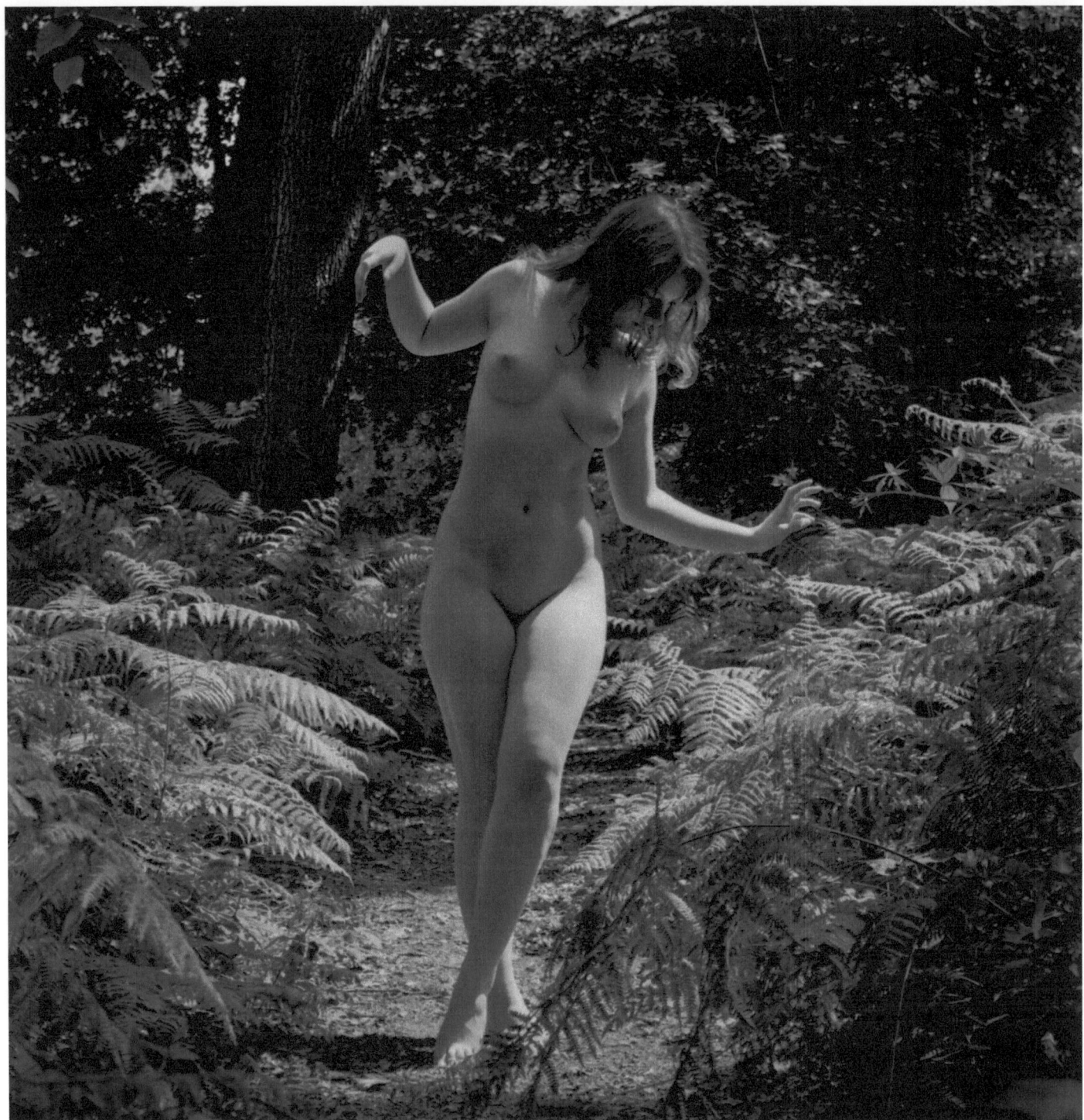

50

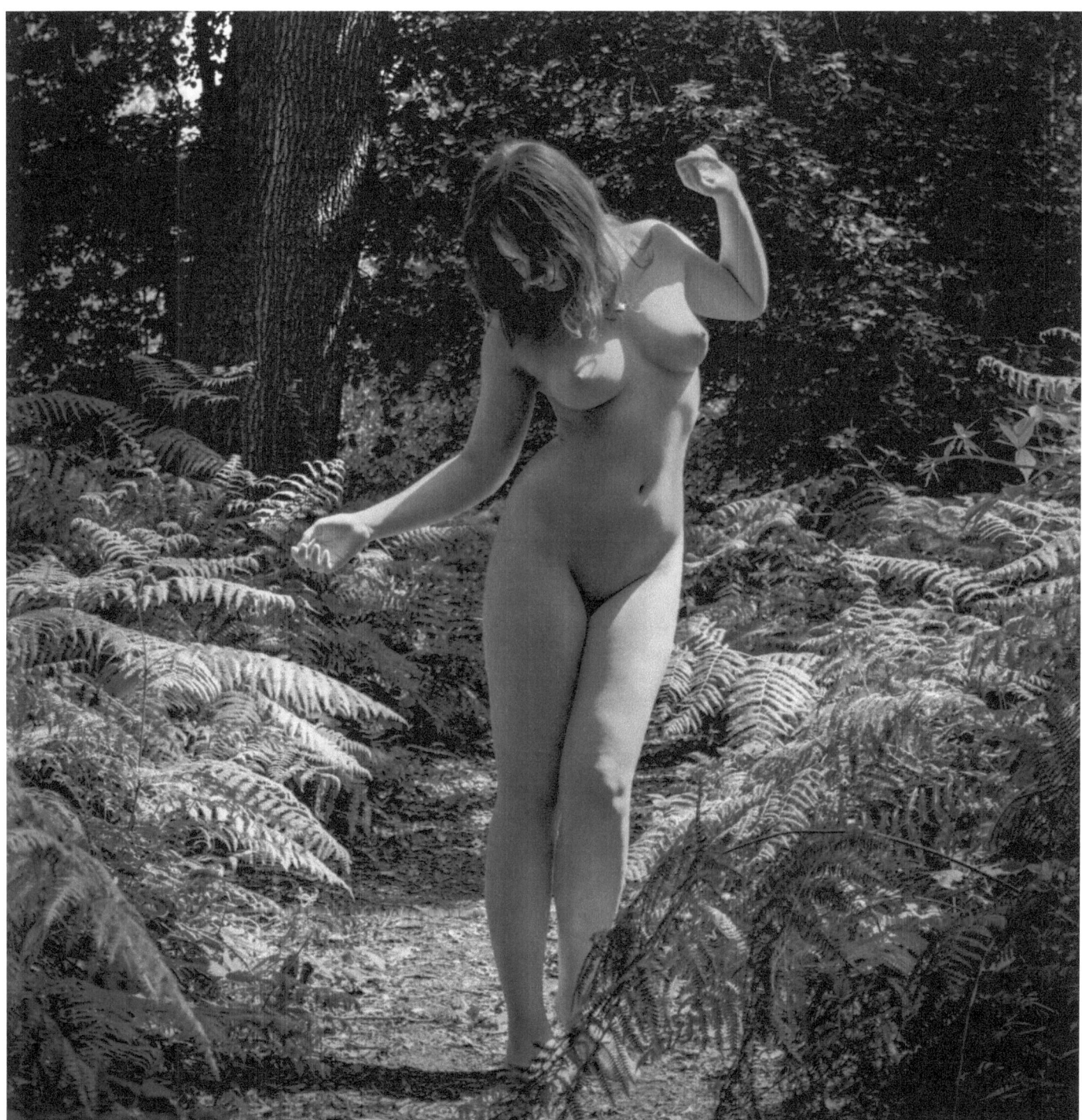

51

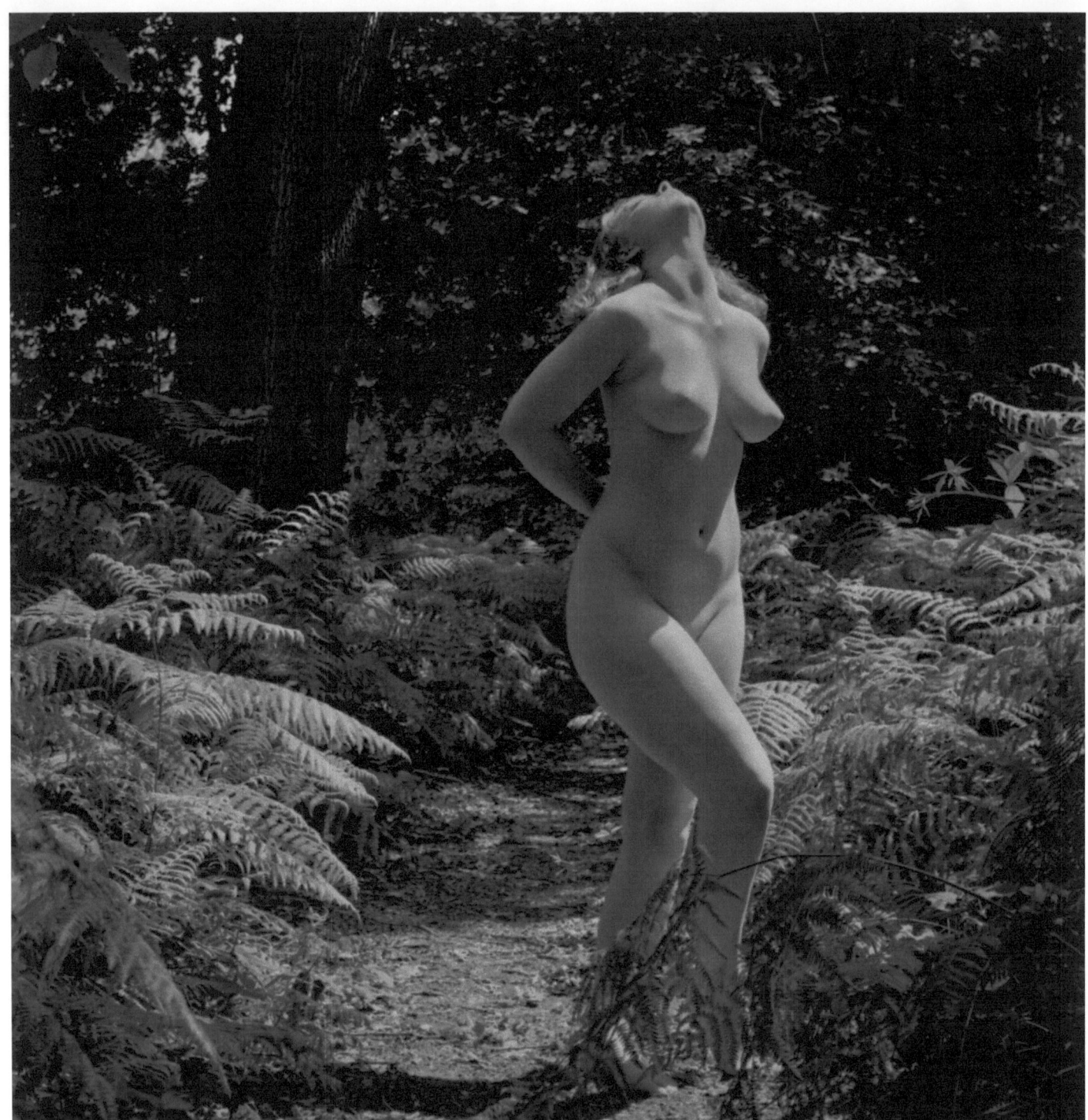

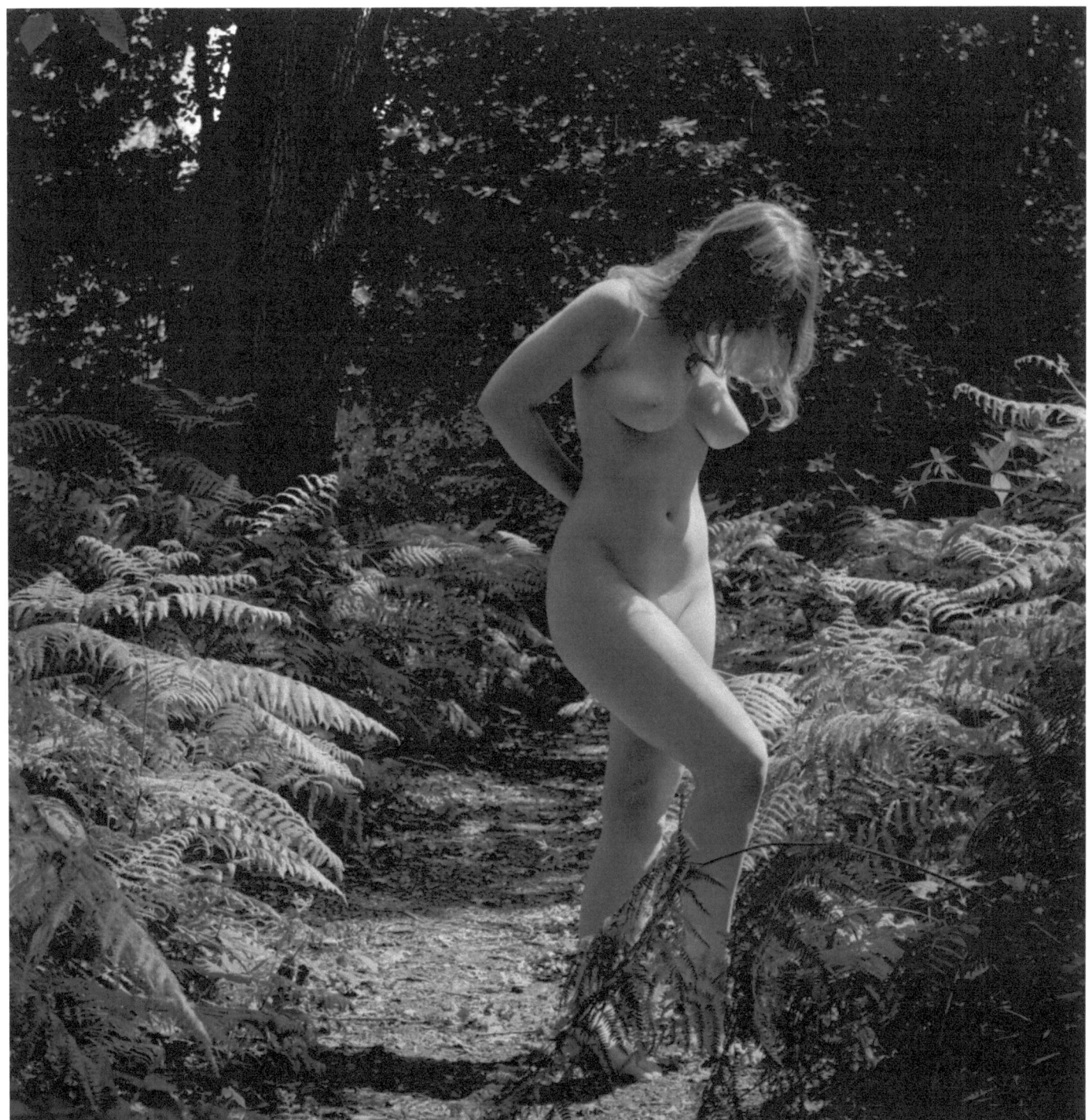

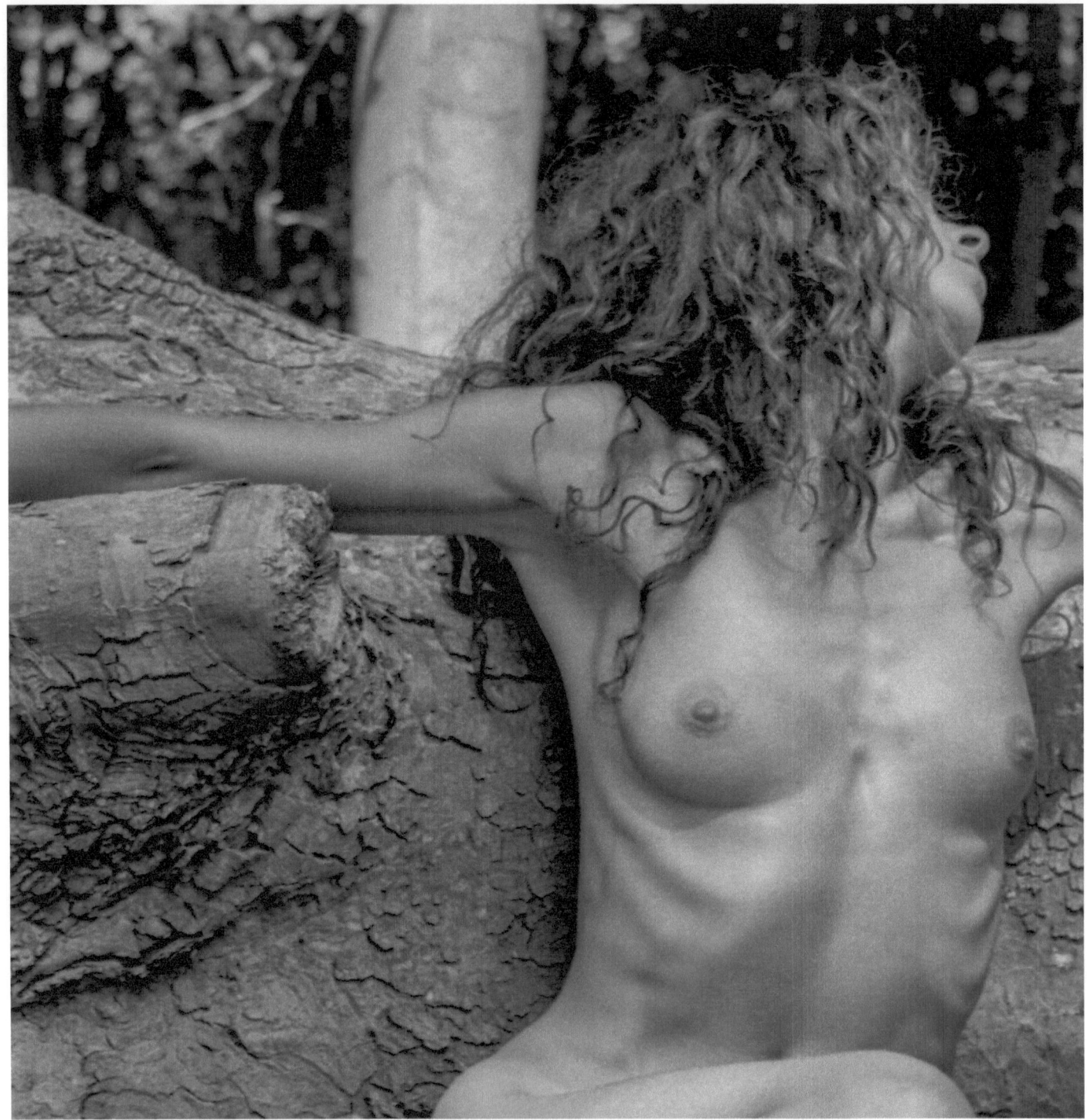

54

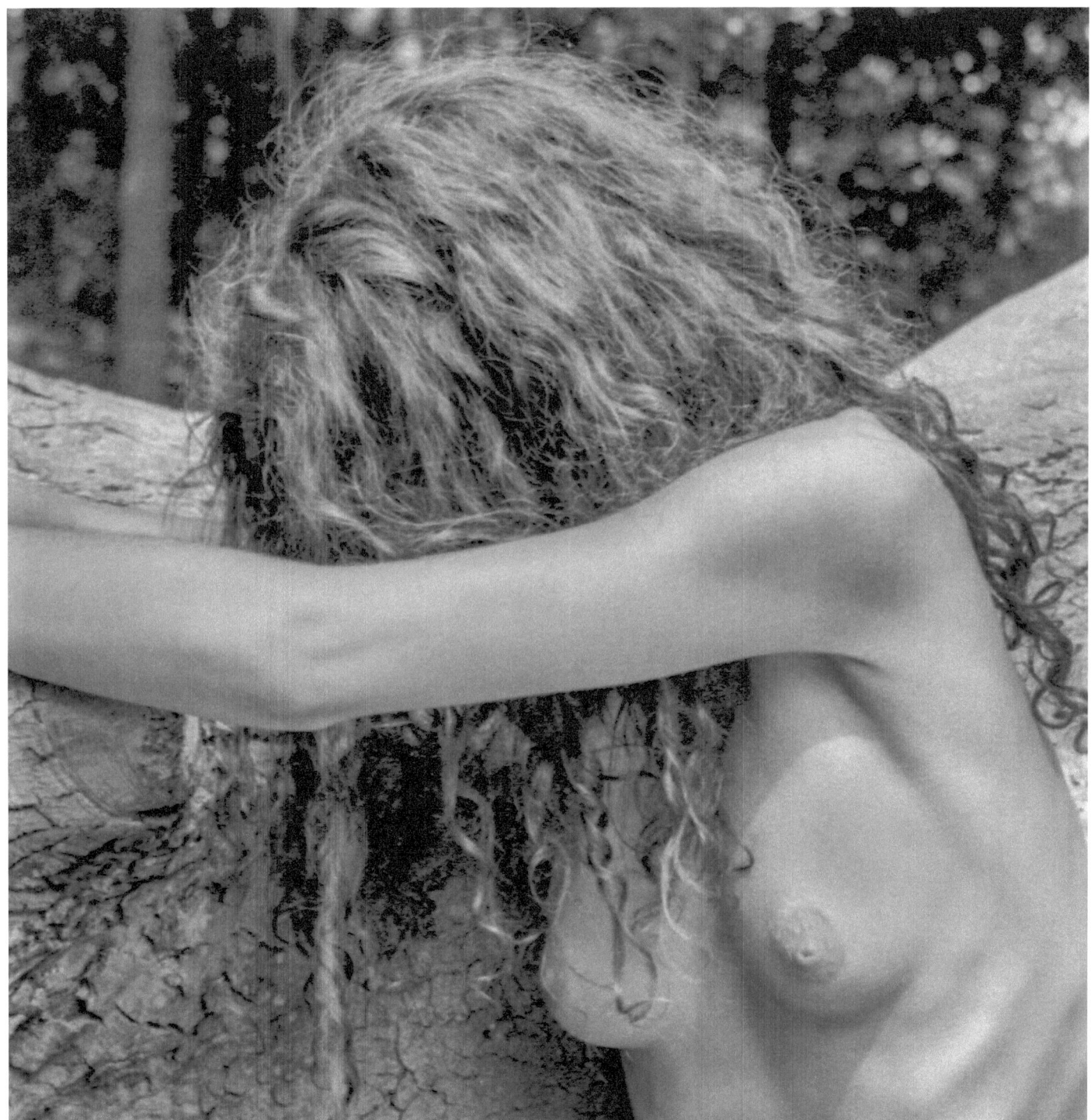

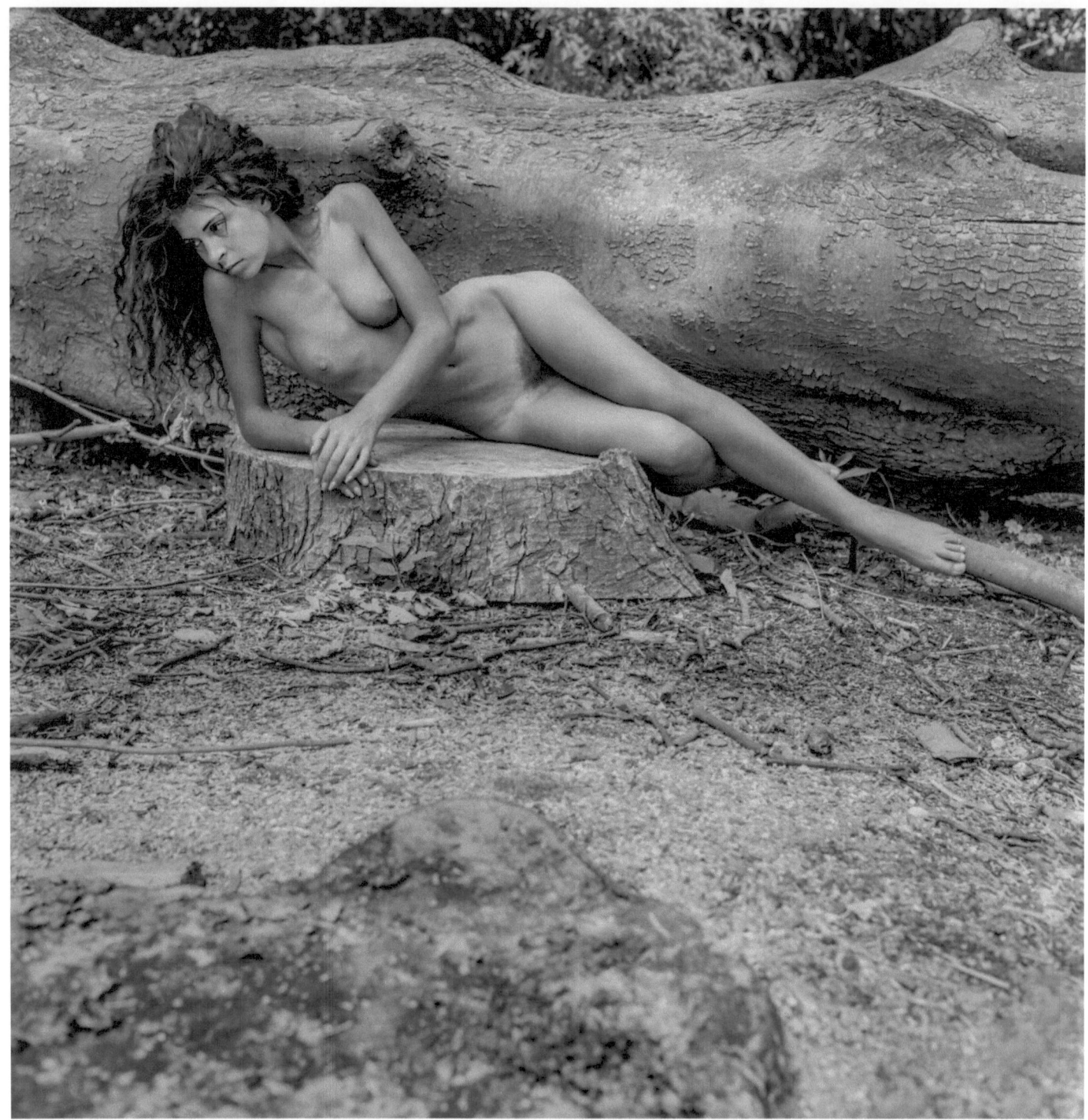

56

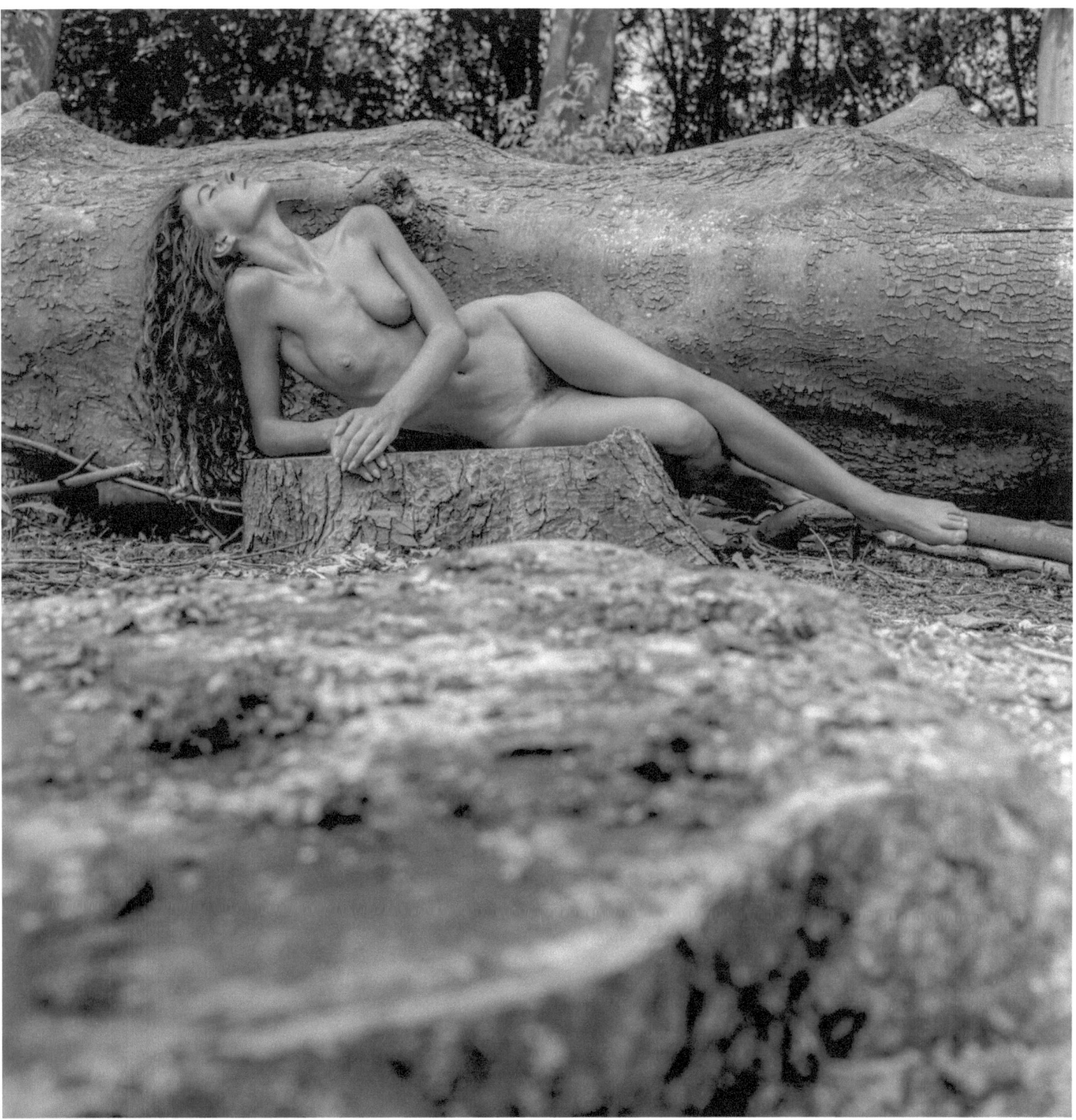

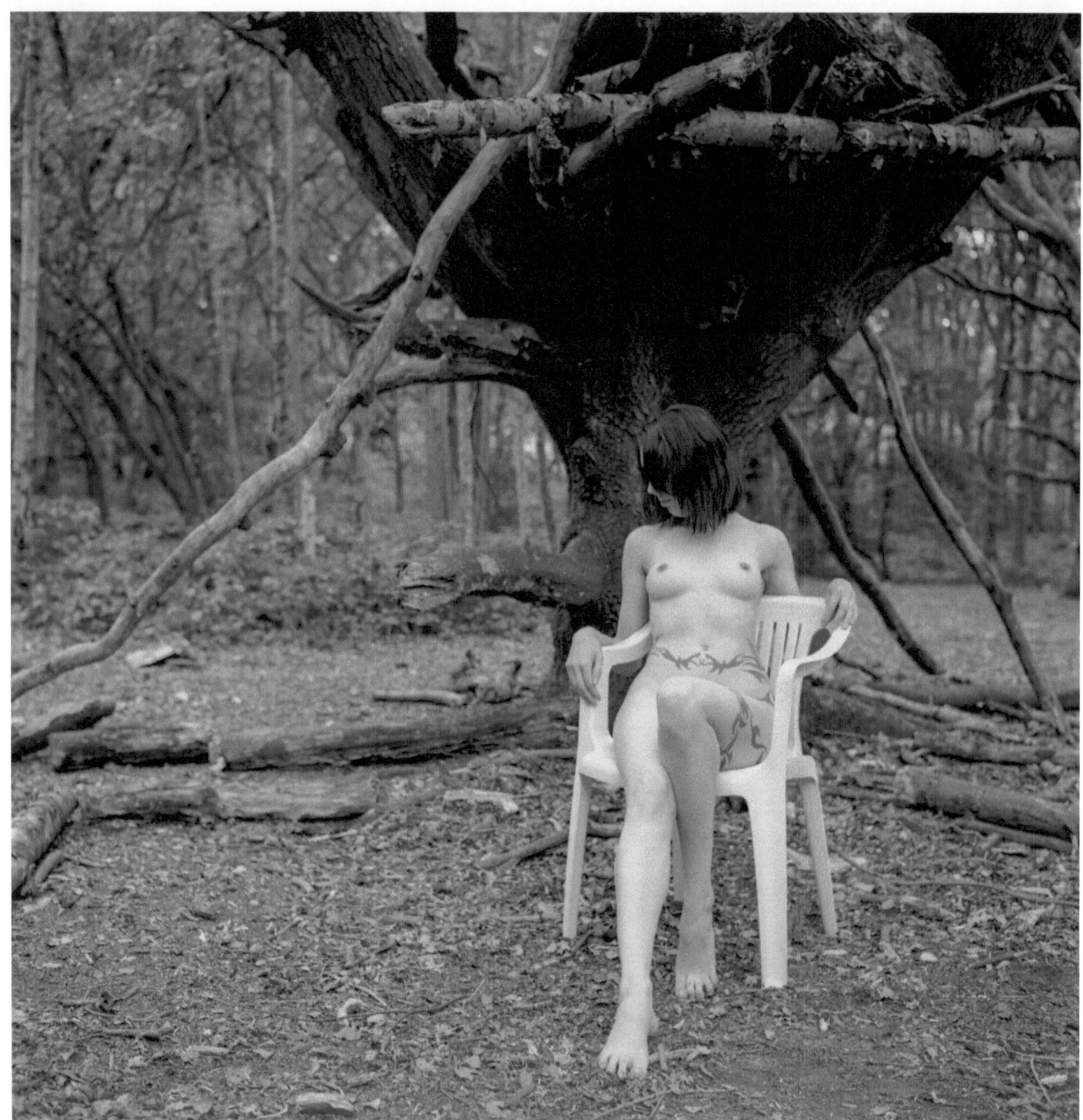

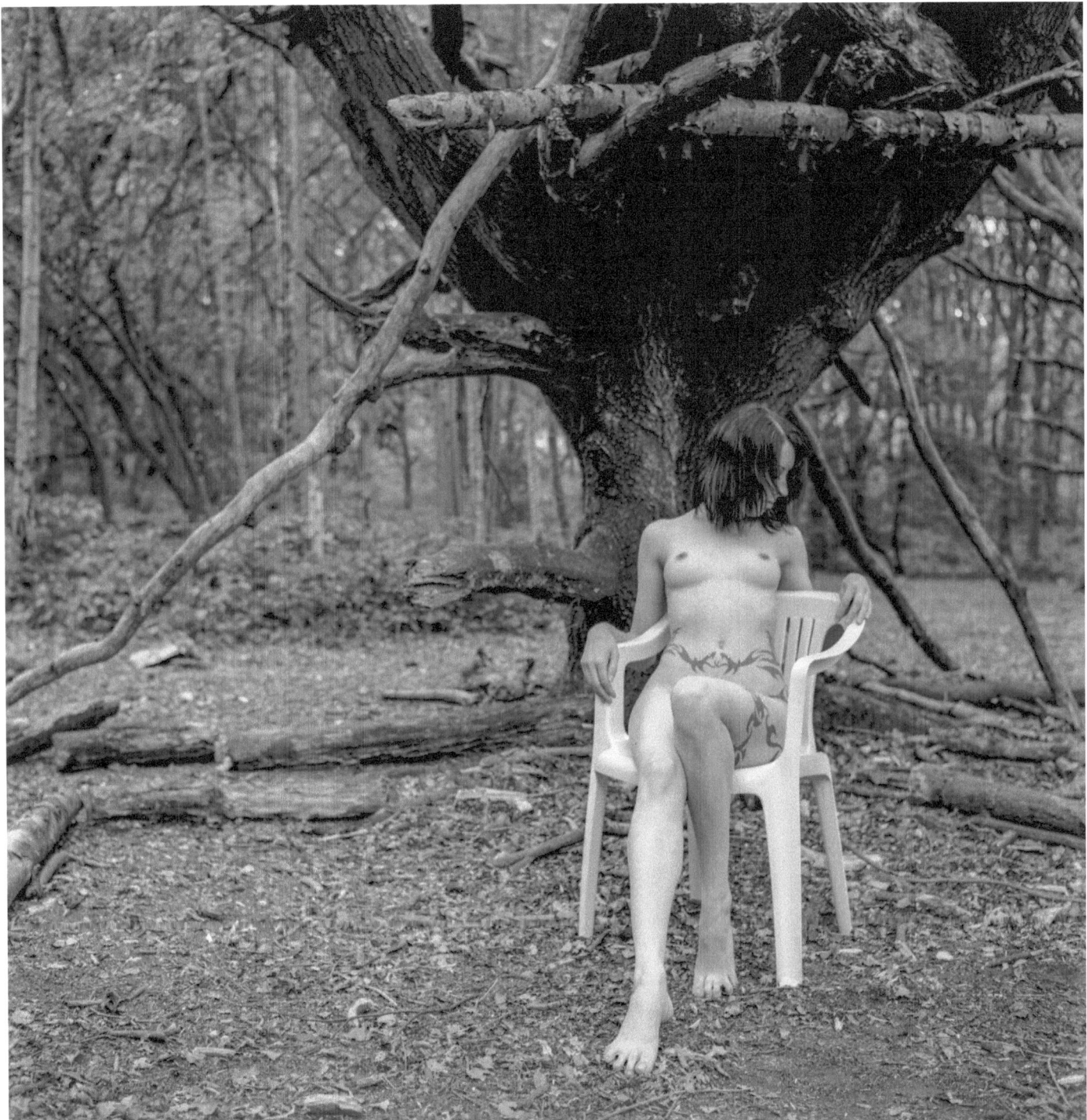

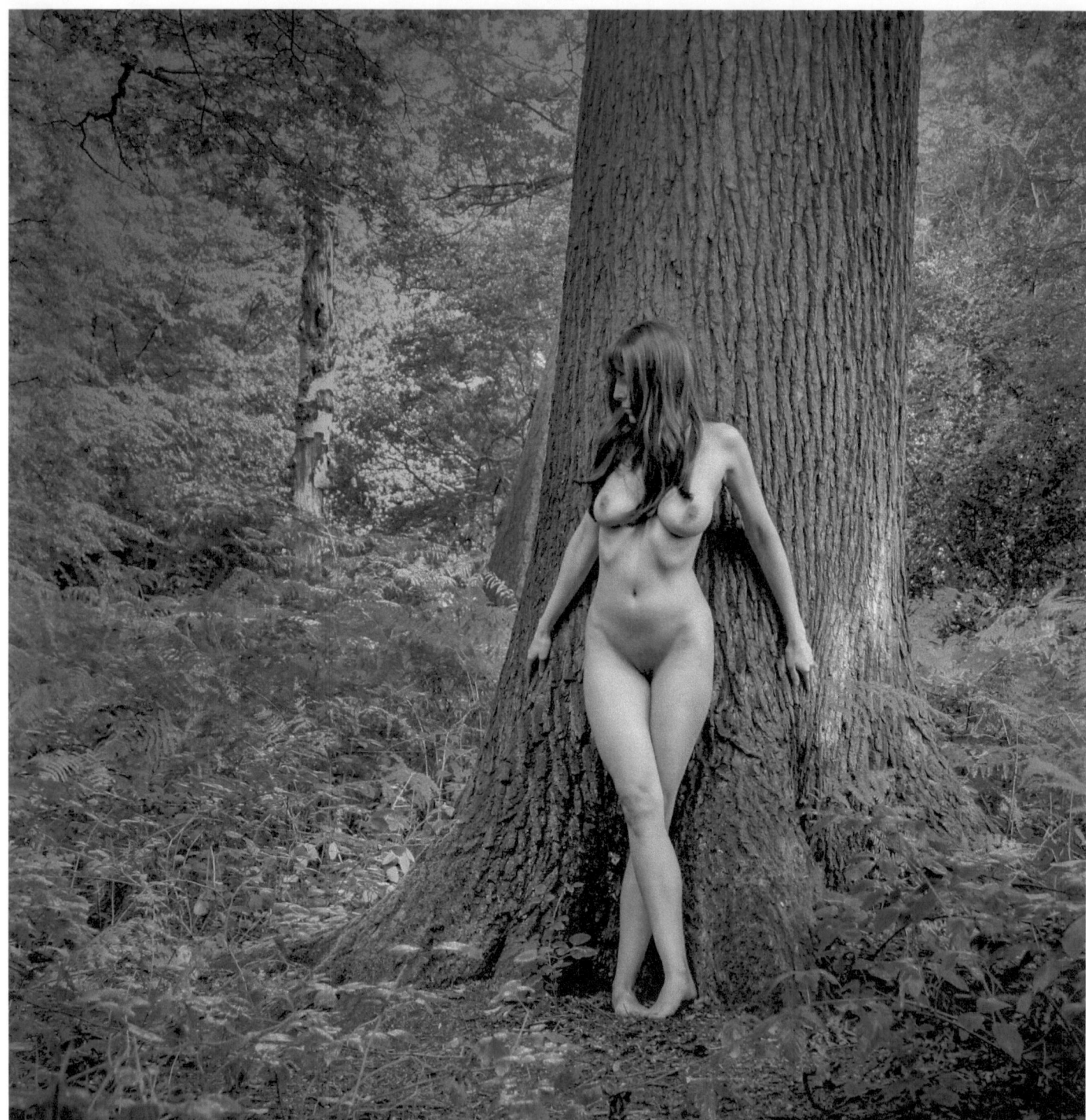

60

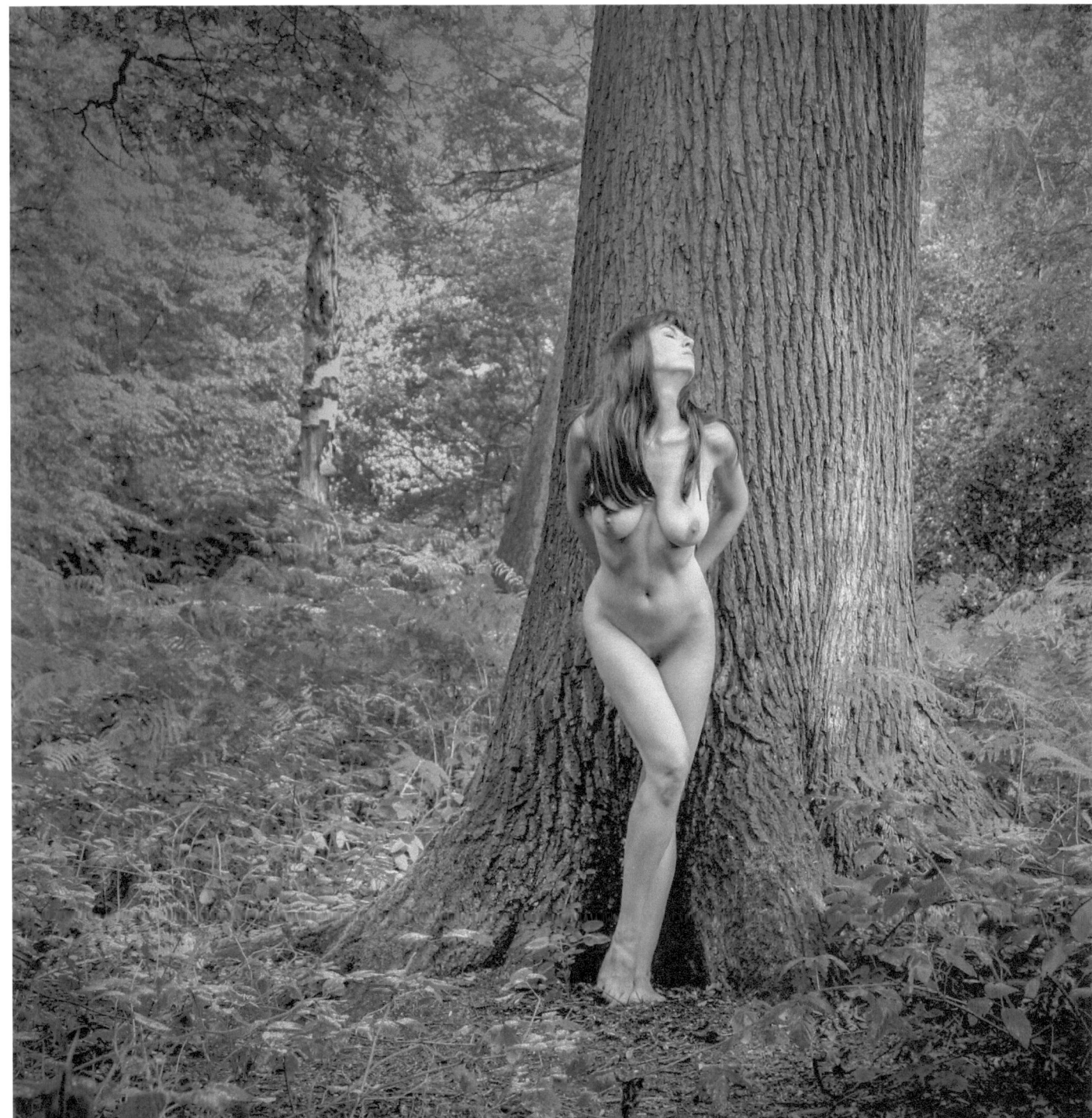

61

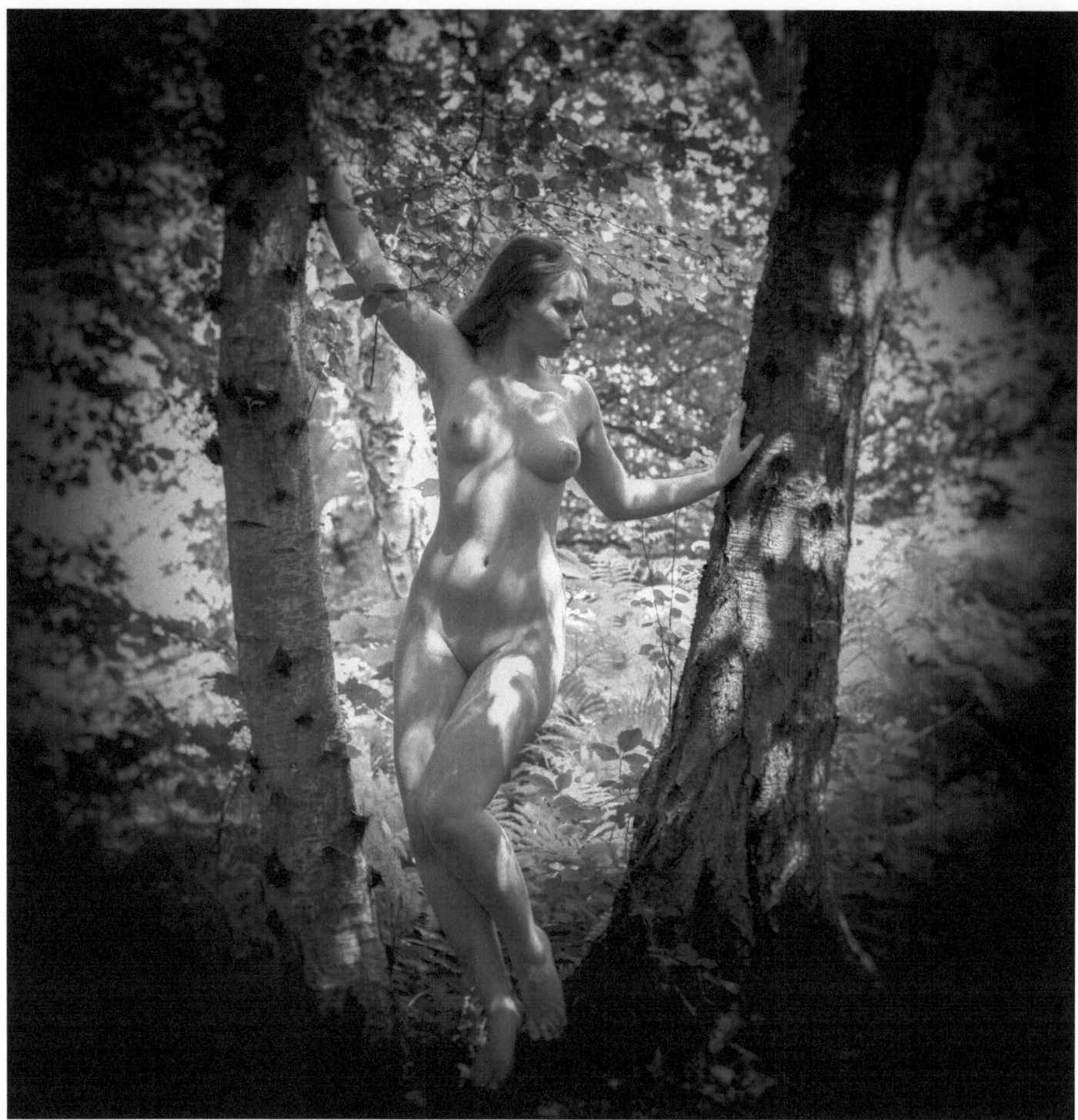

62

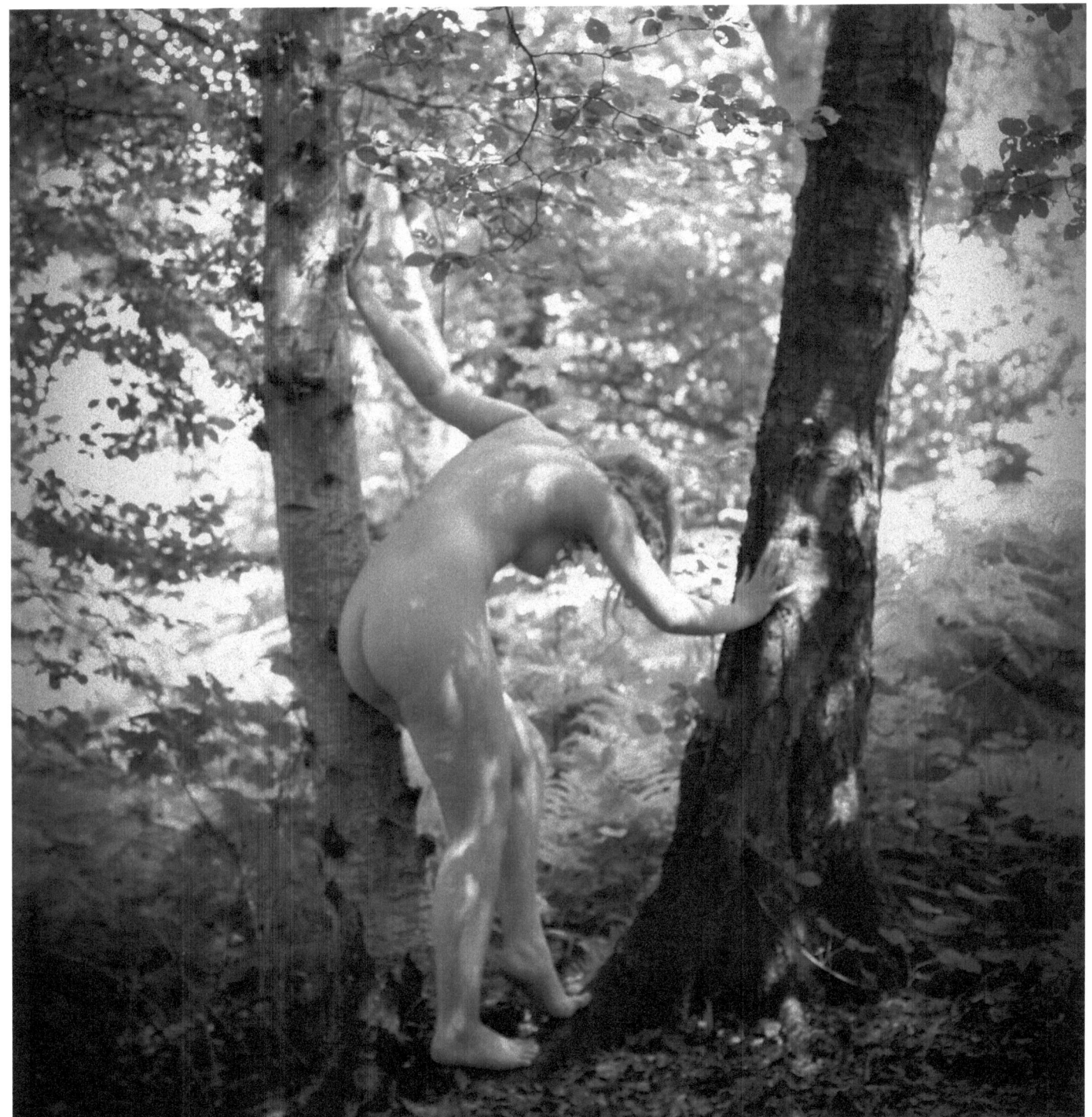

63

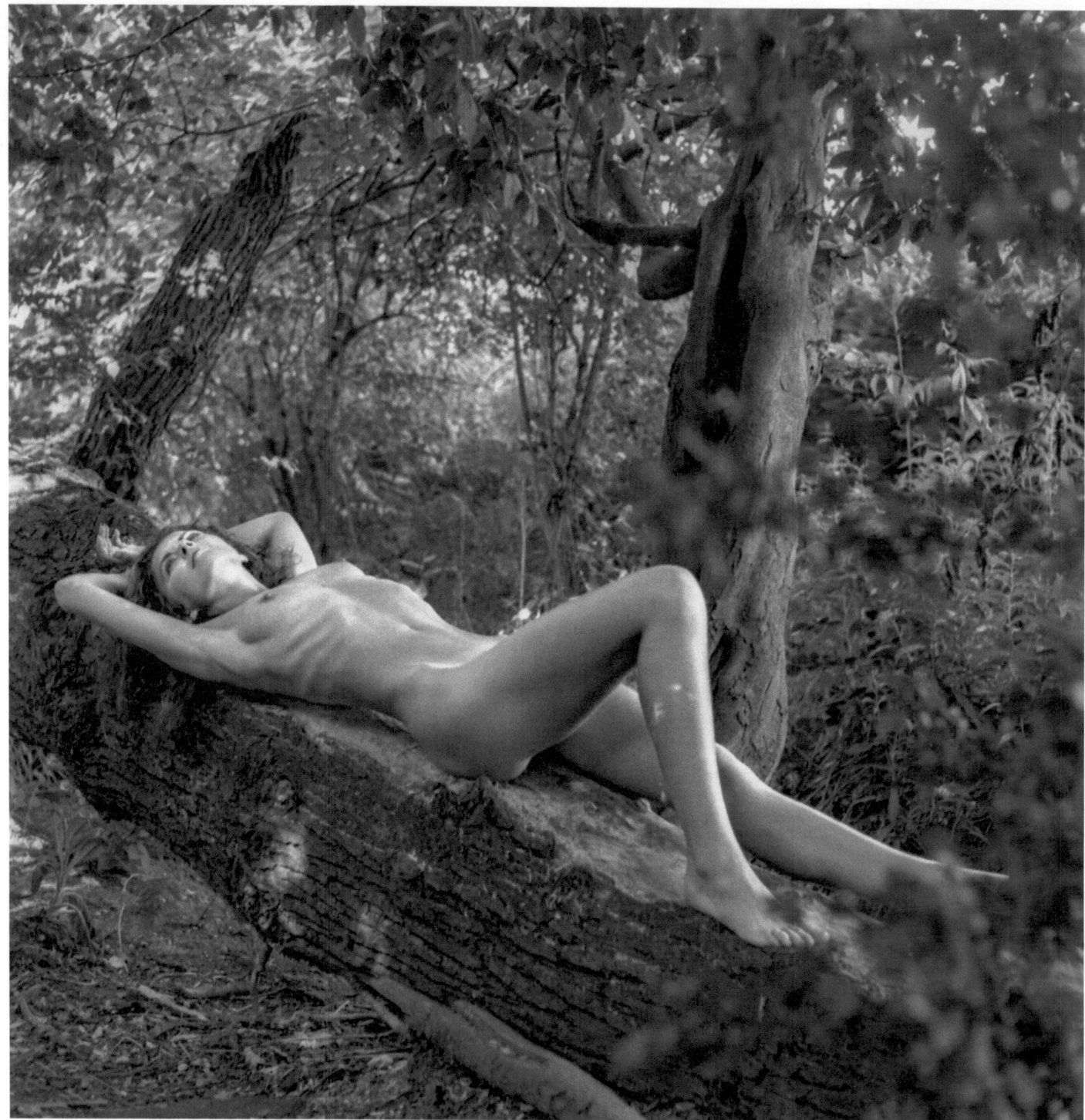

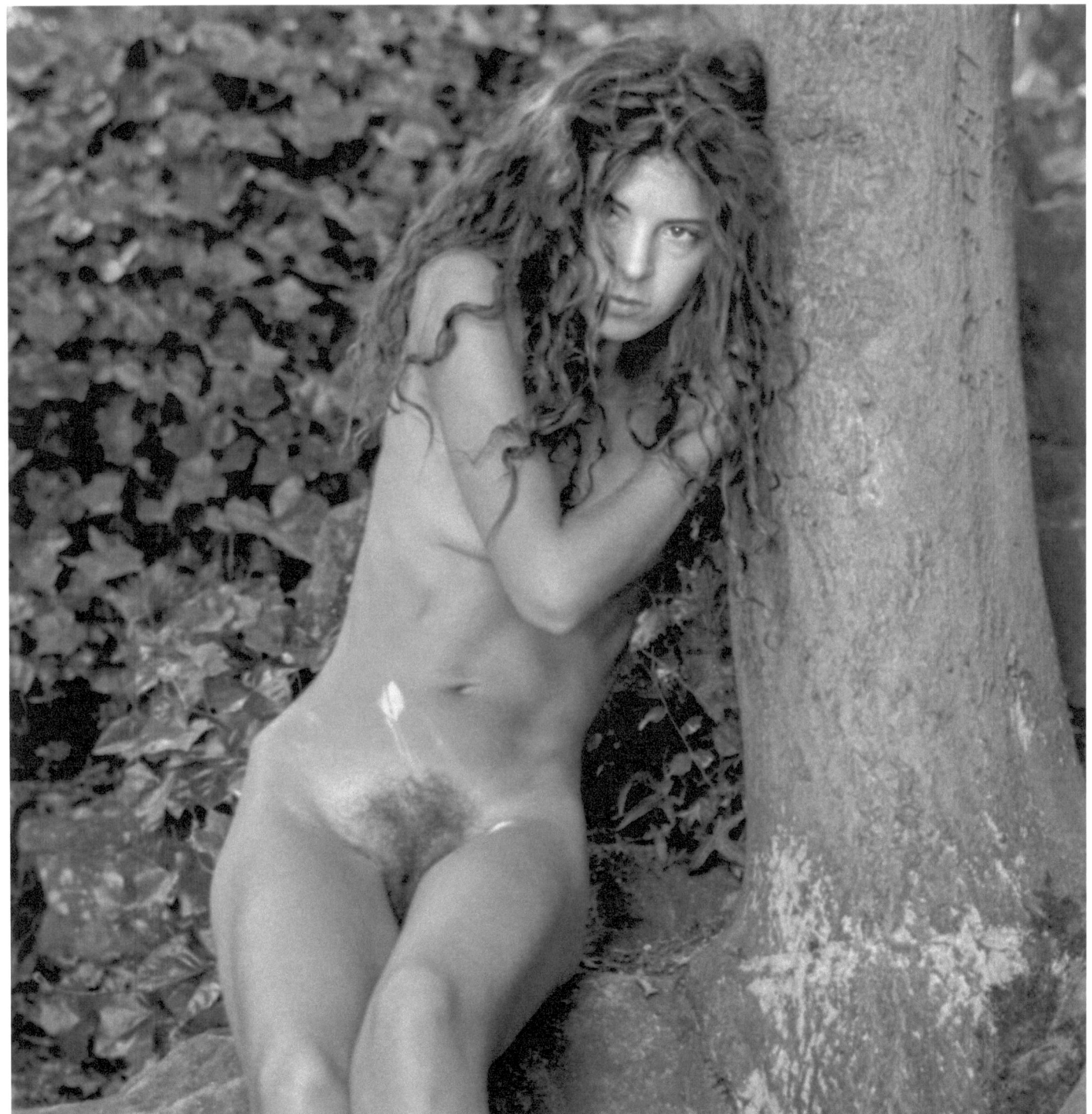

65

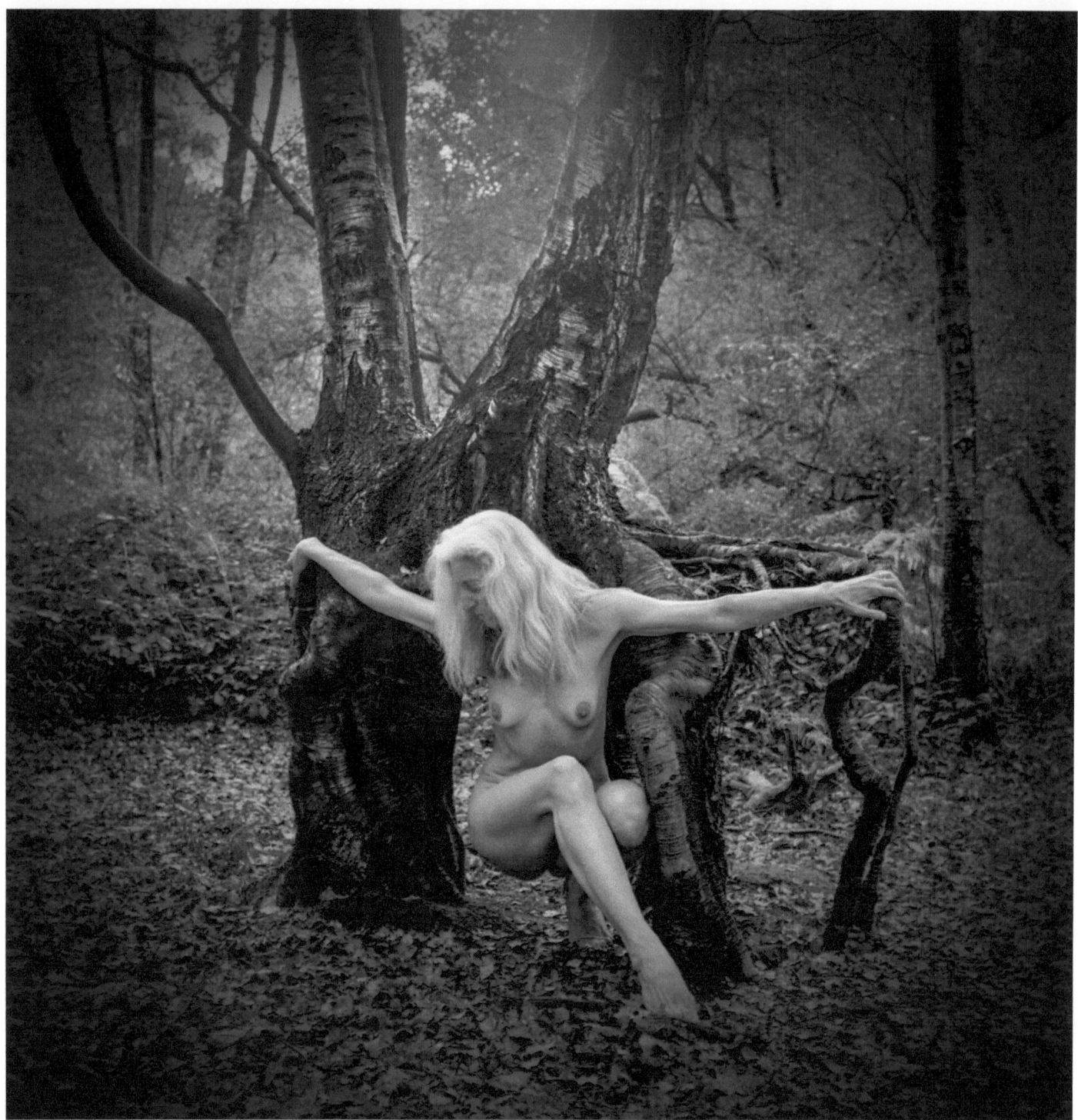

66

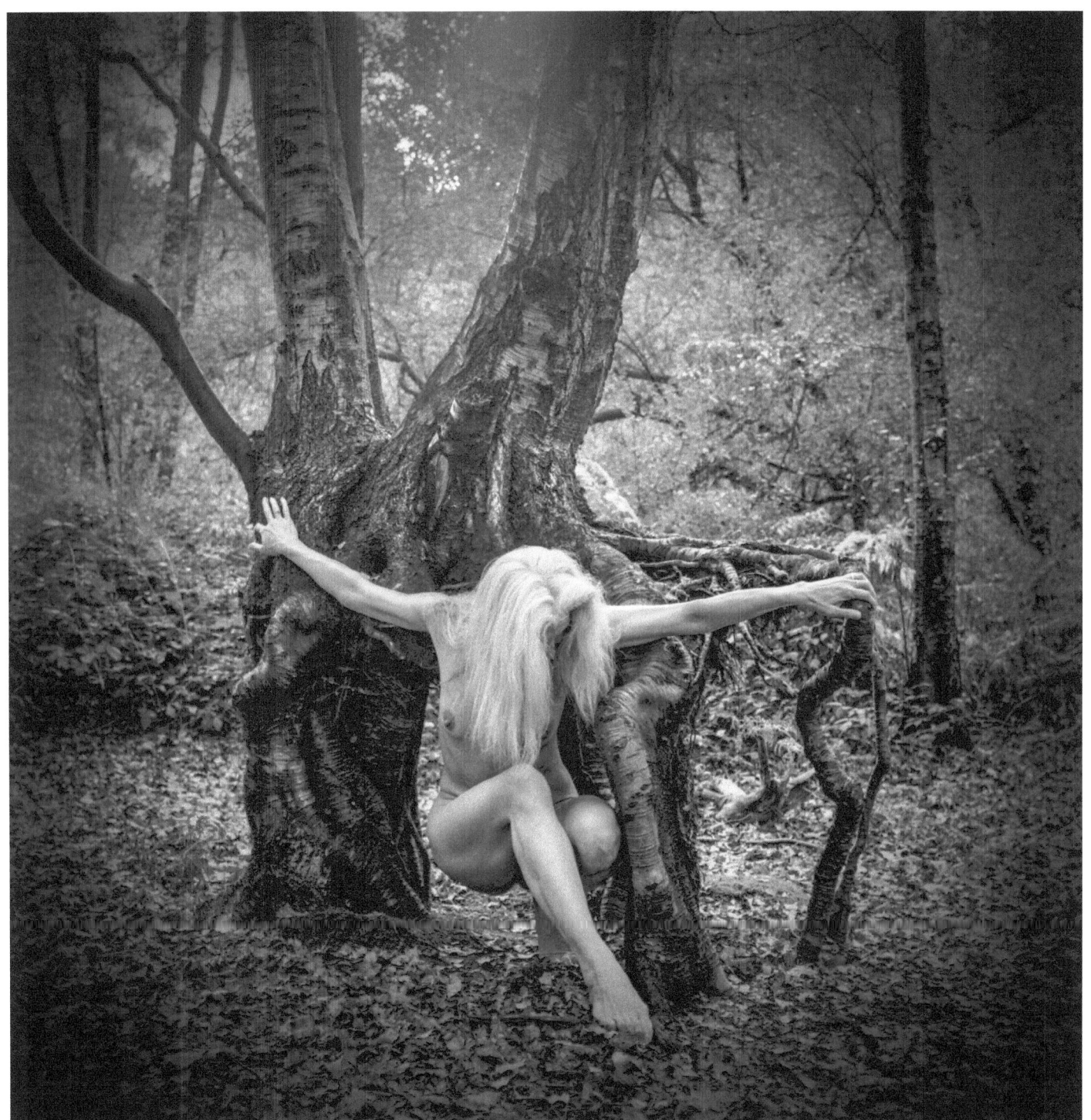

67

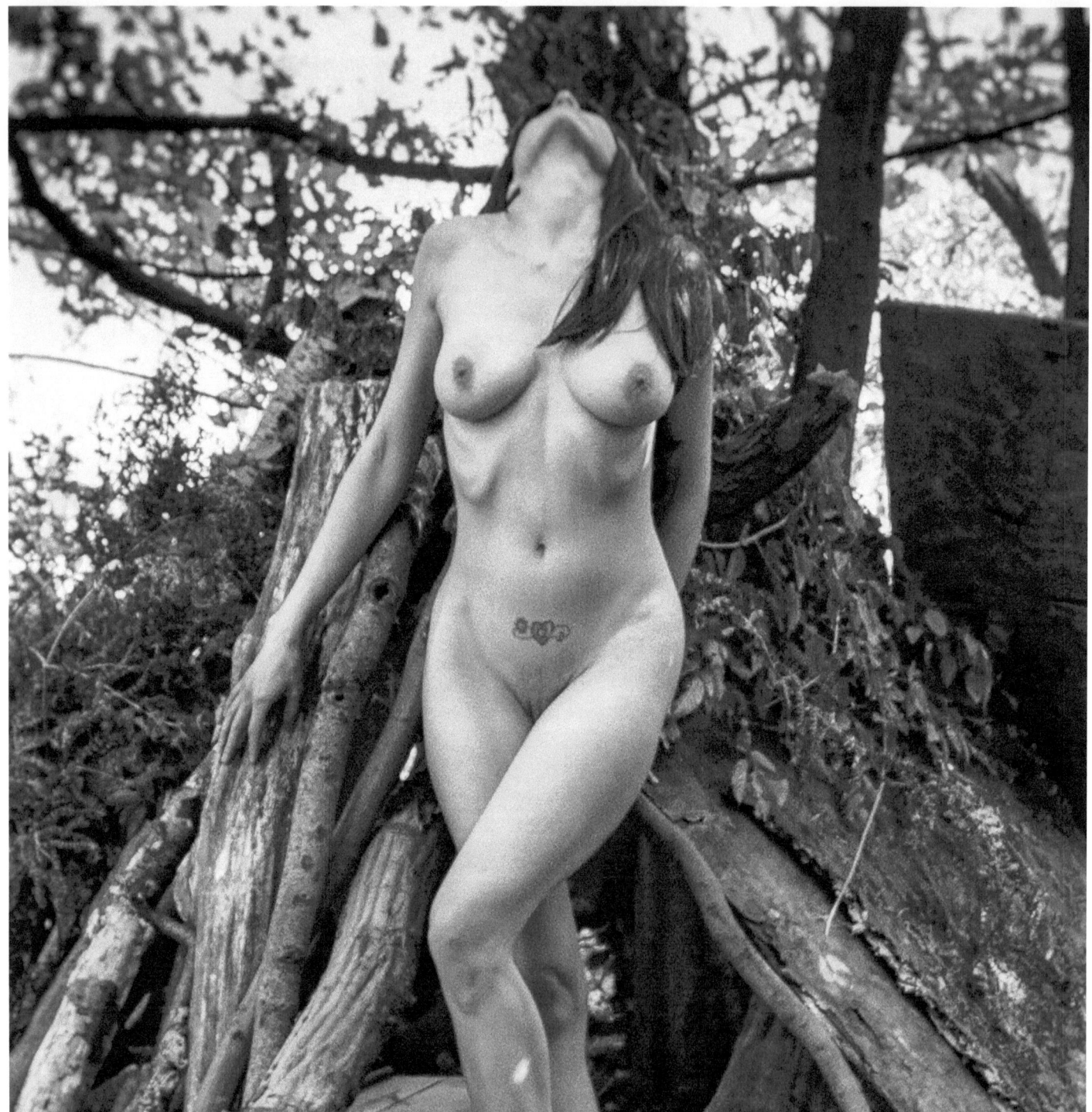

68

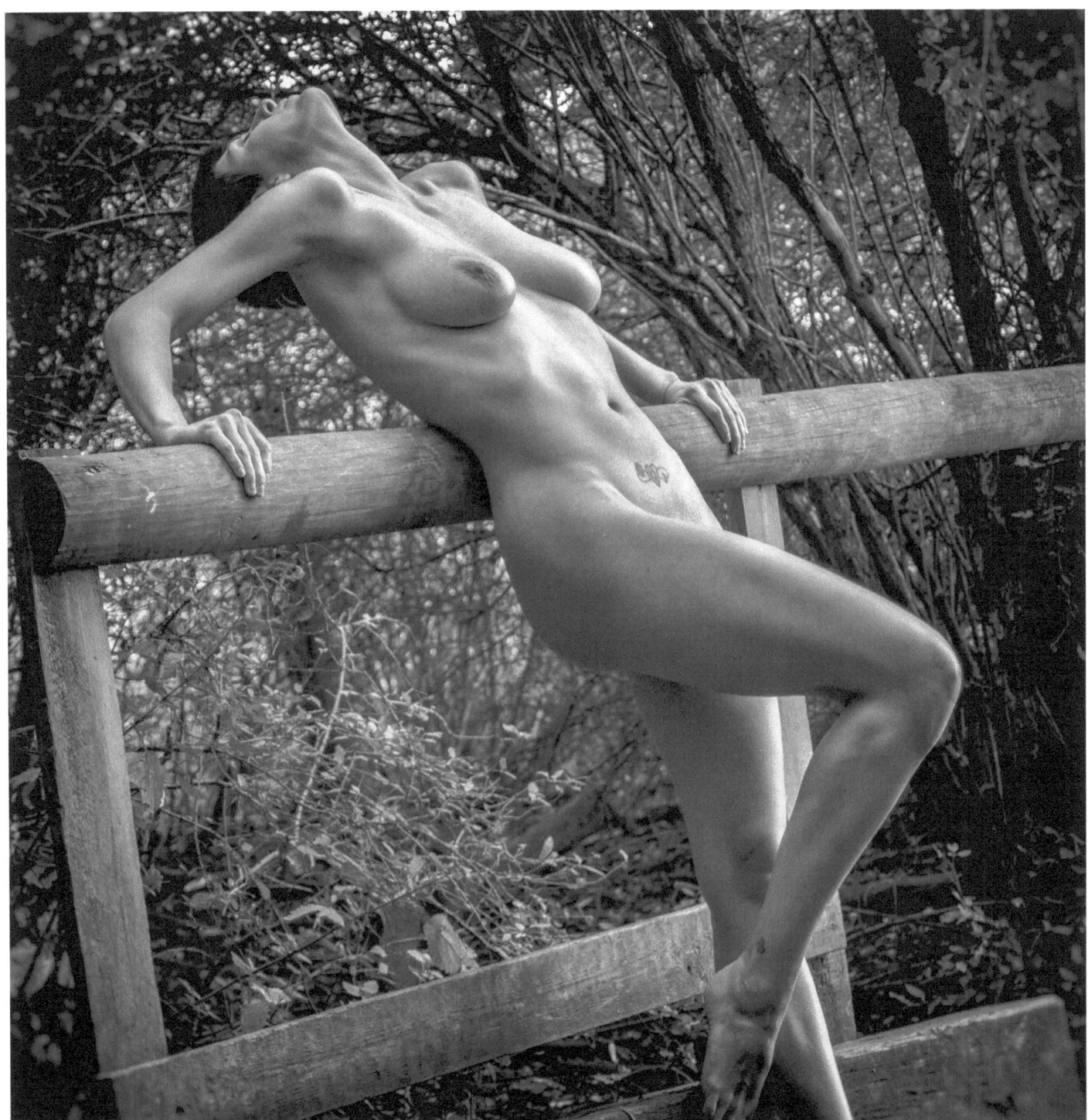

69

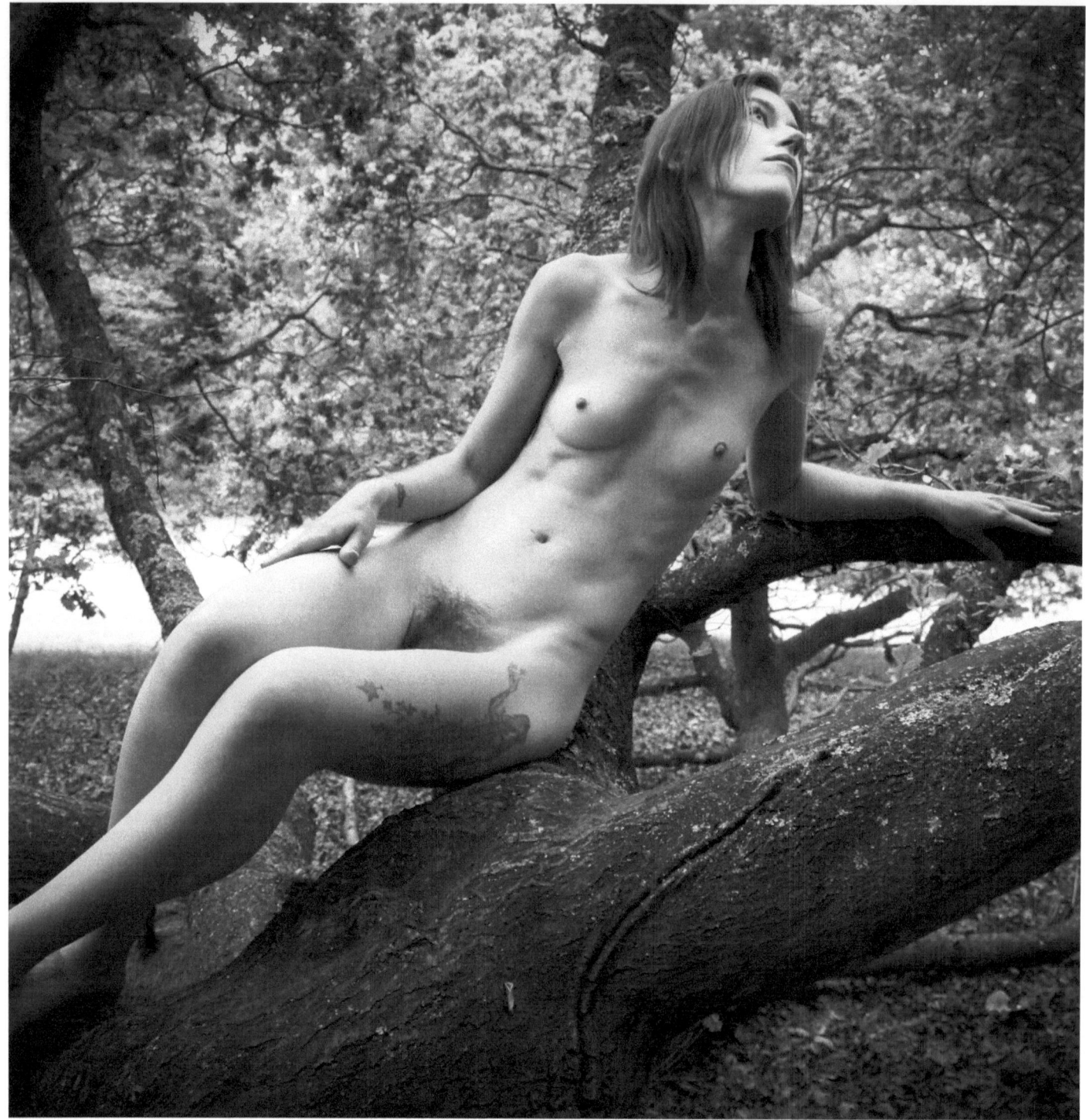

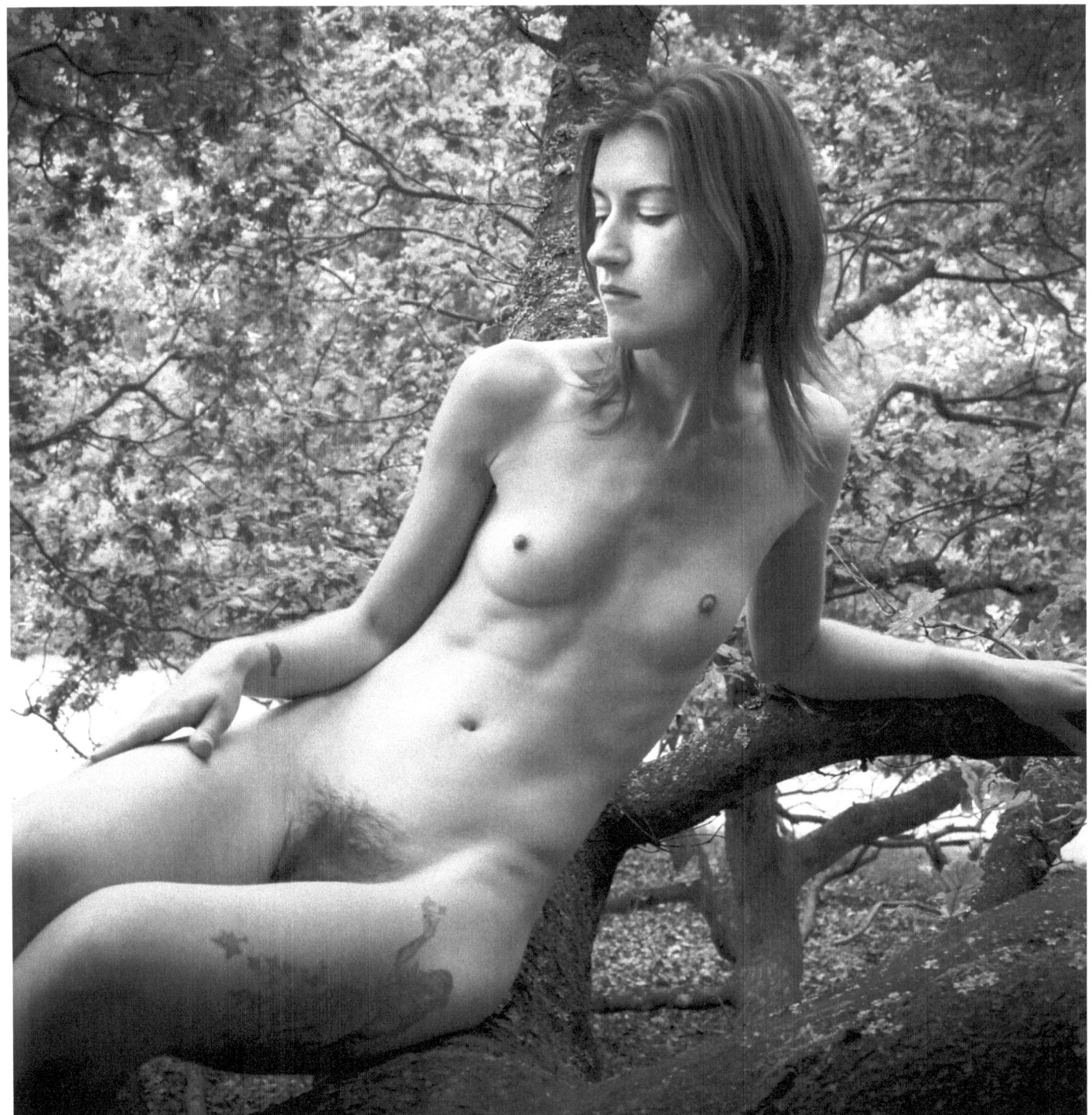

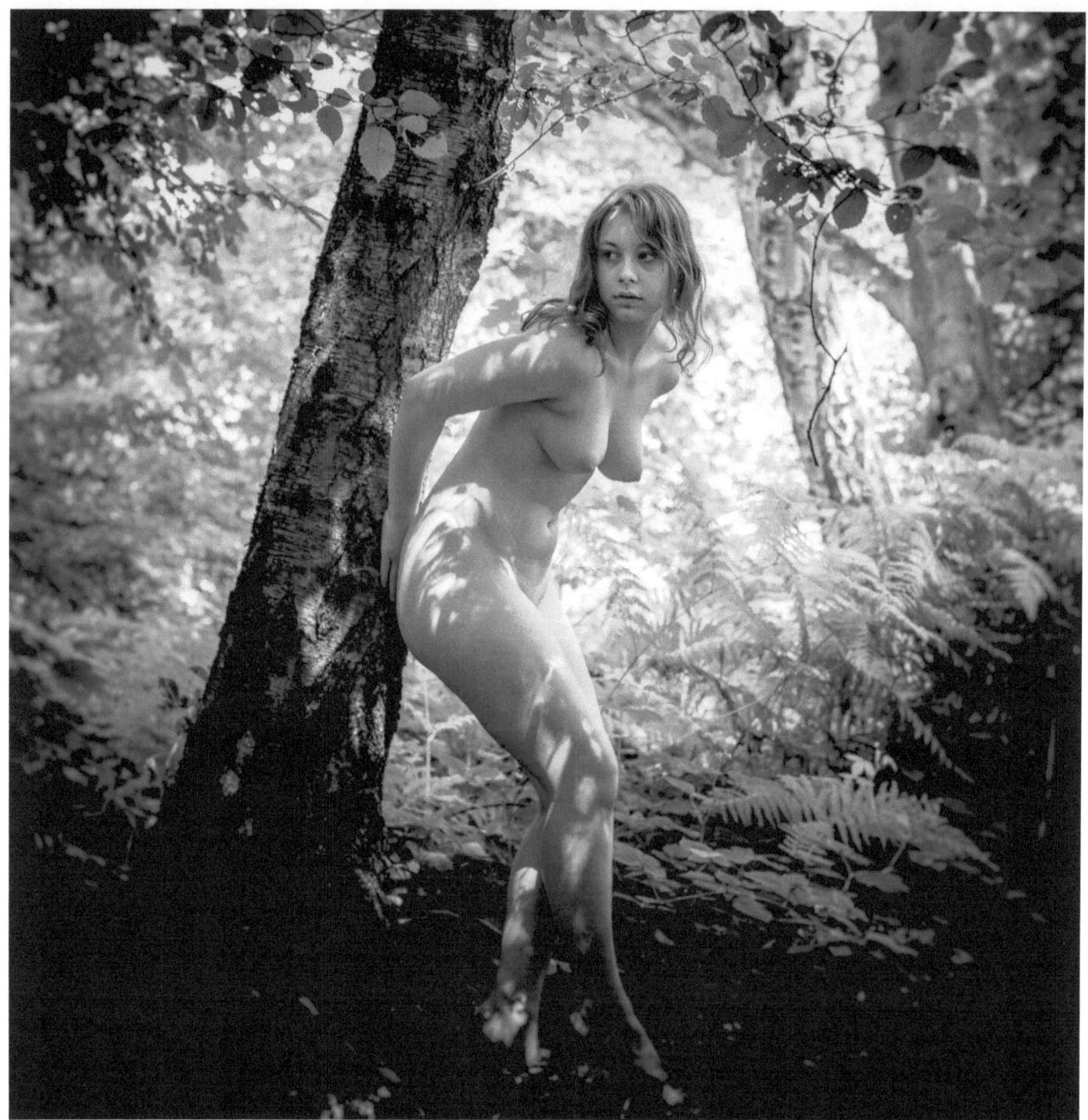

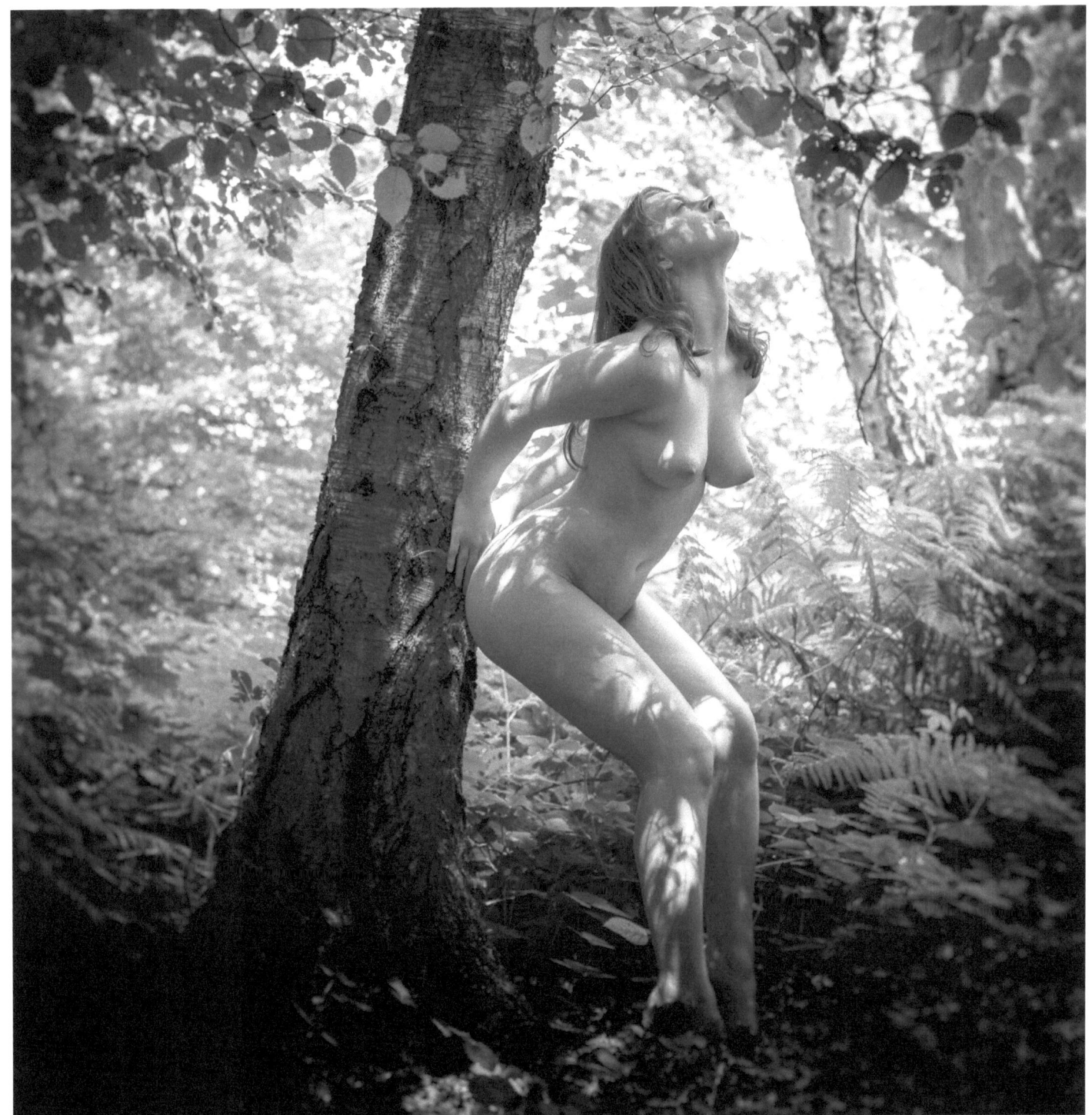

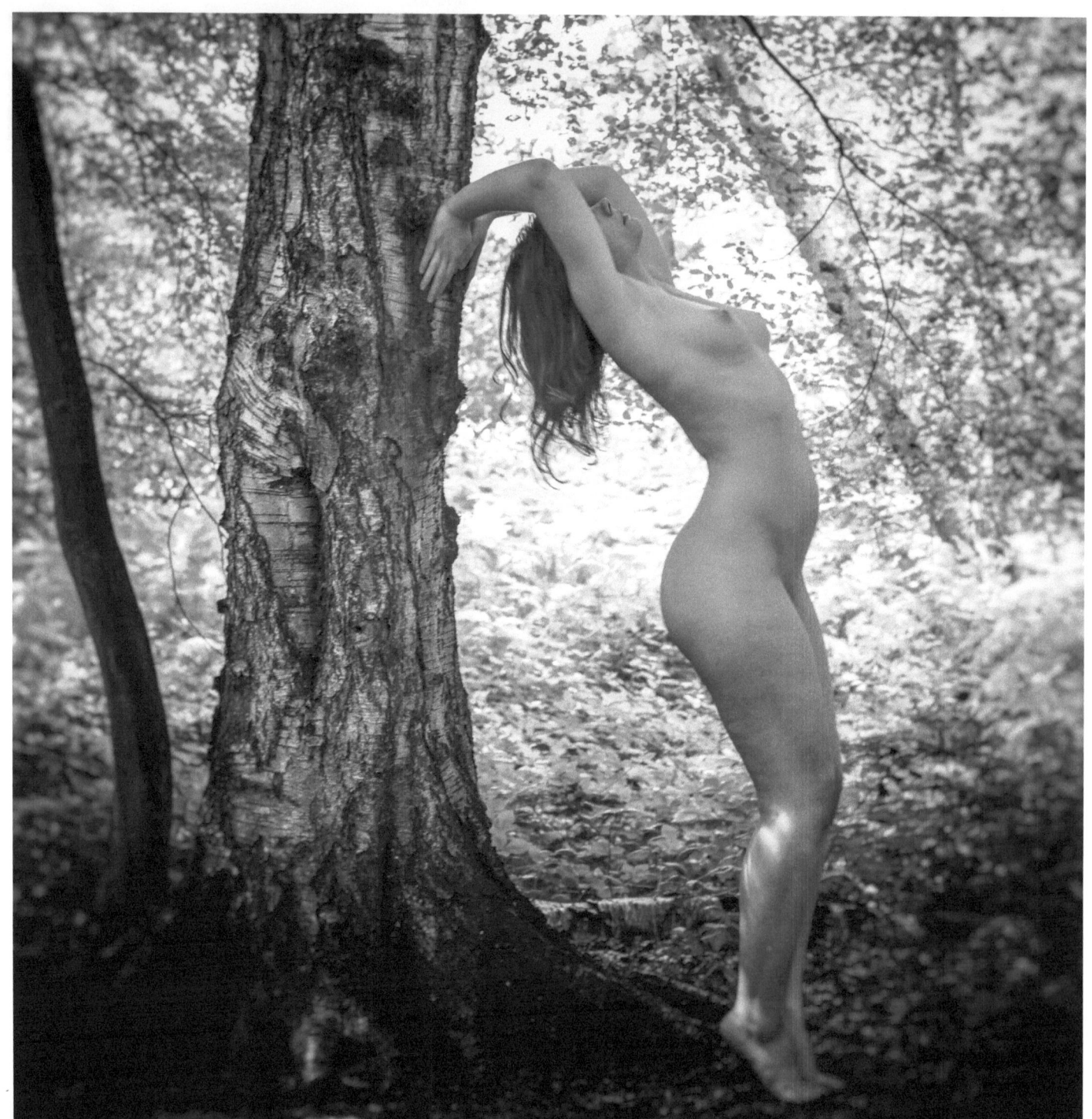

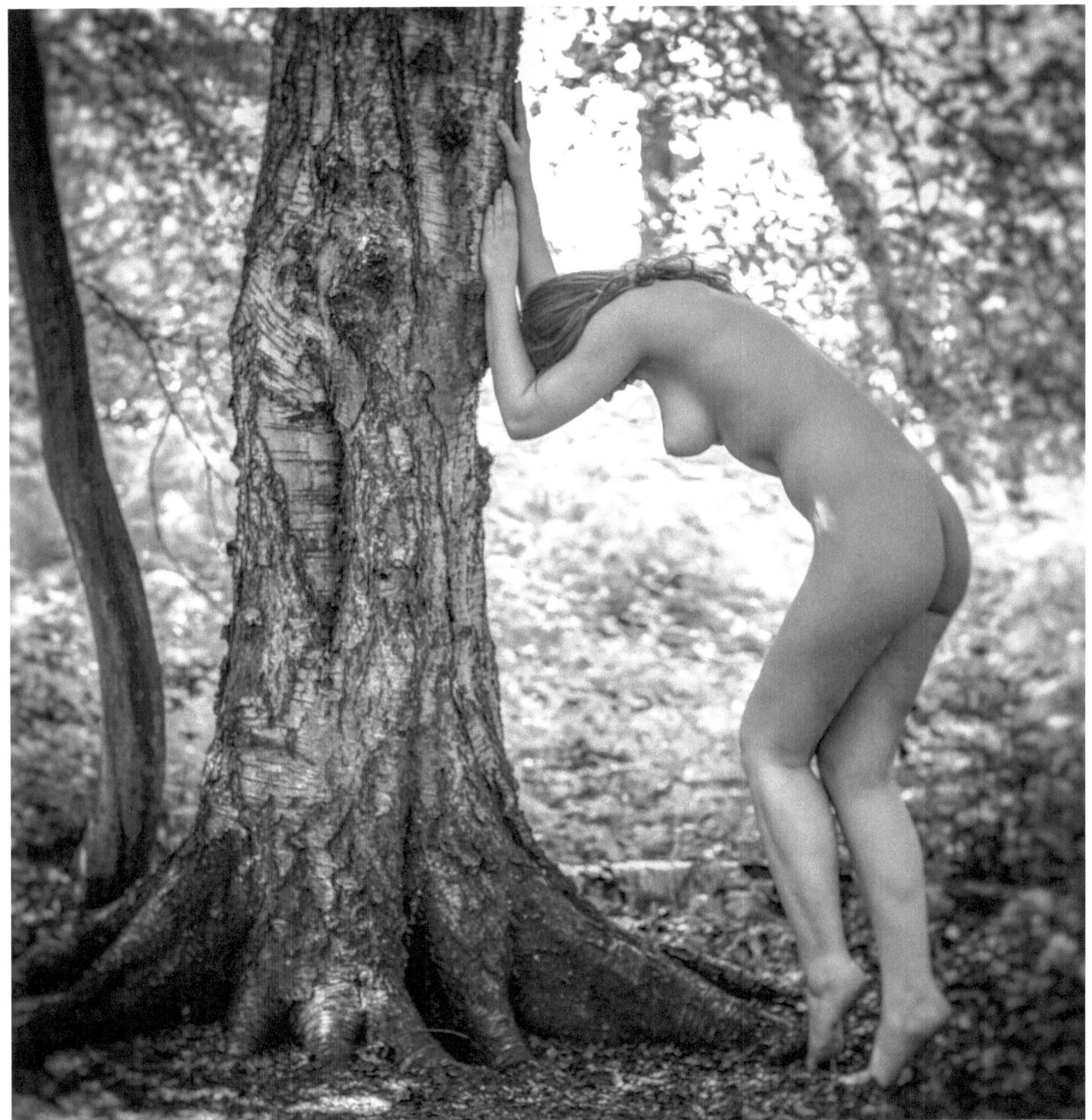

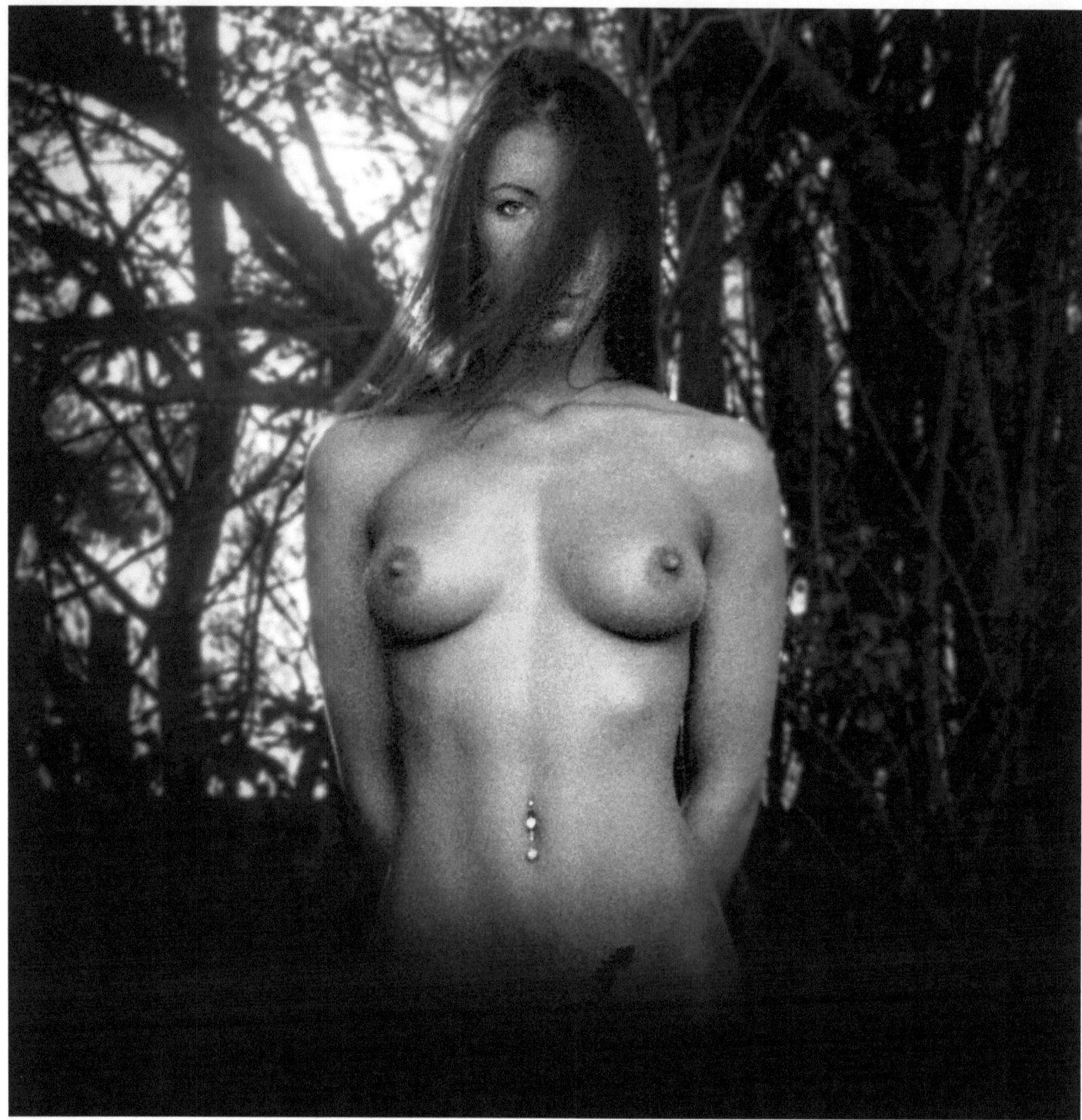

76

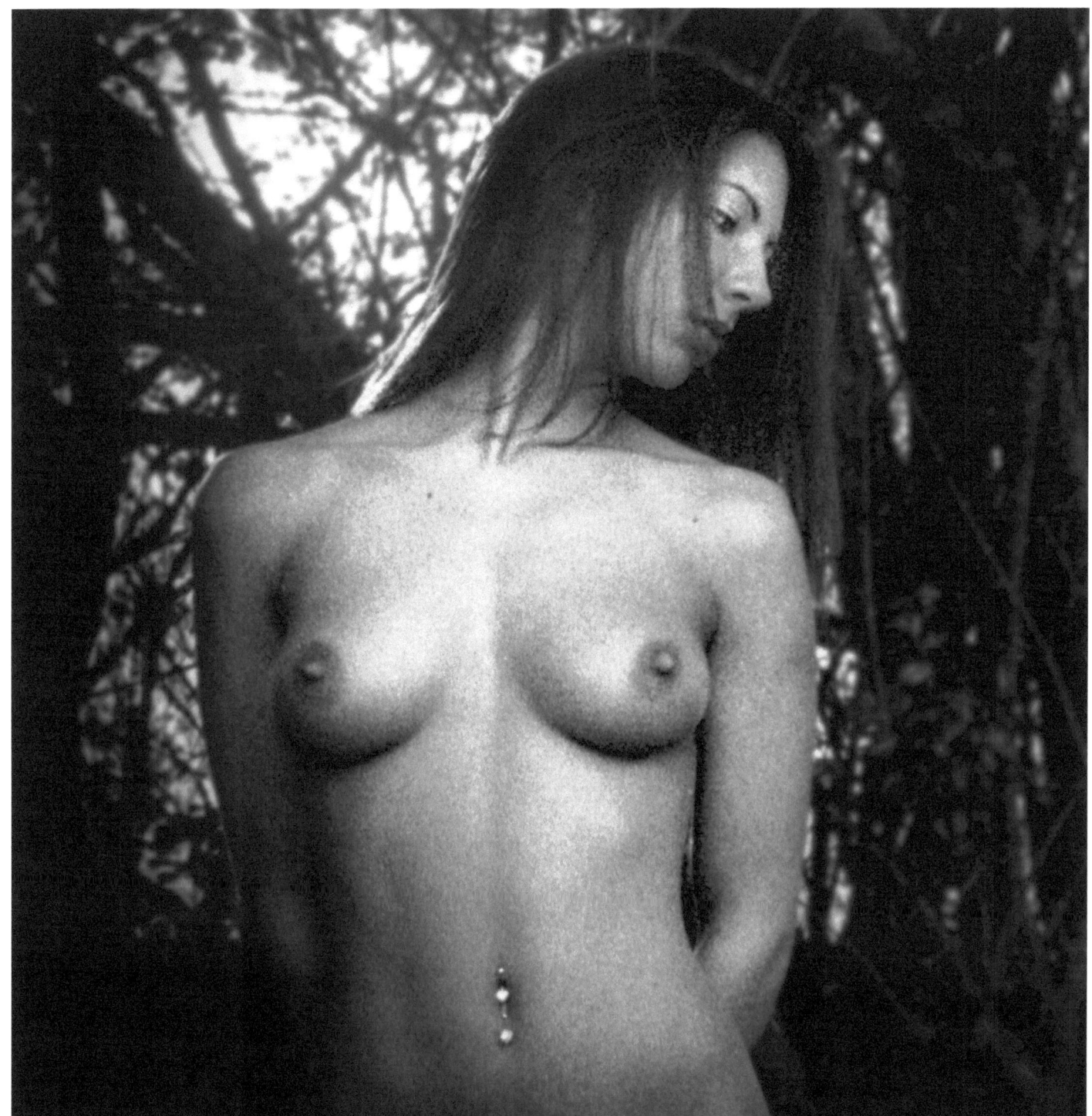

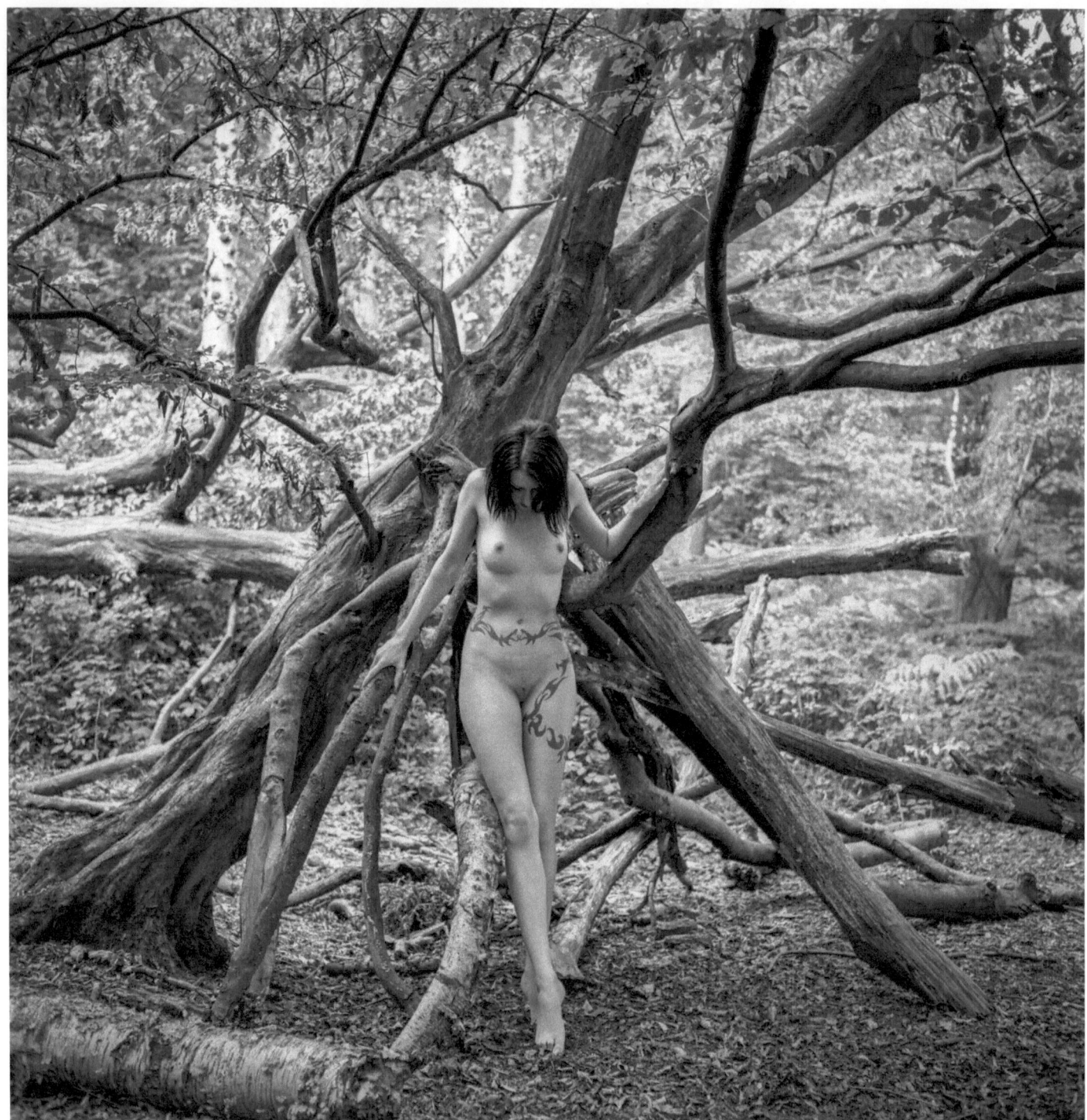

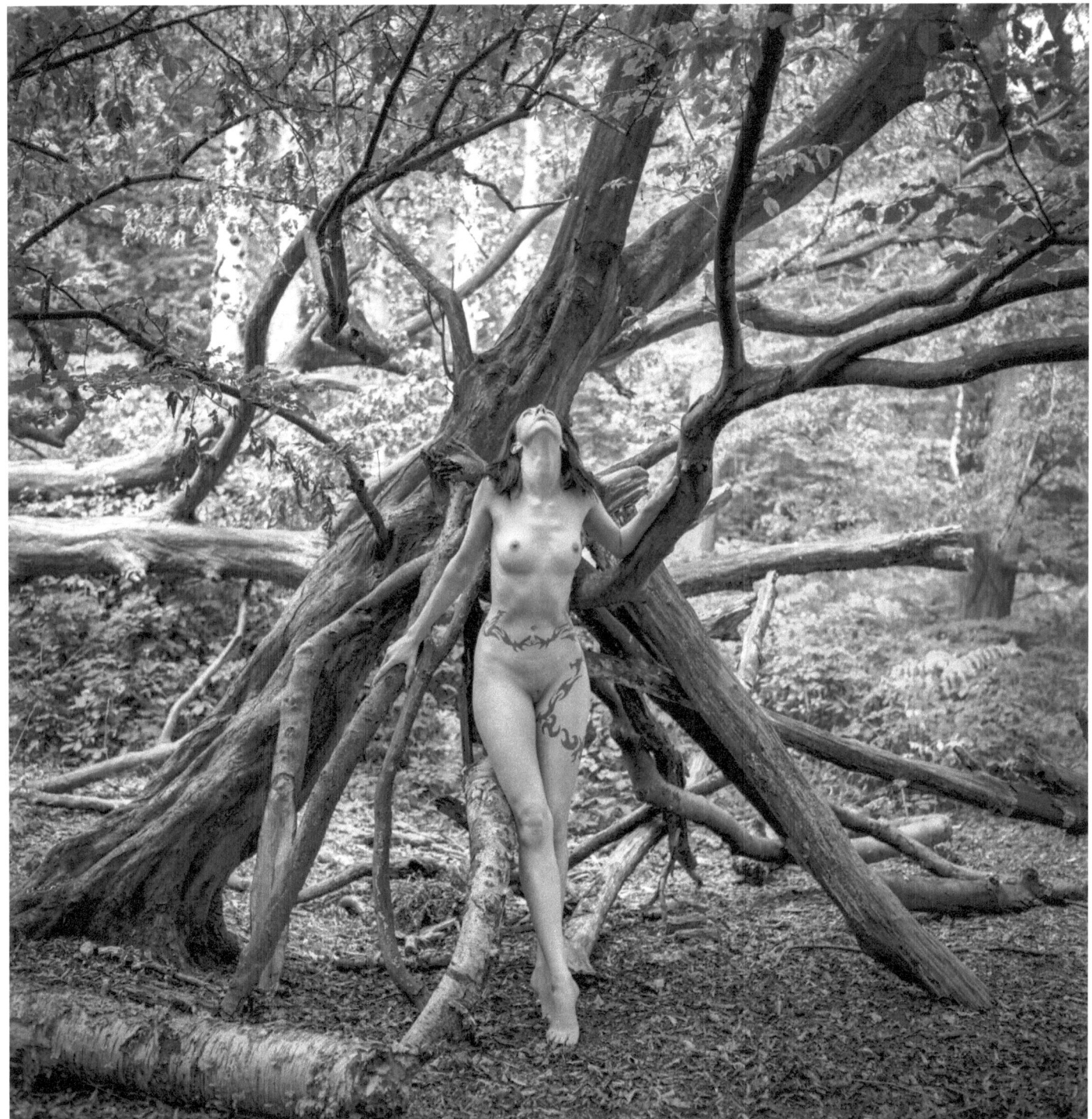

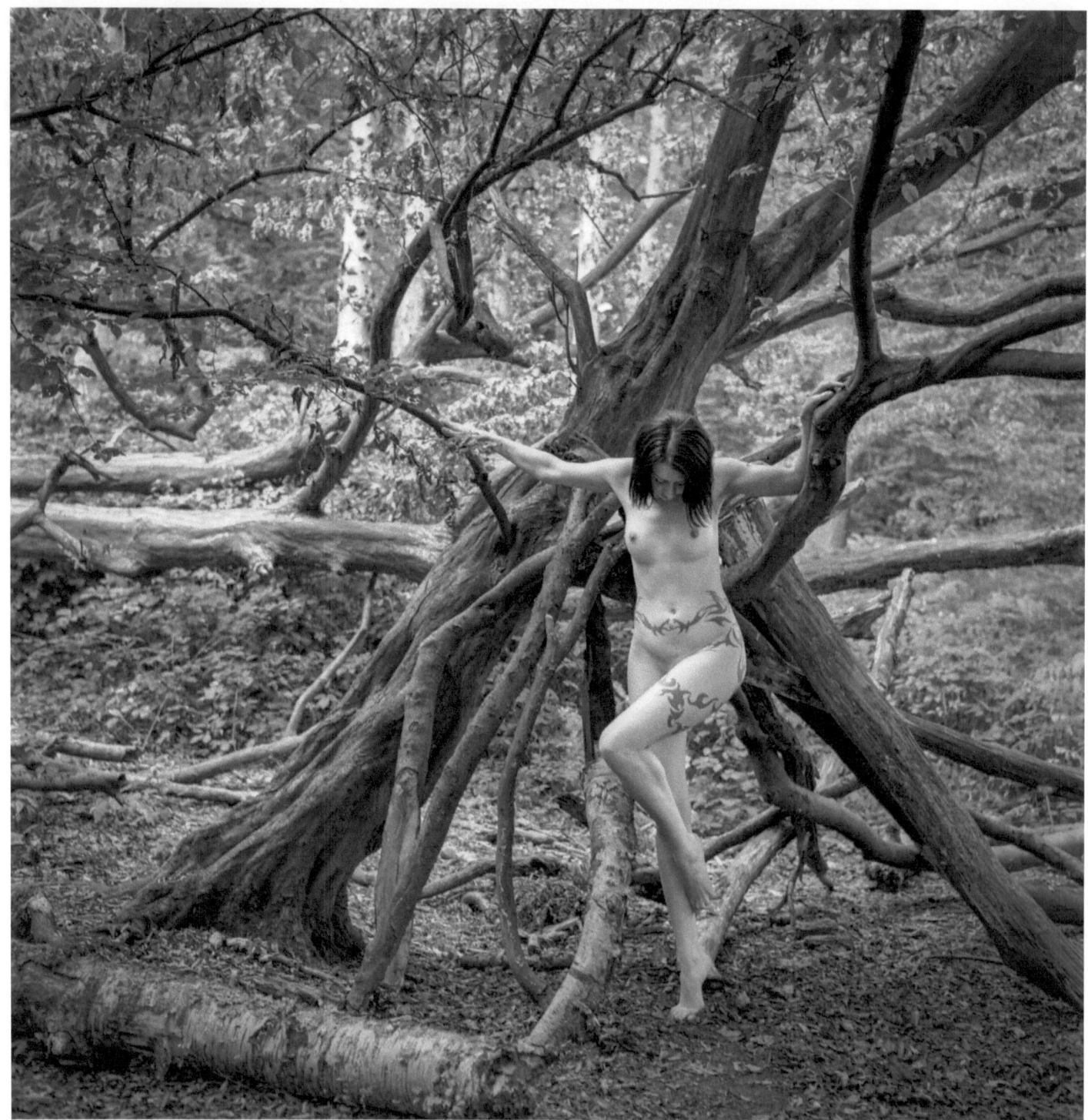

80

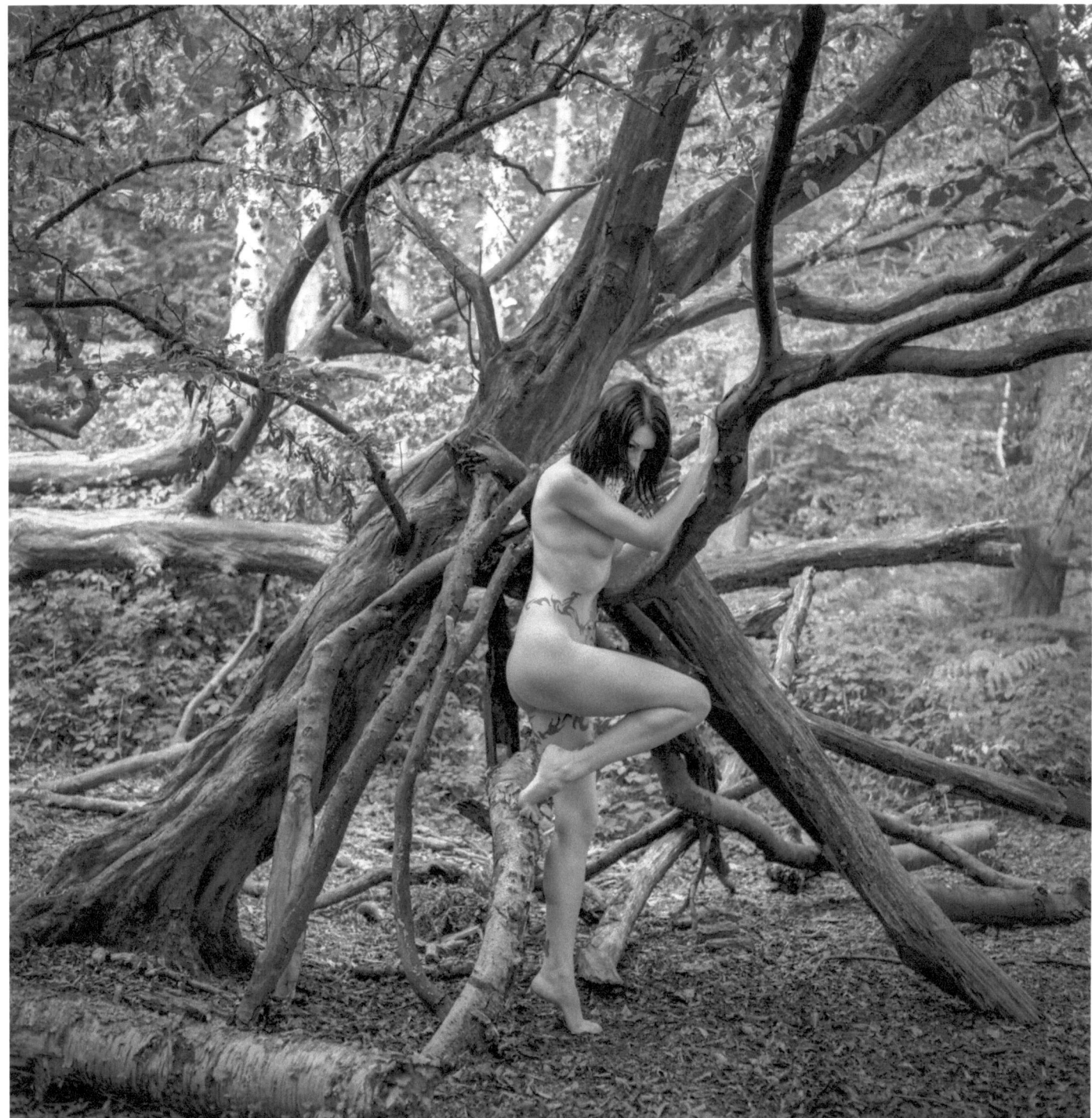

81

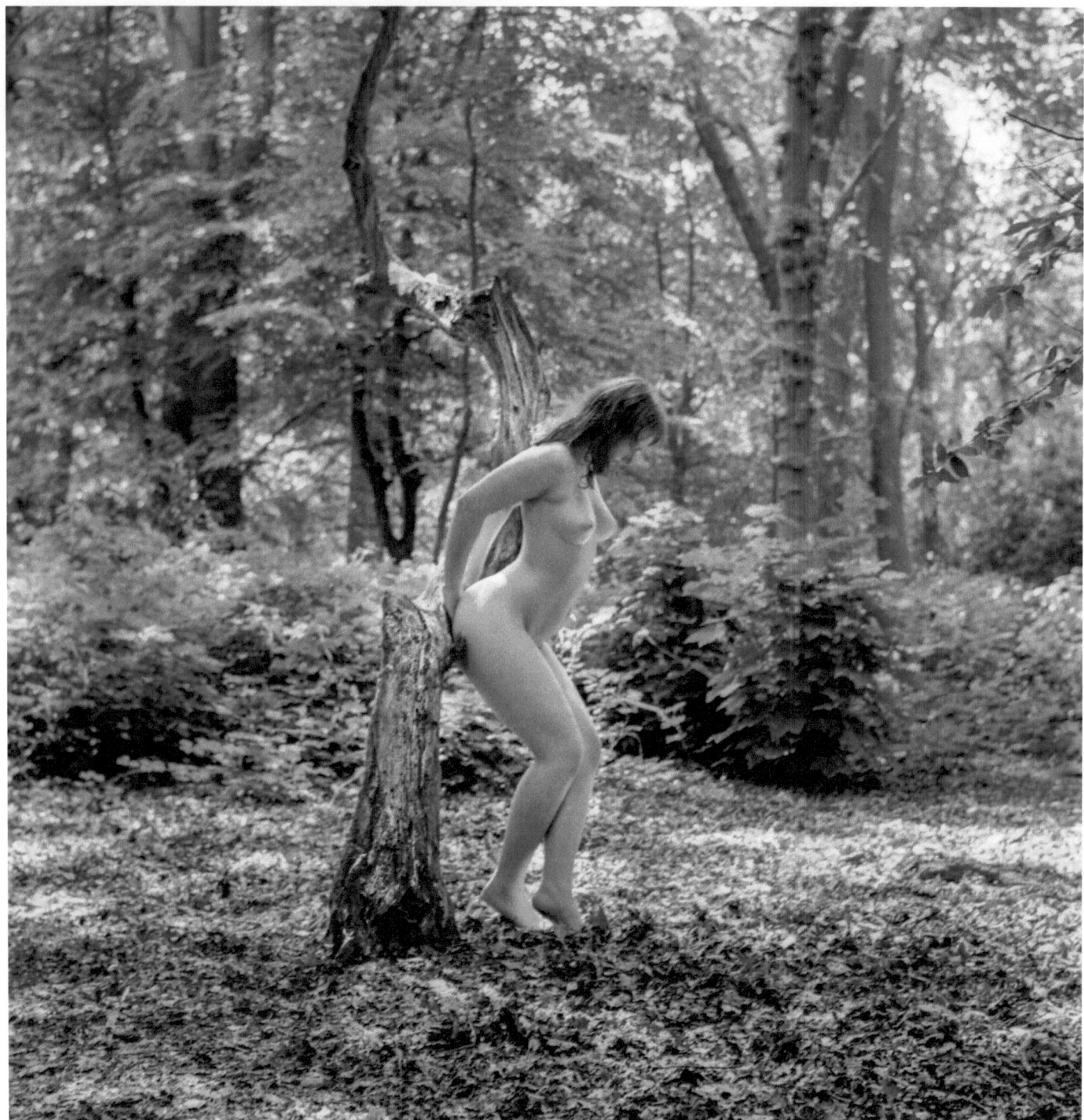

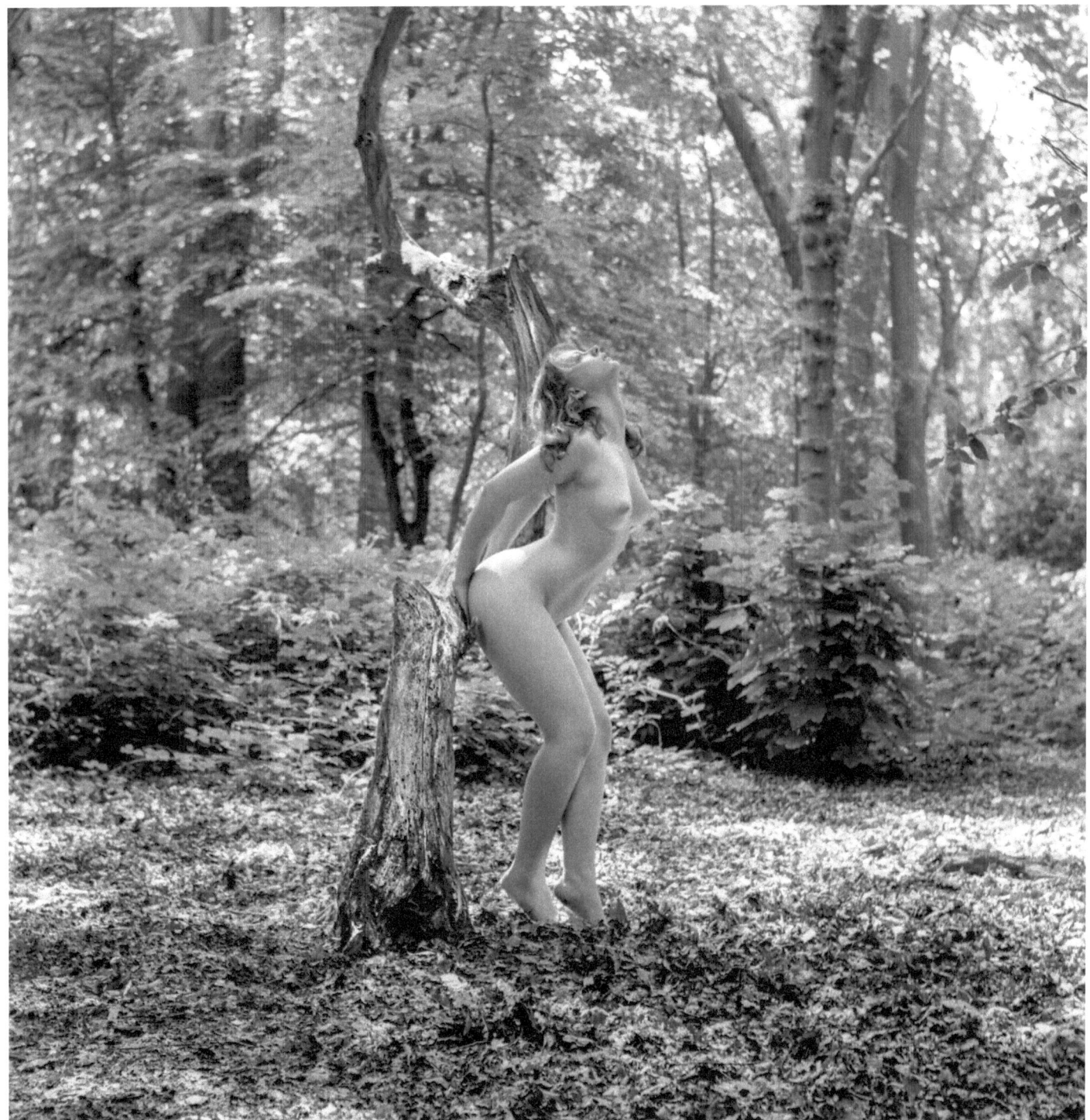

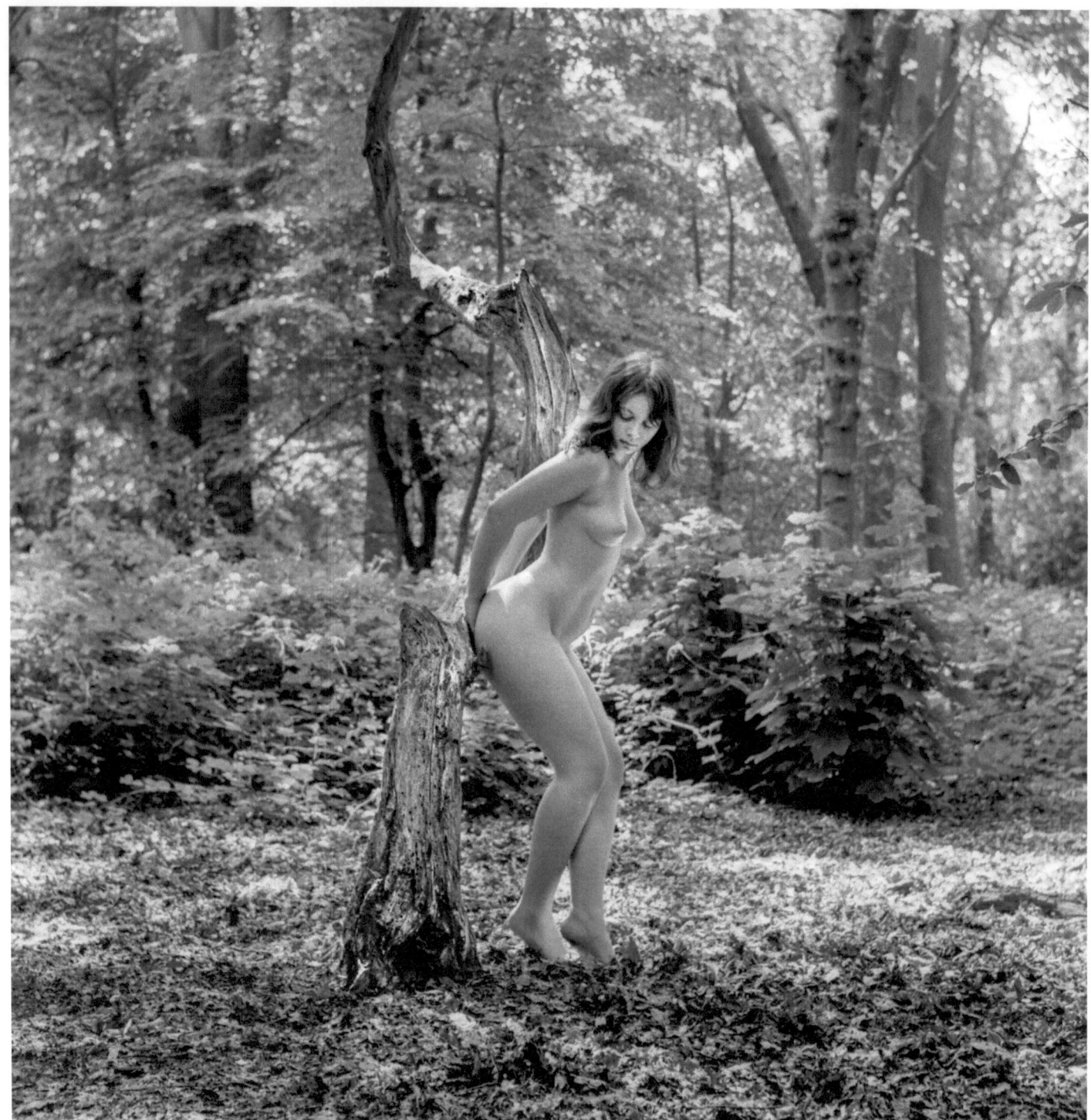

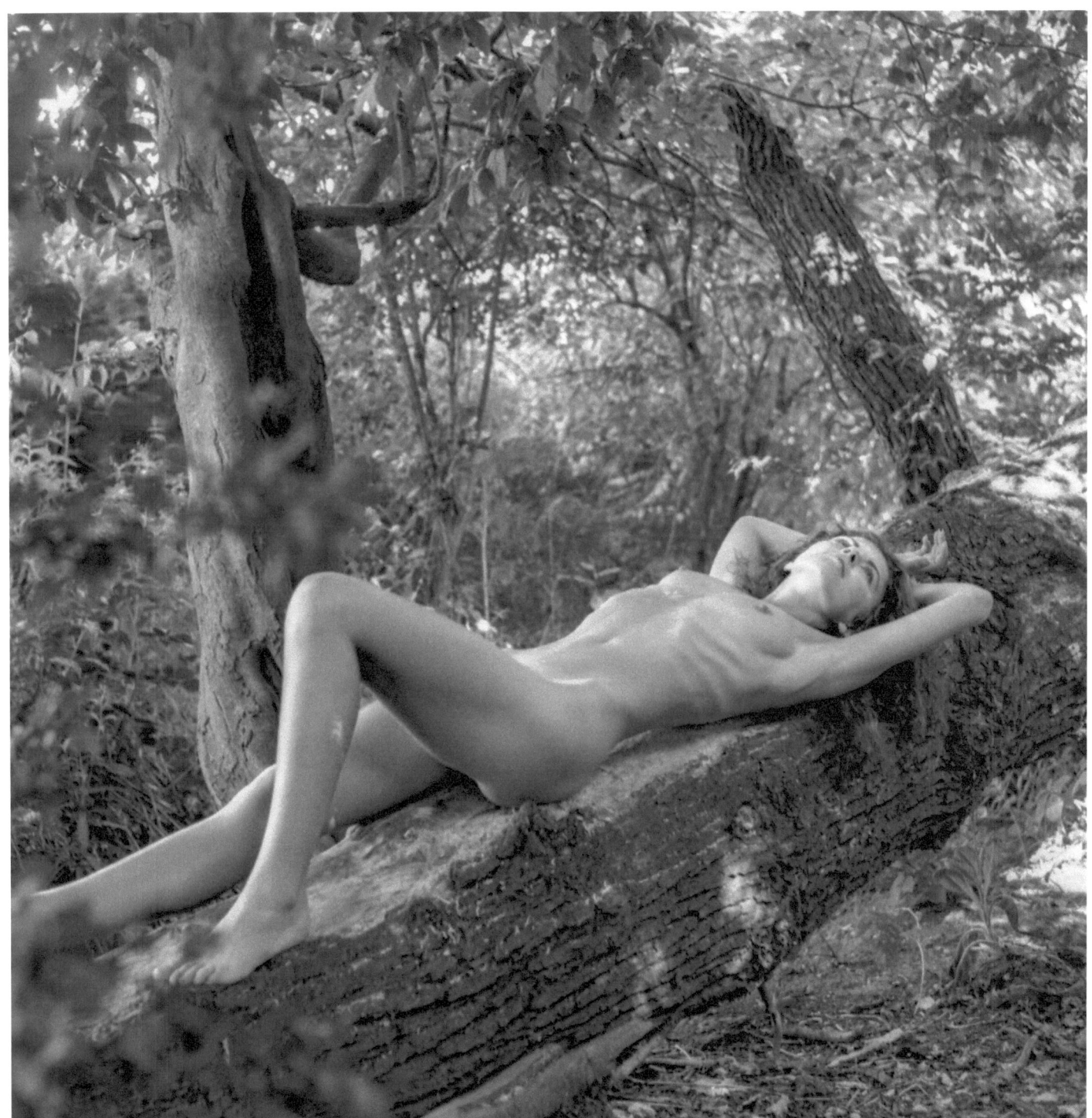

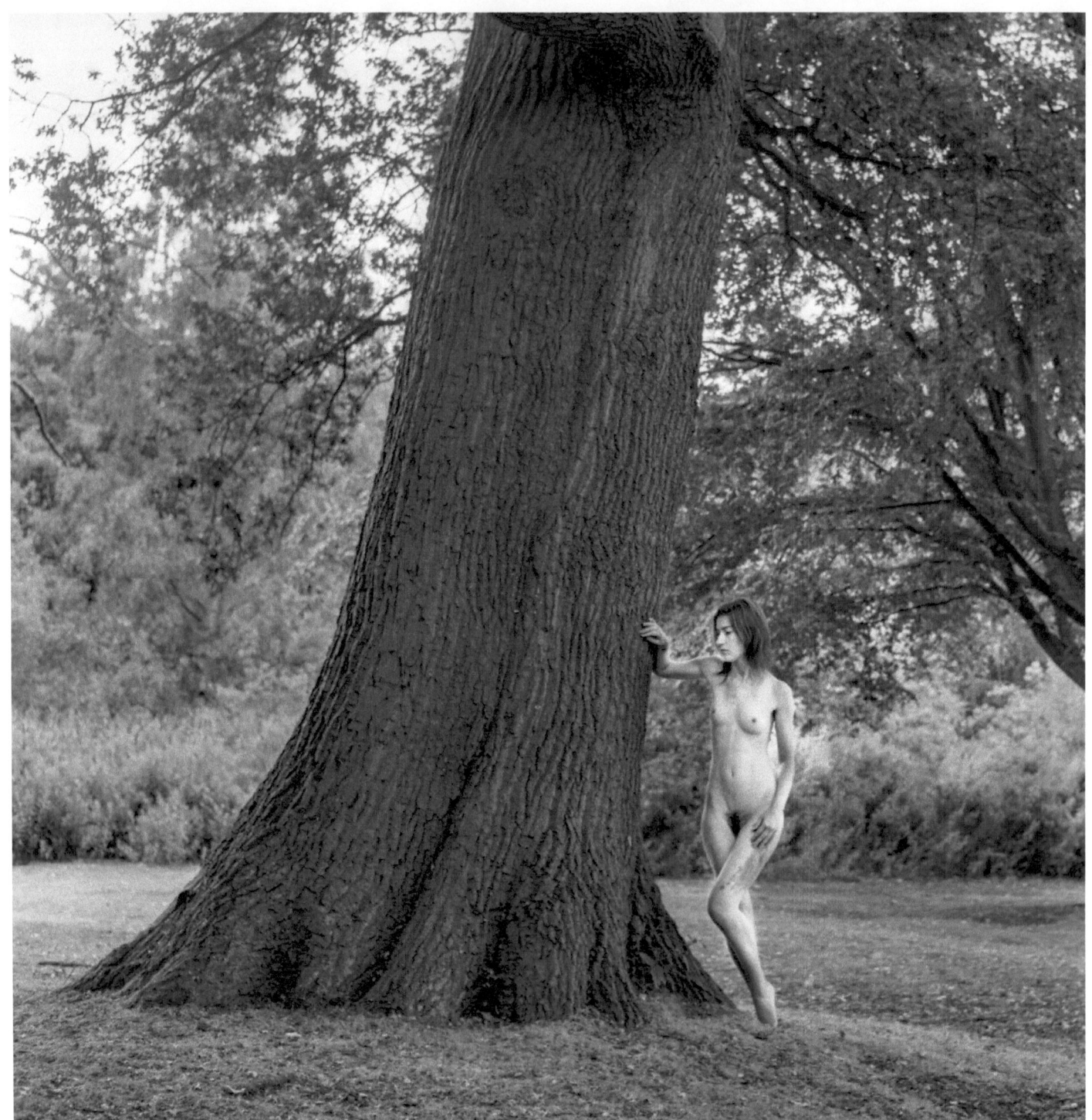

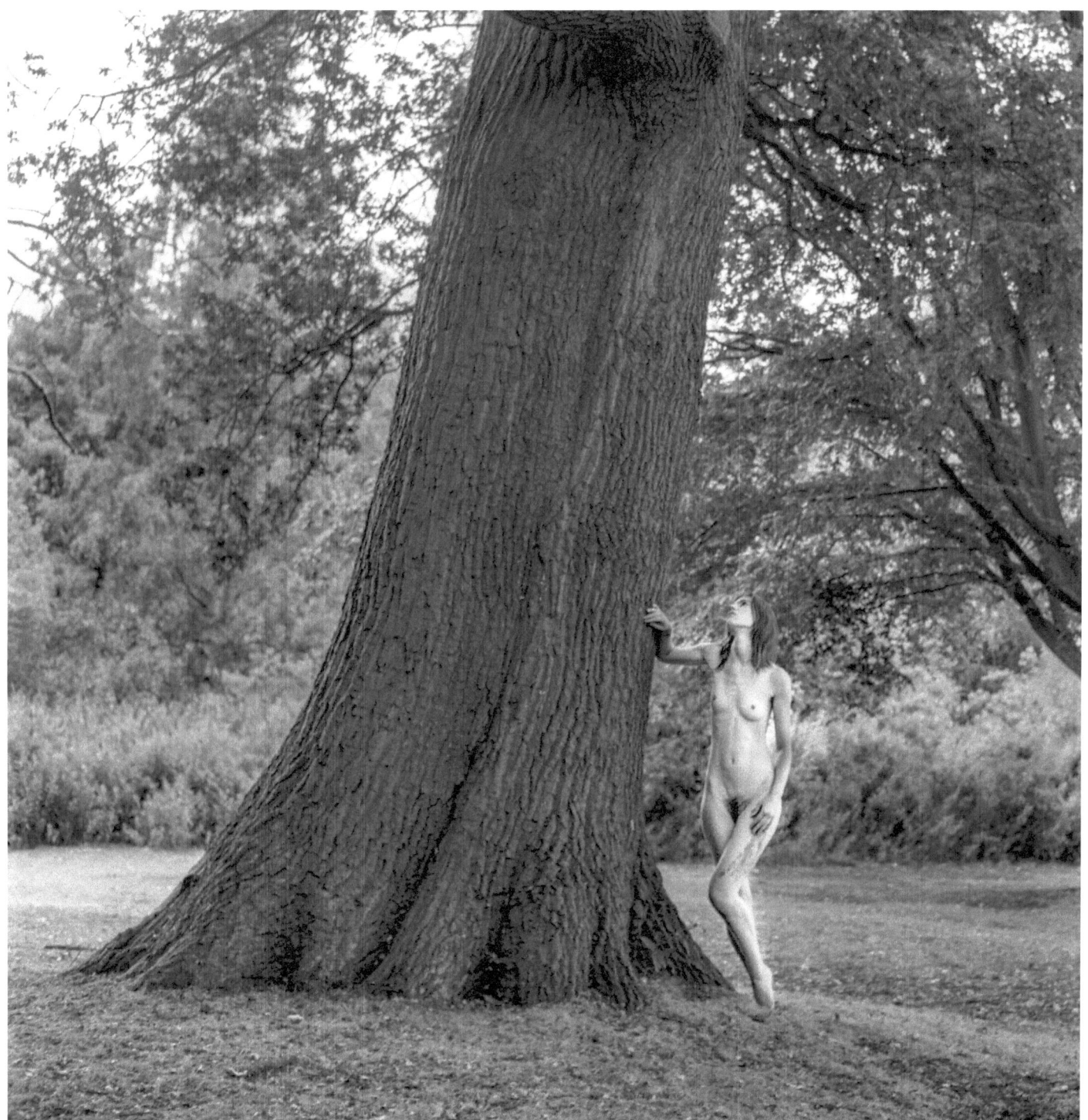

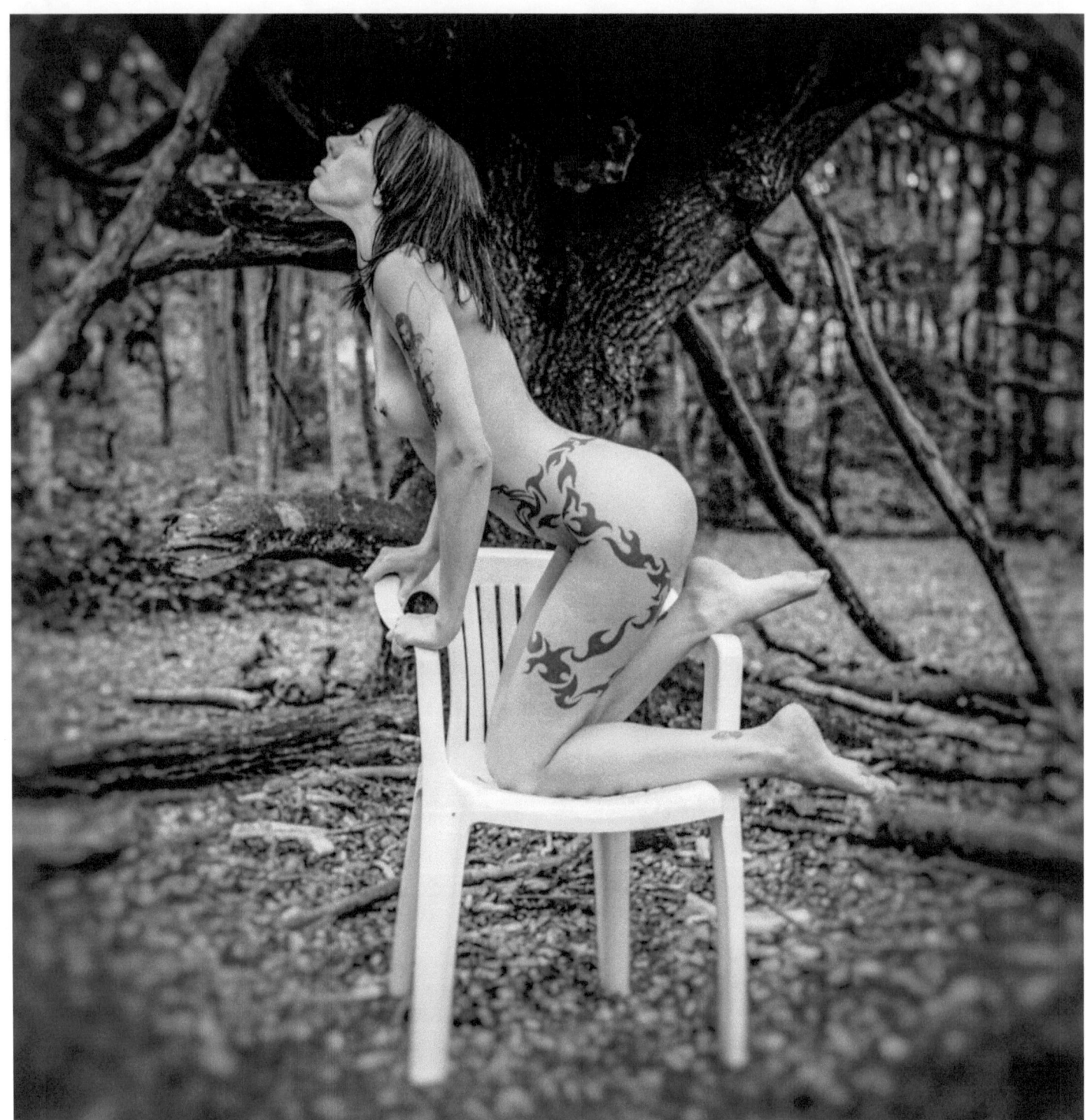

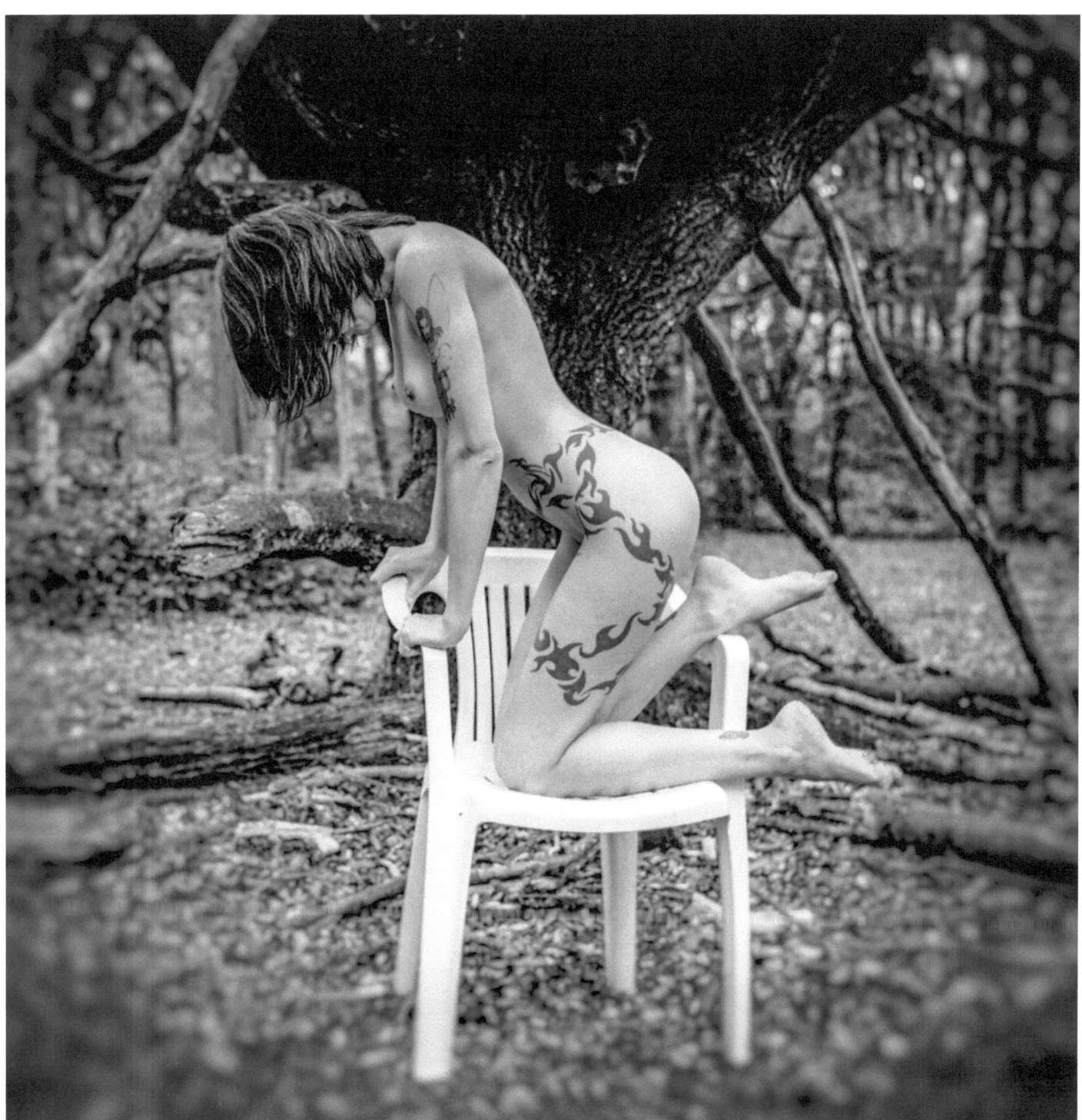

89

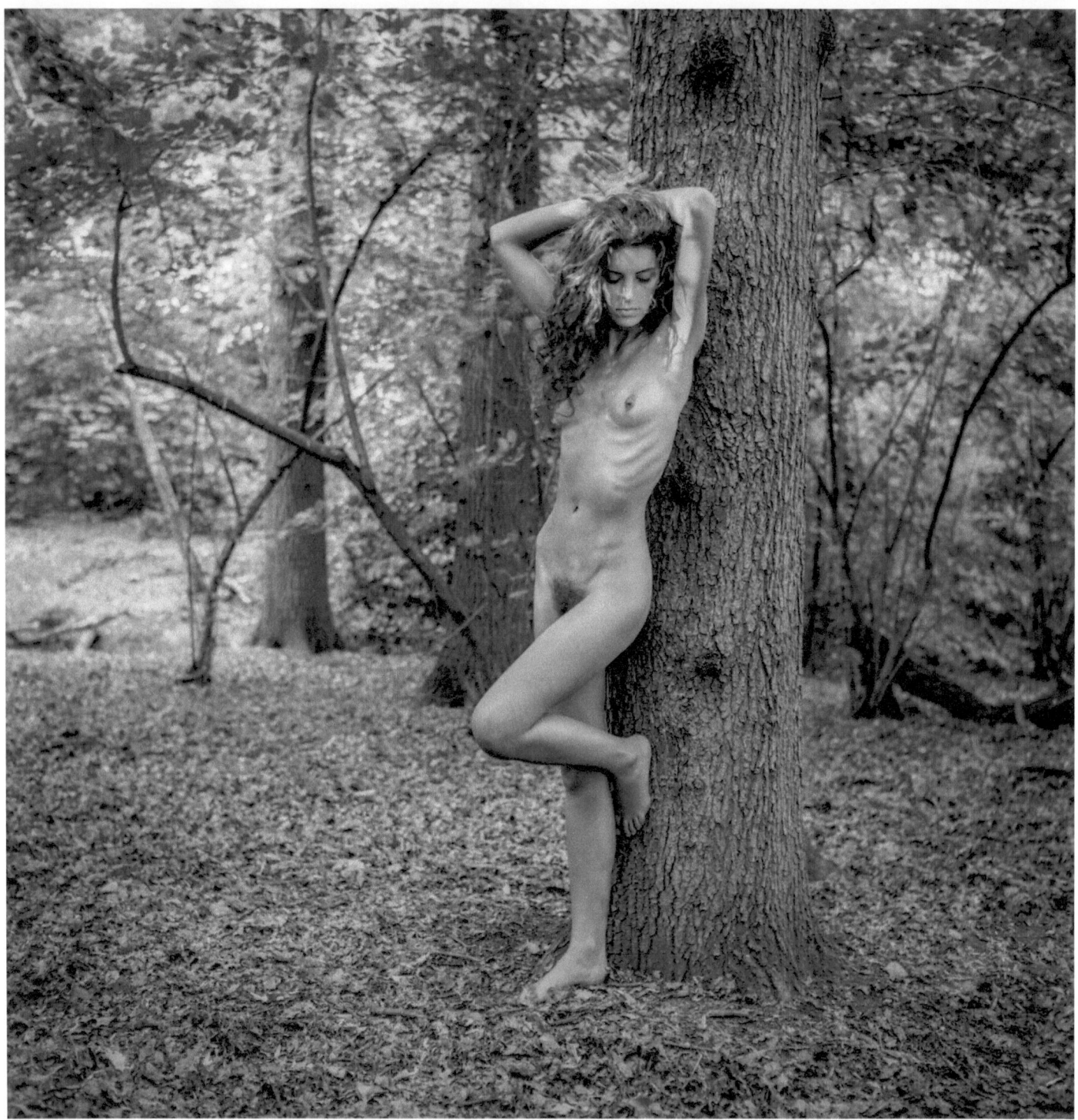

90

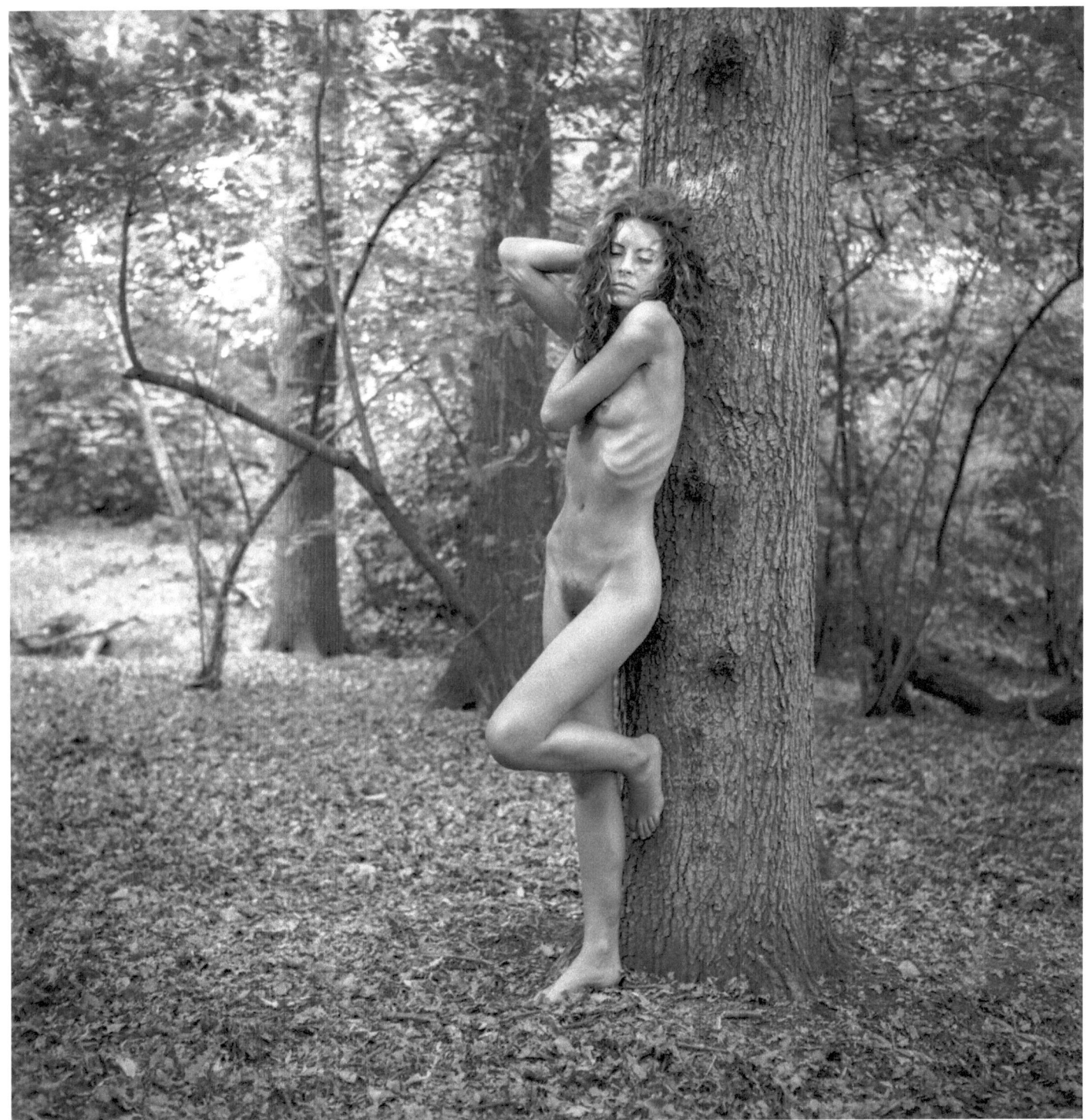

91

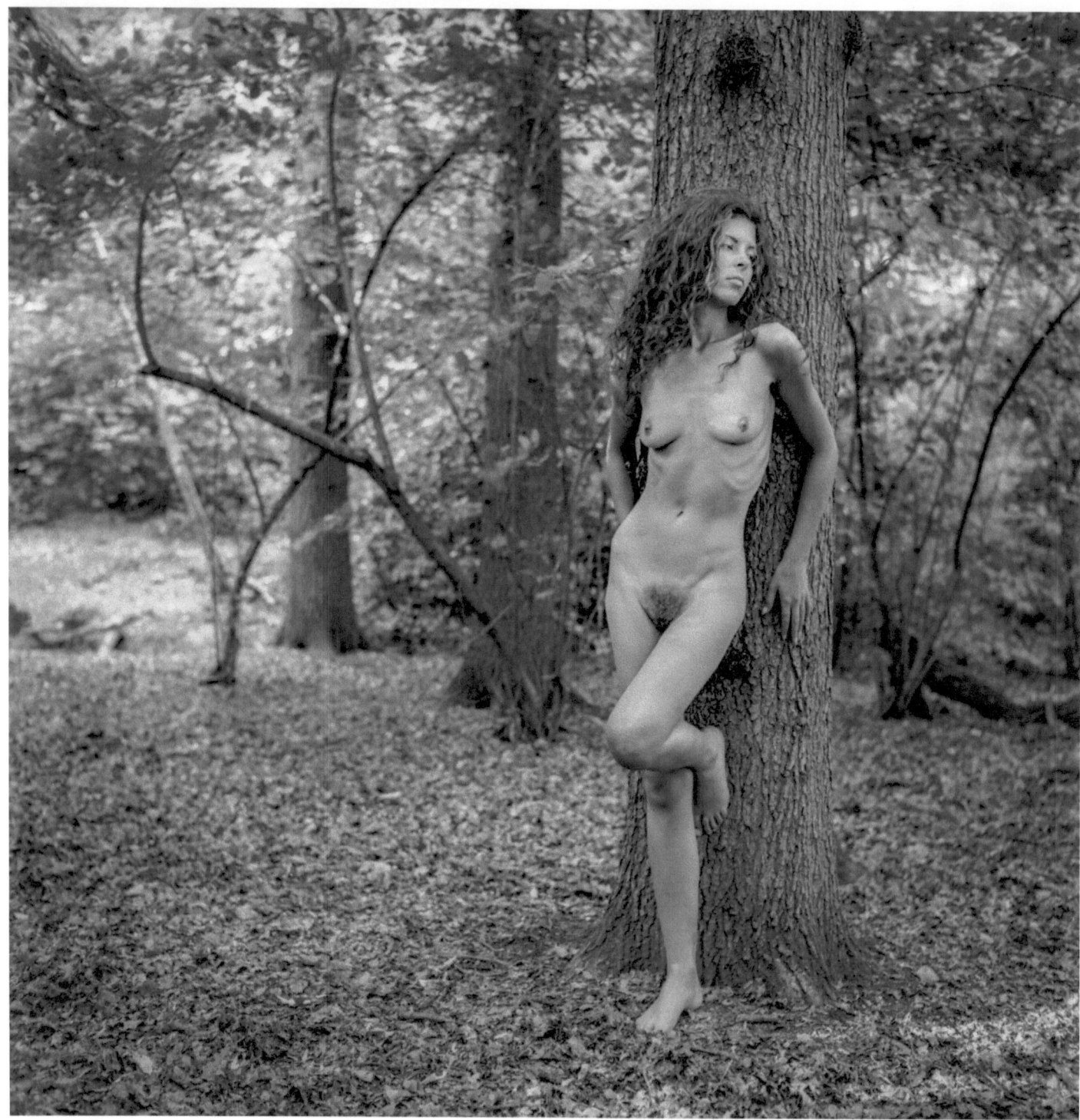

92

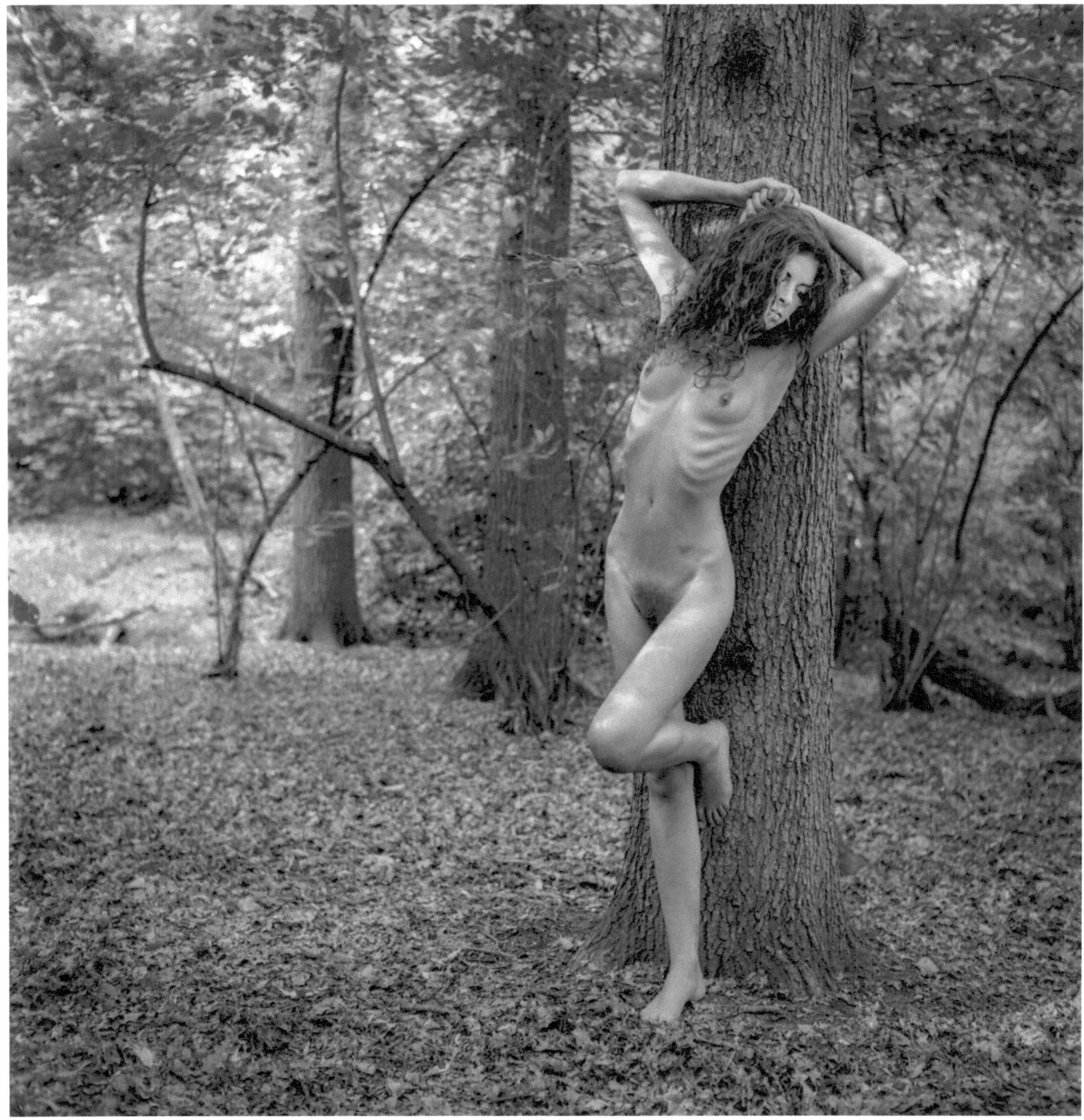

93

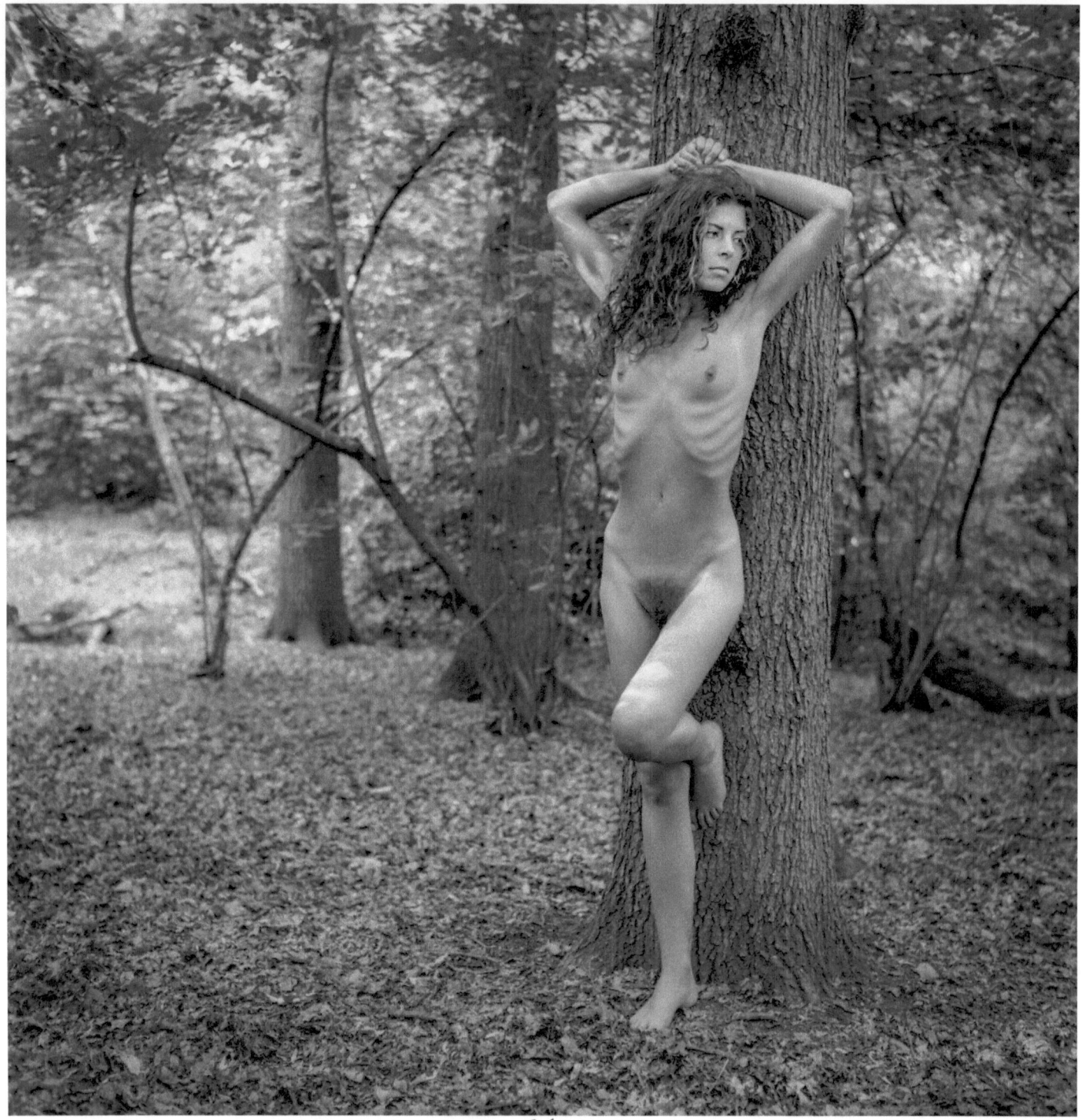

94

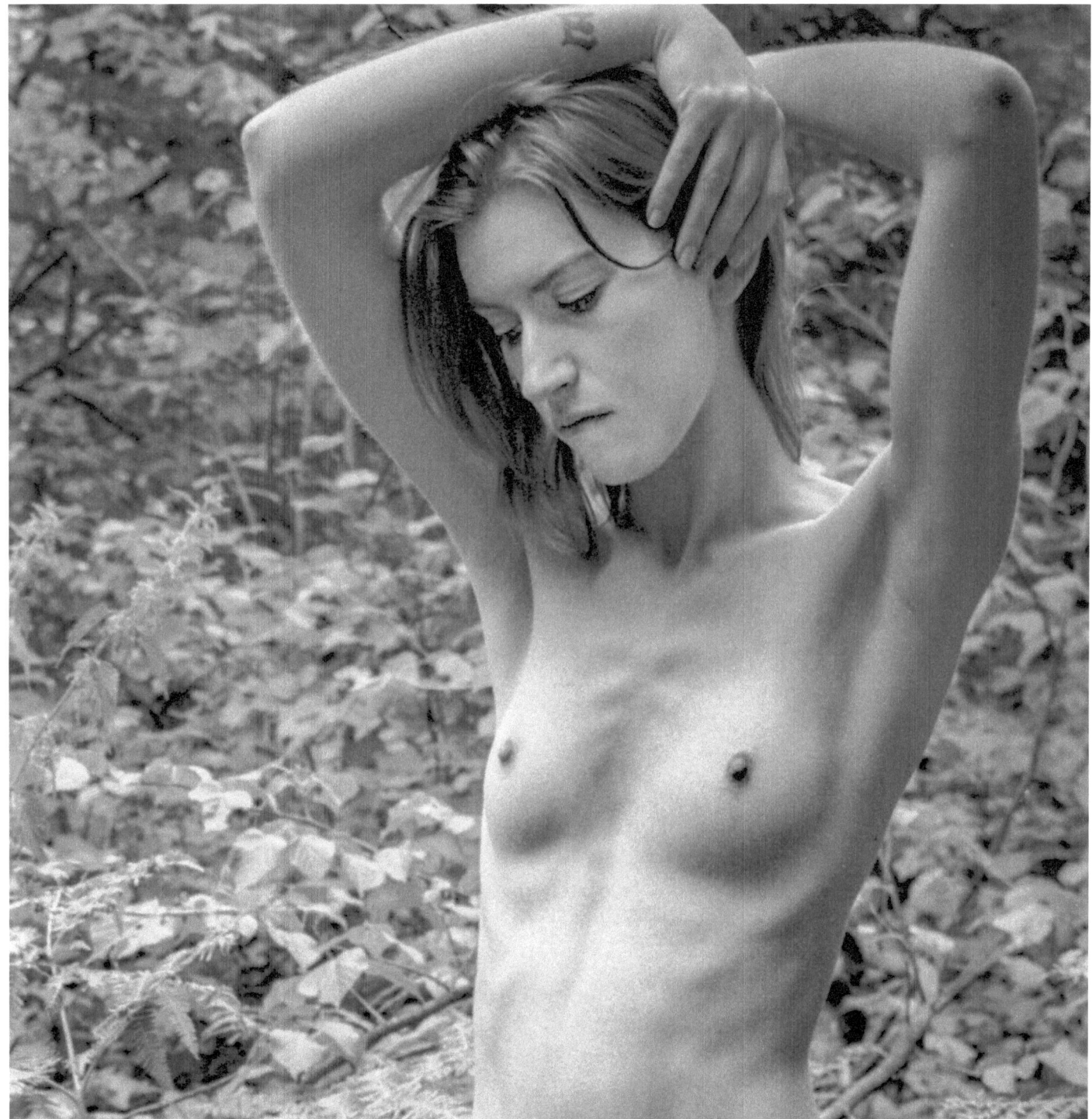

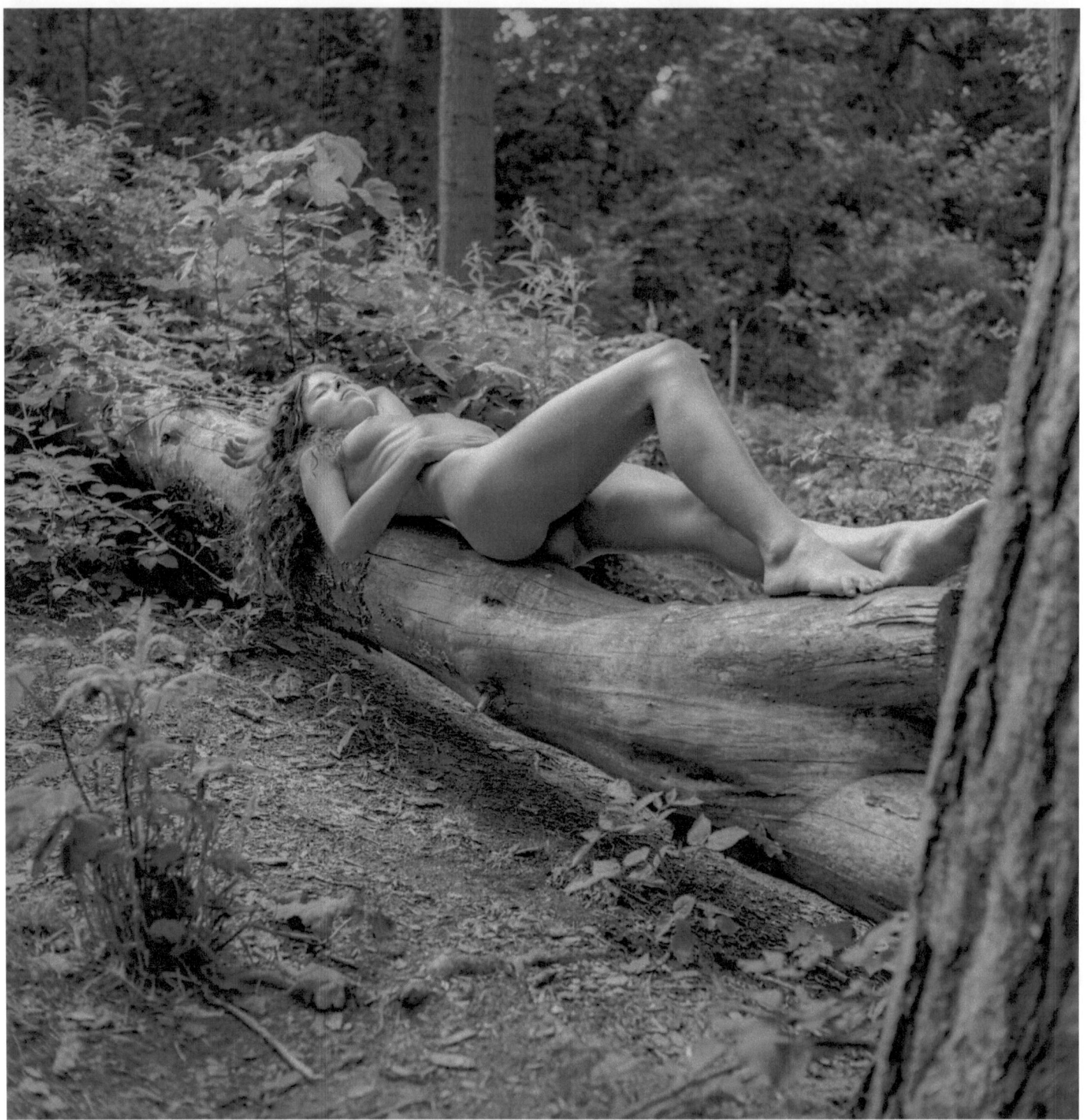

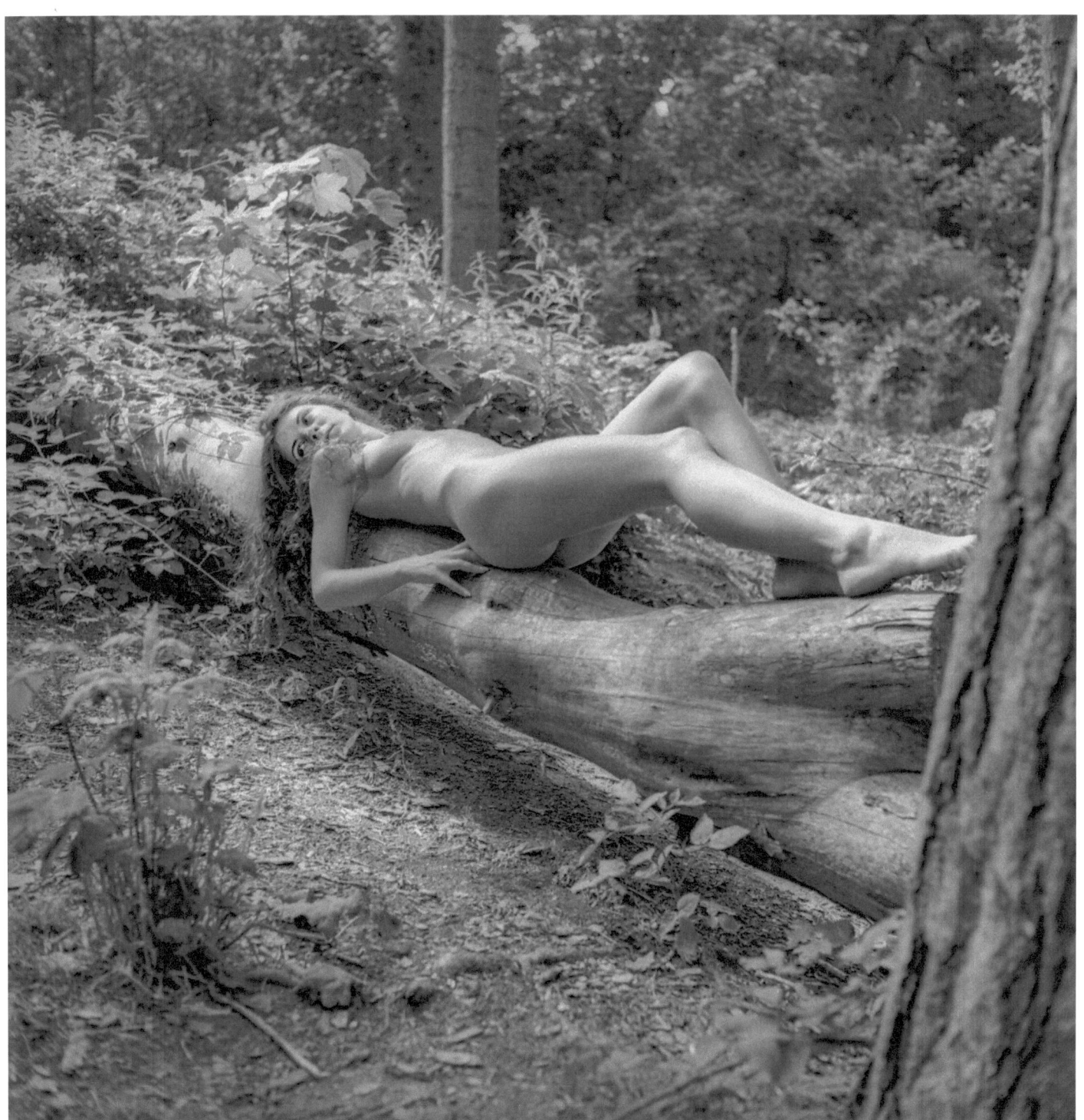

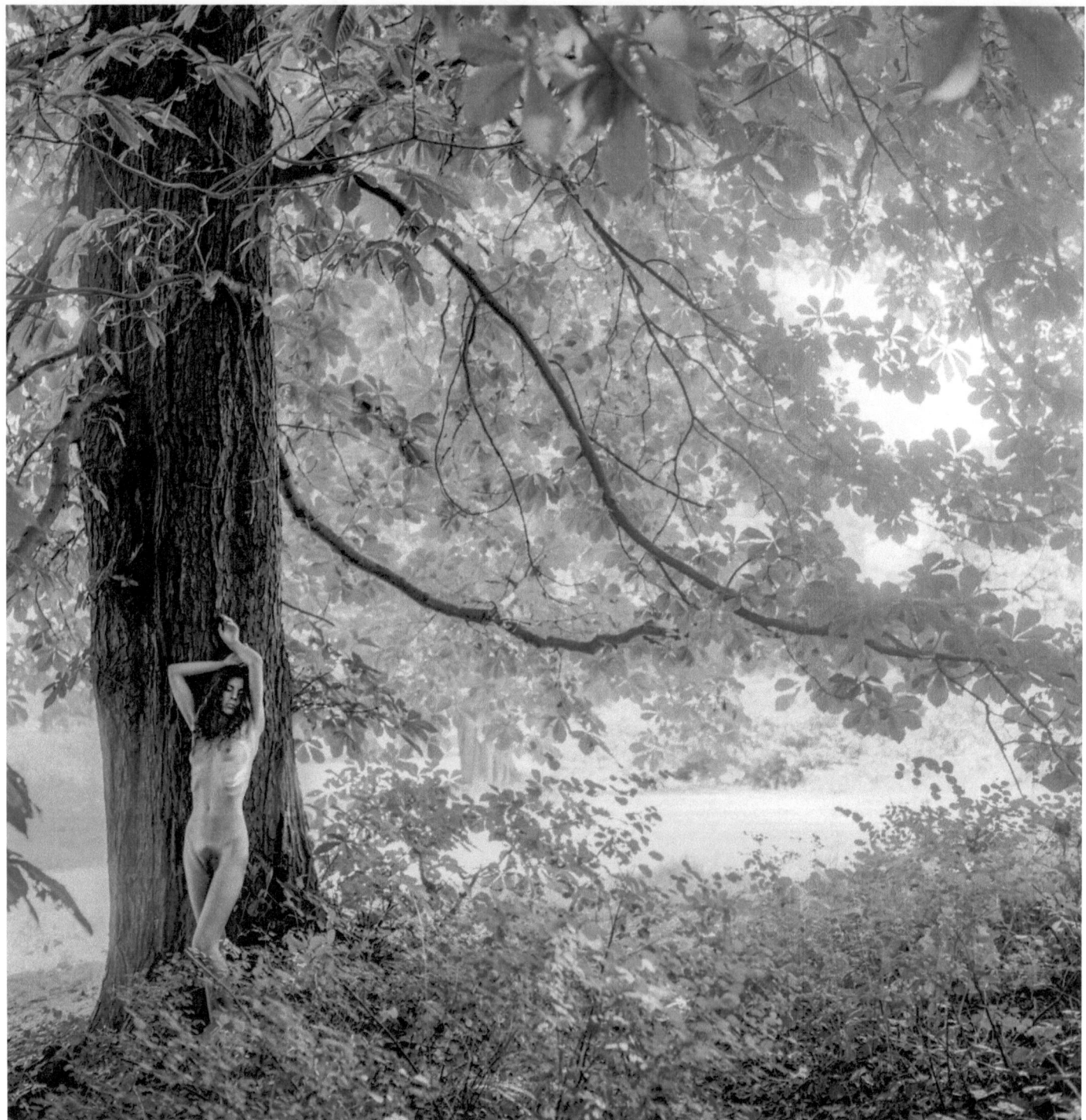

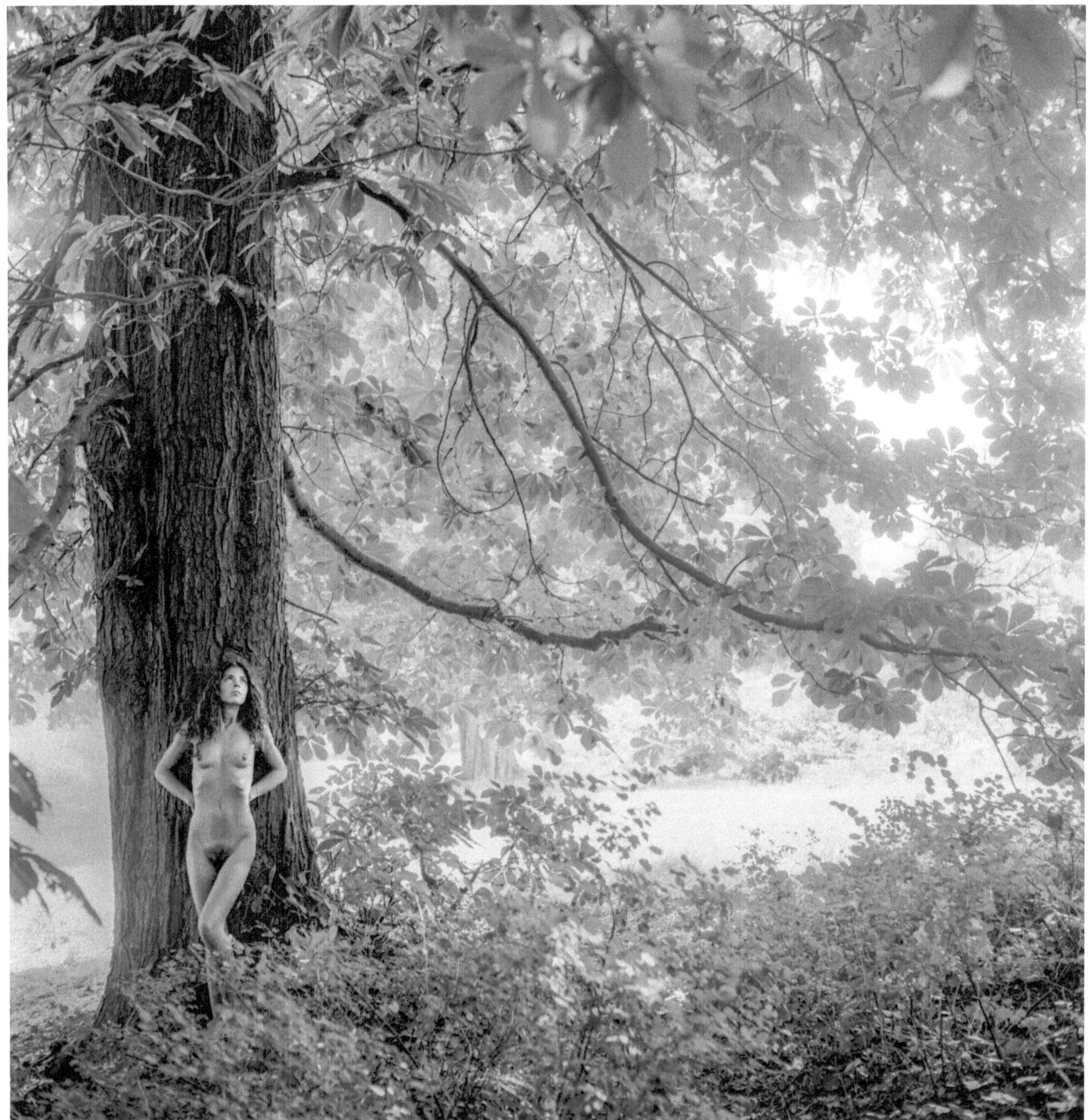

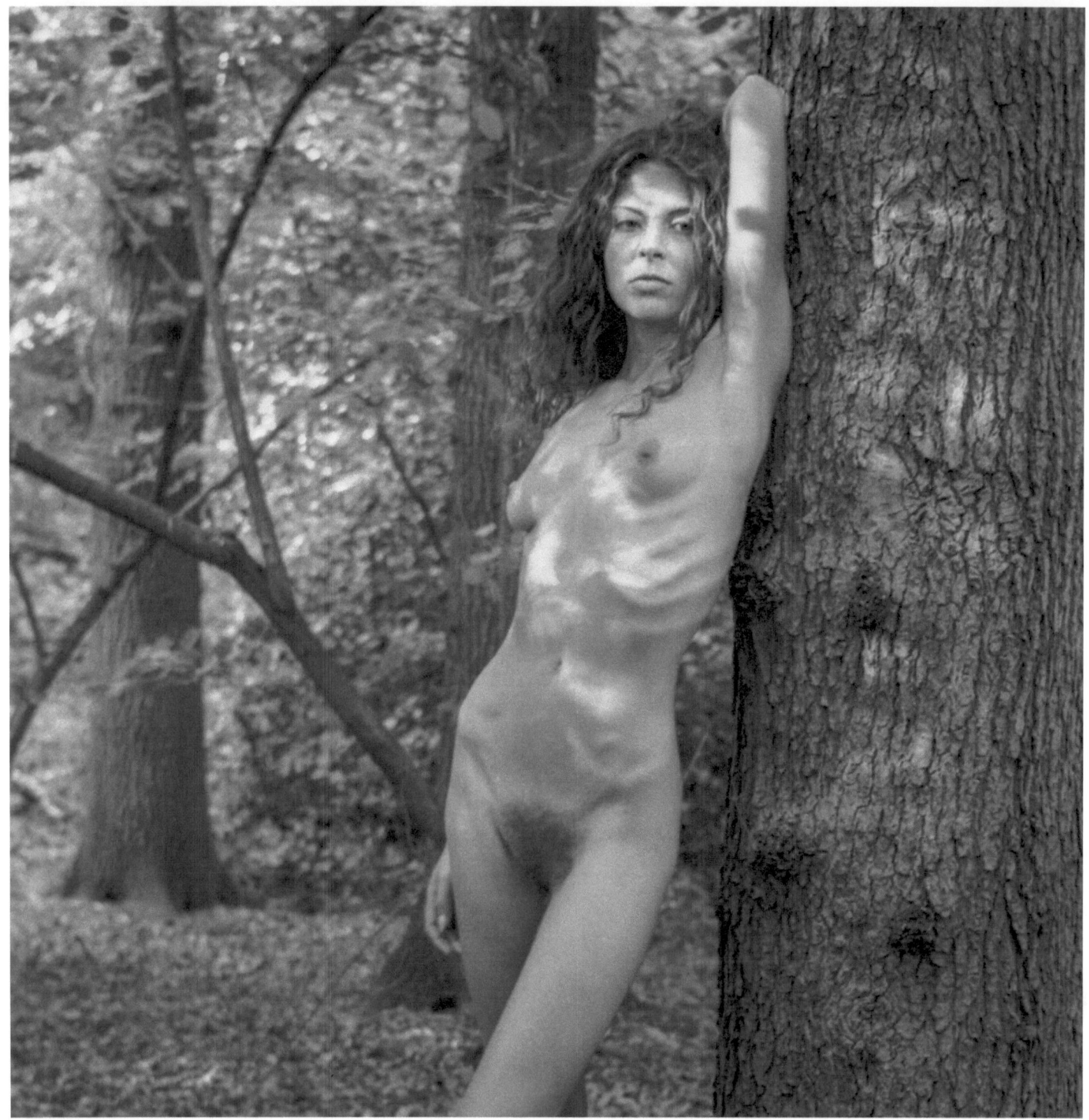

100

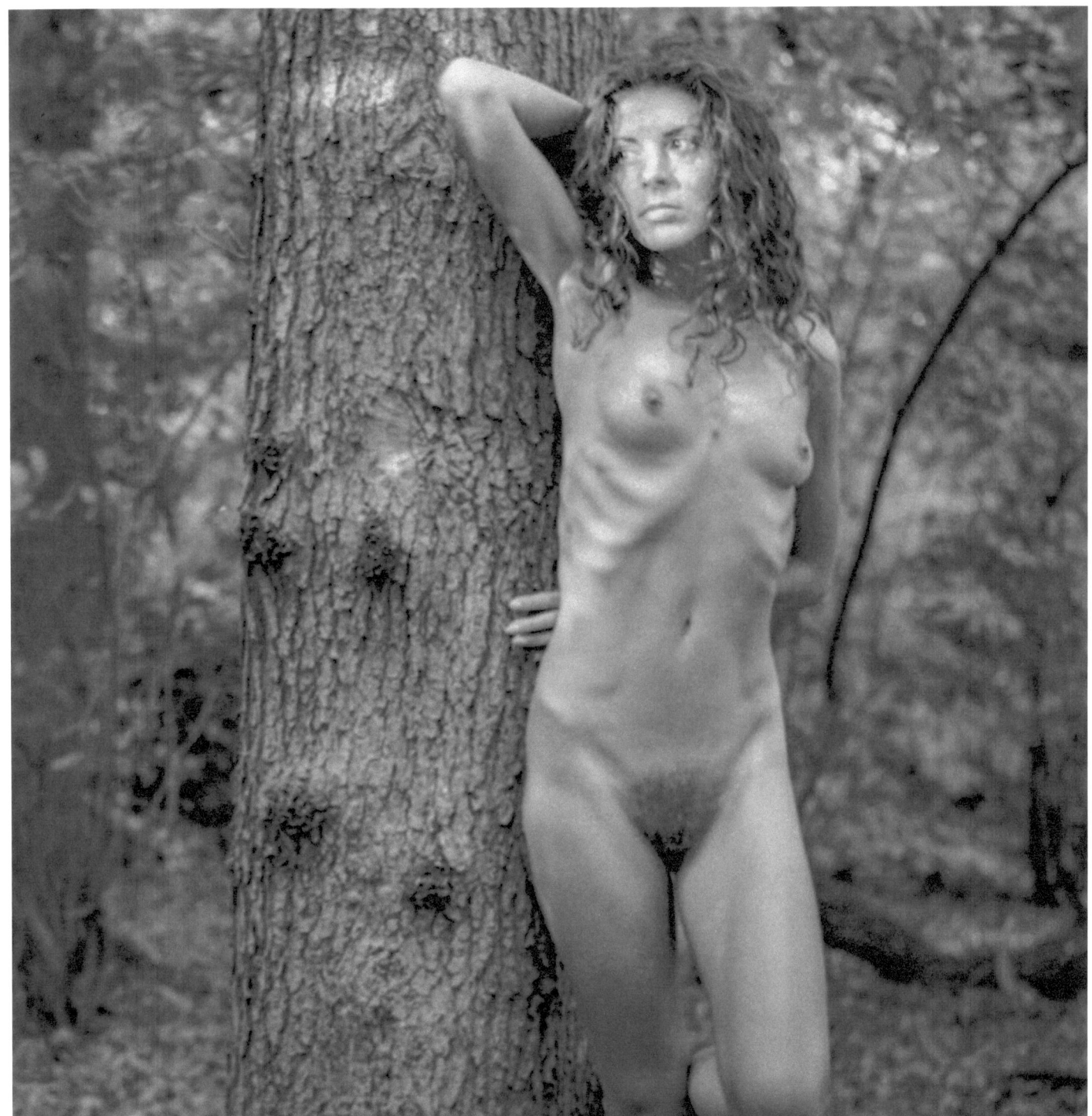

101

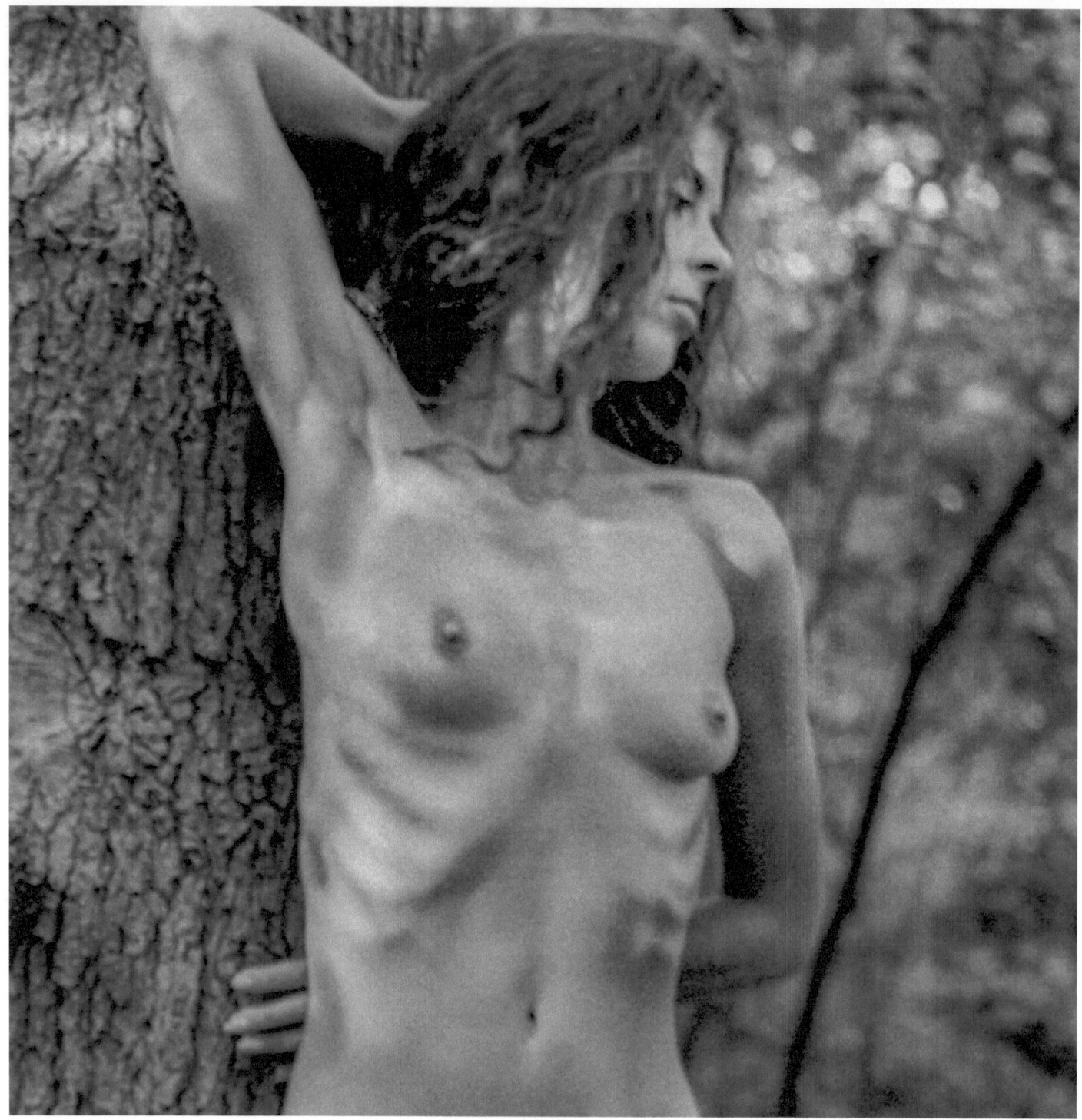

102

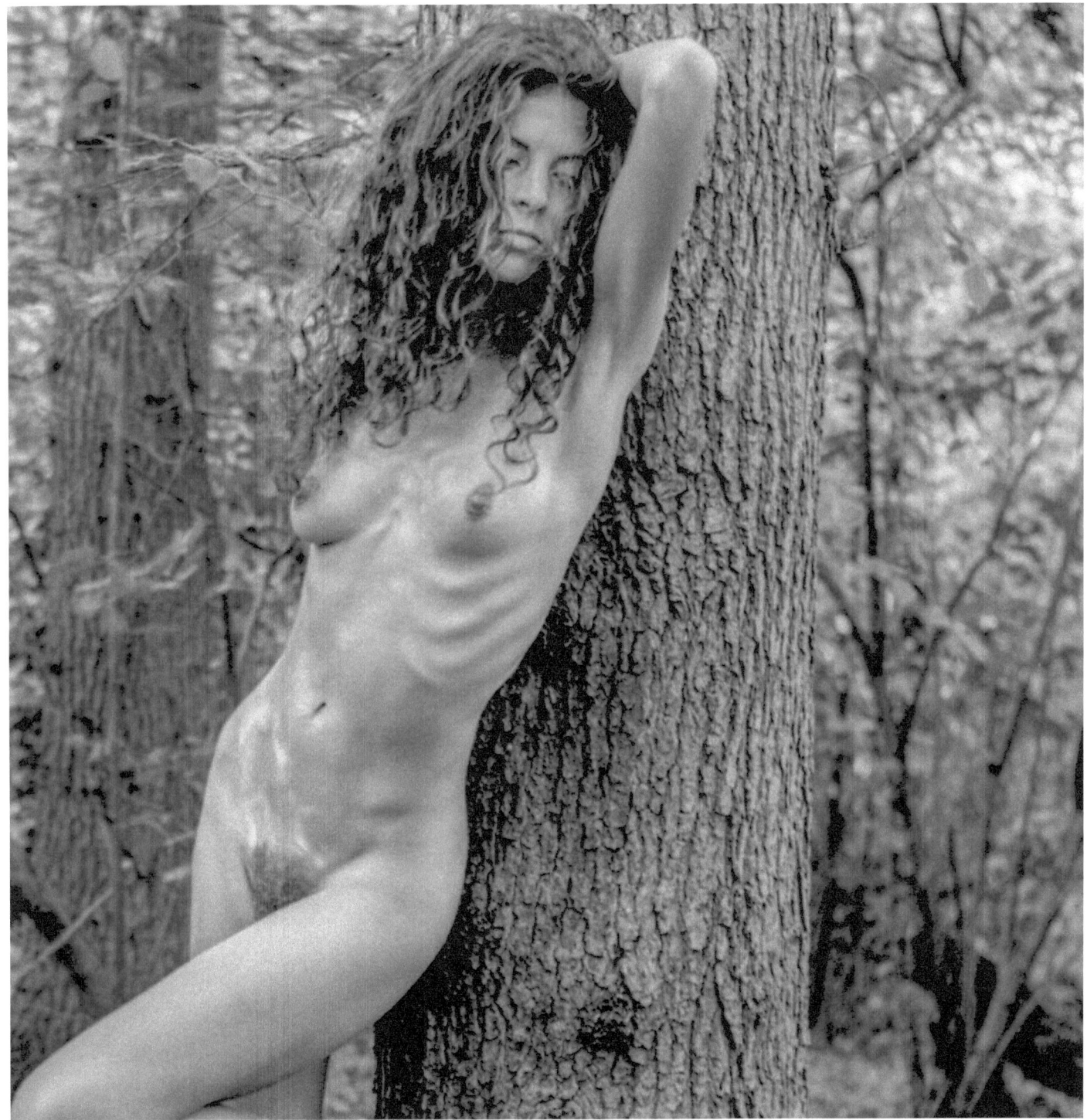

103

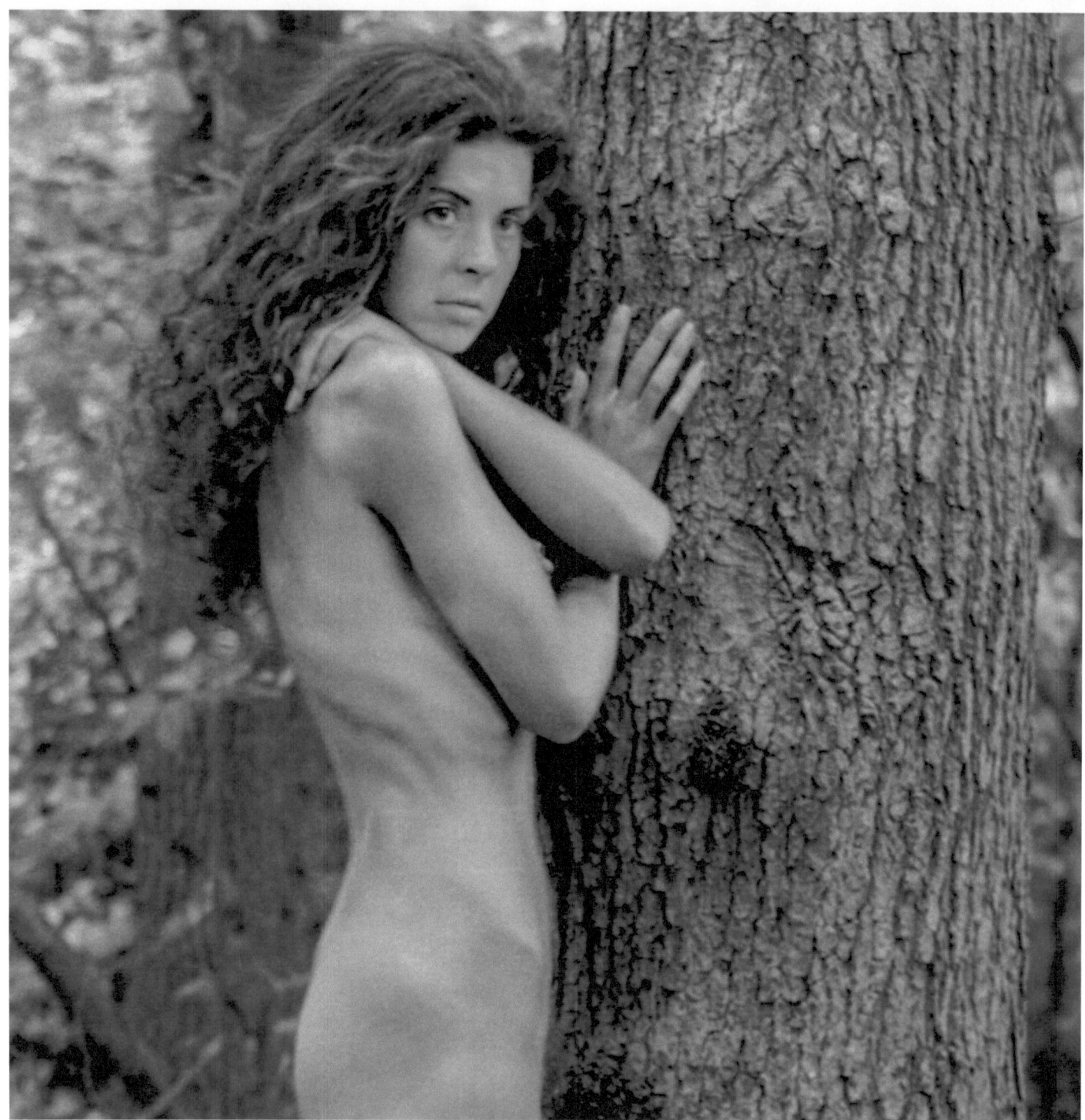

104

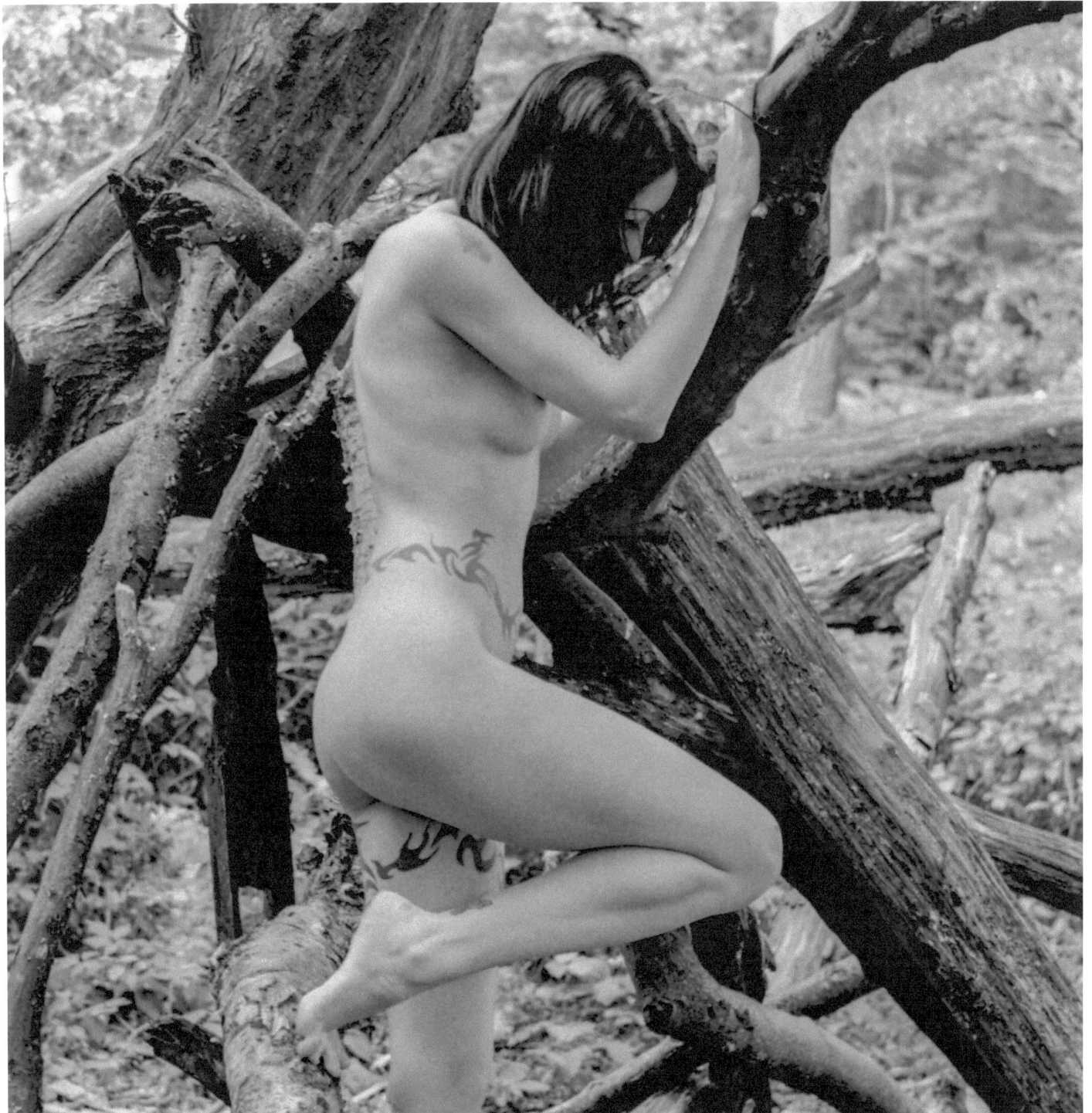

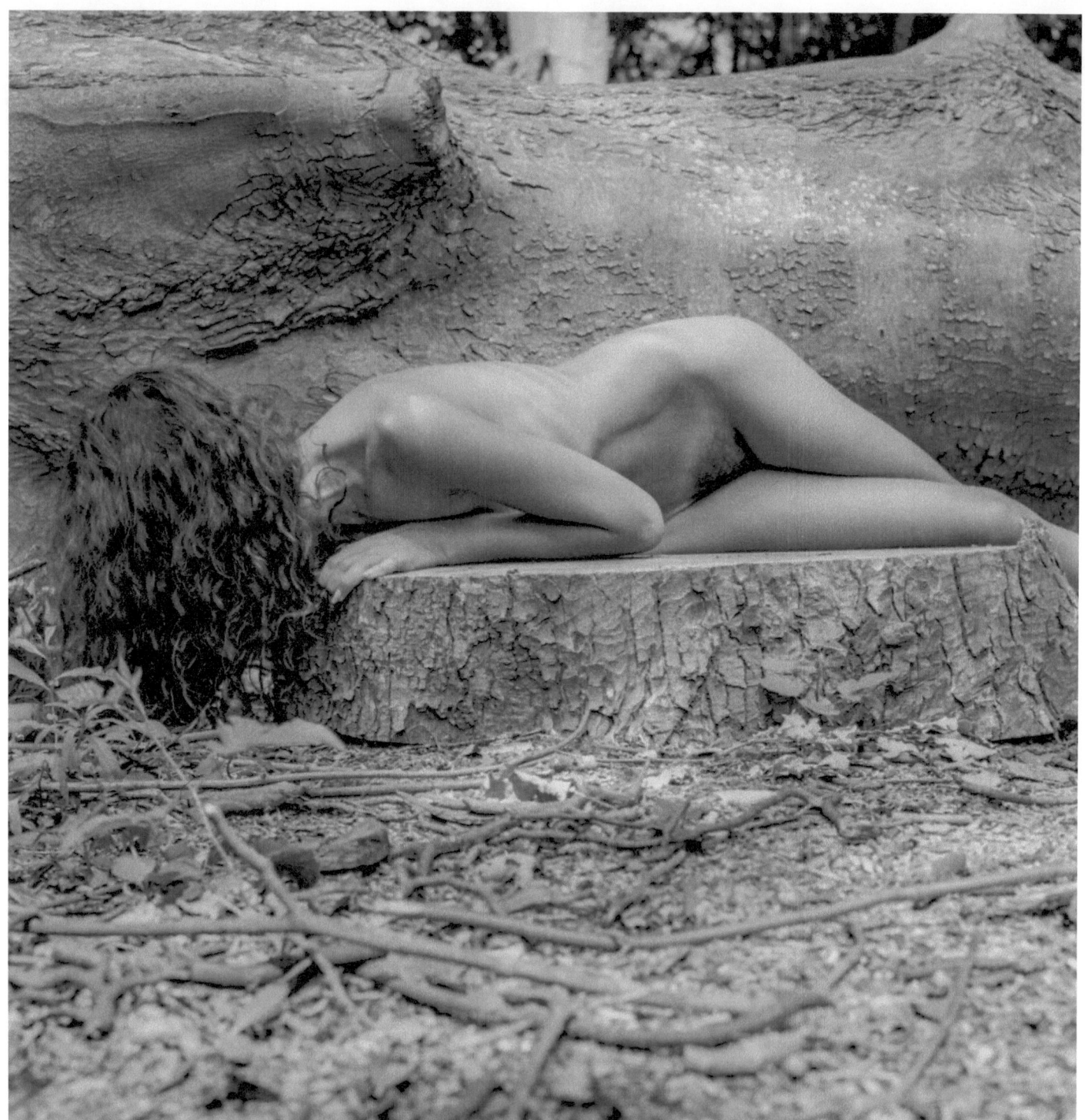

106

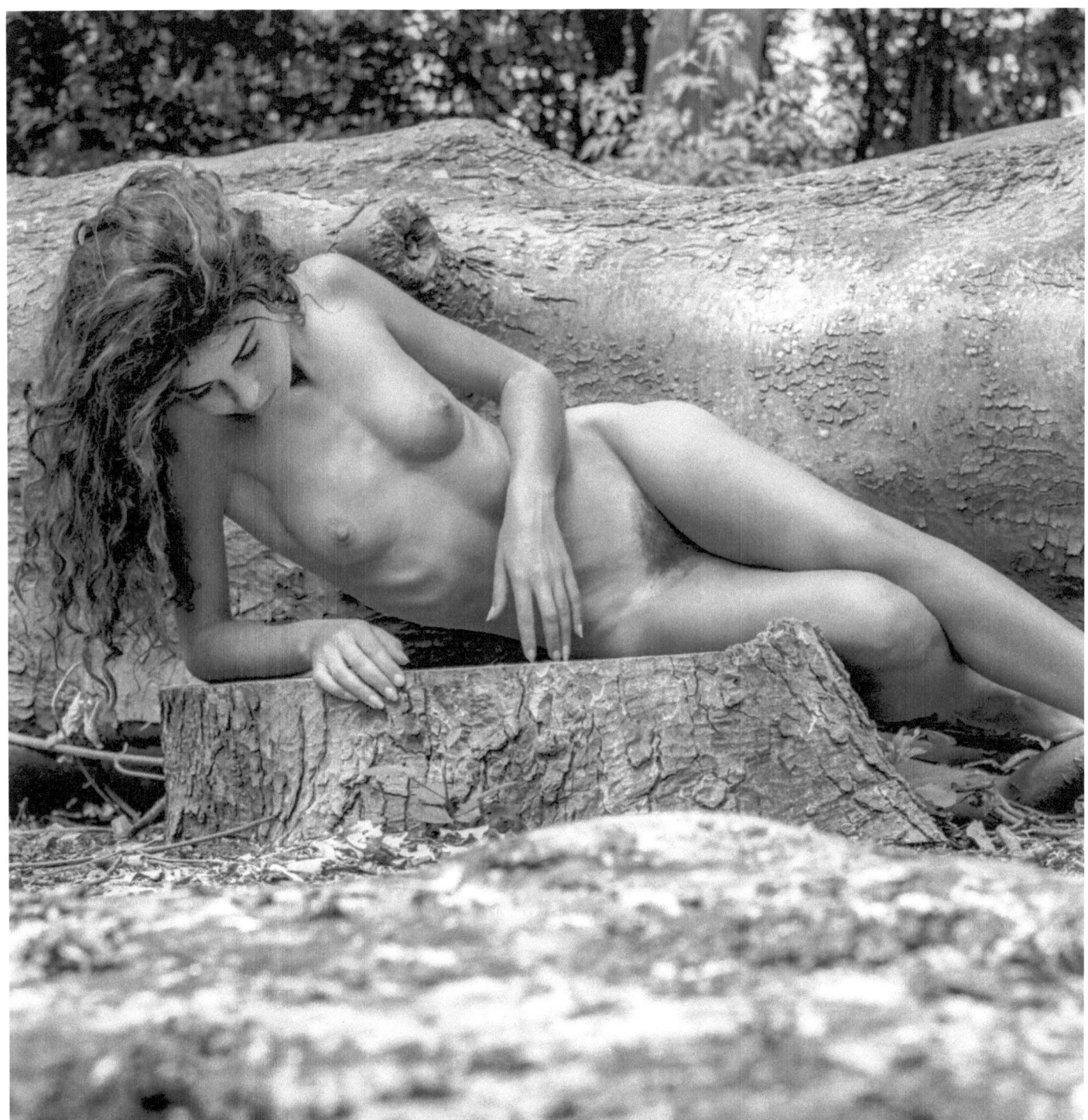

107

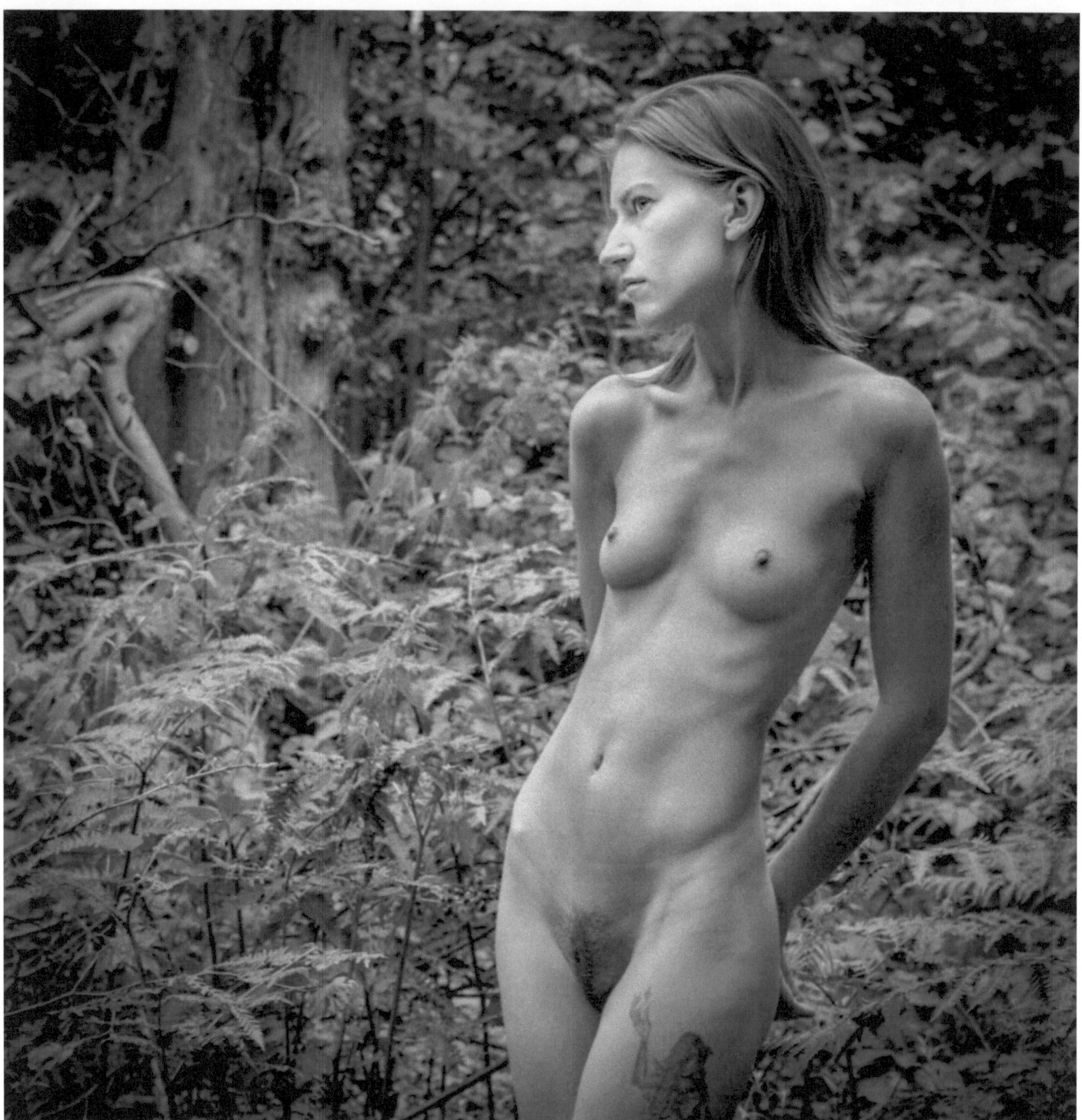

108

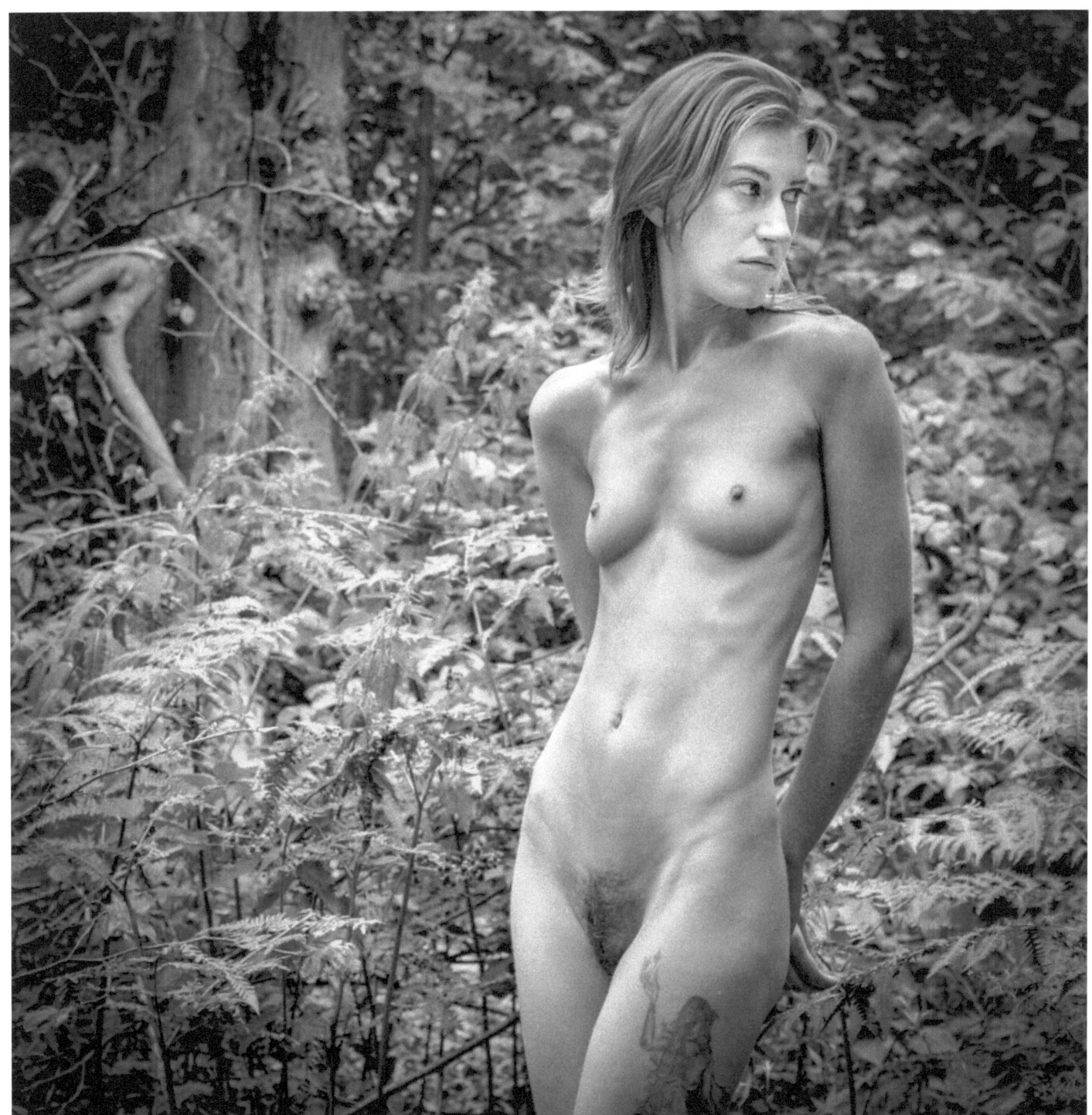

109

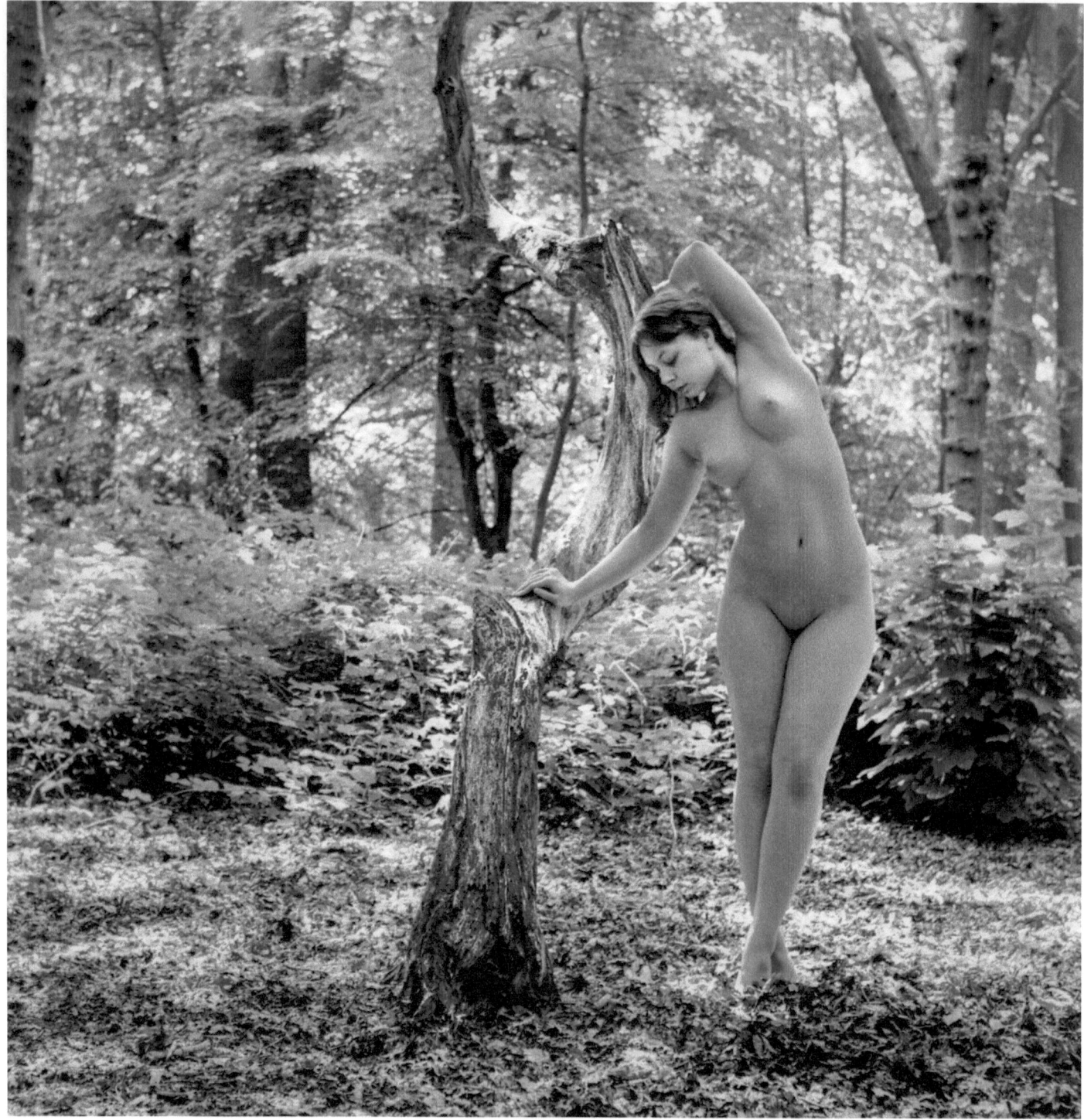

110

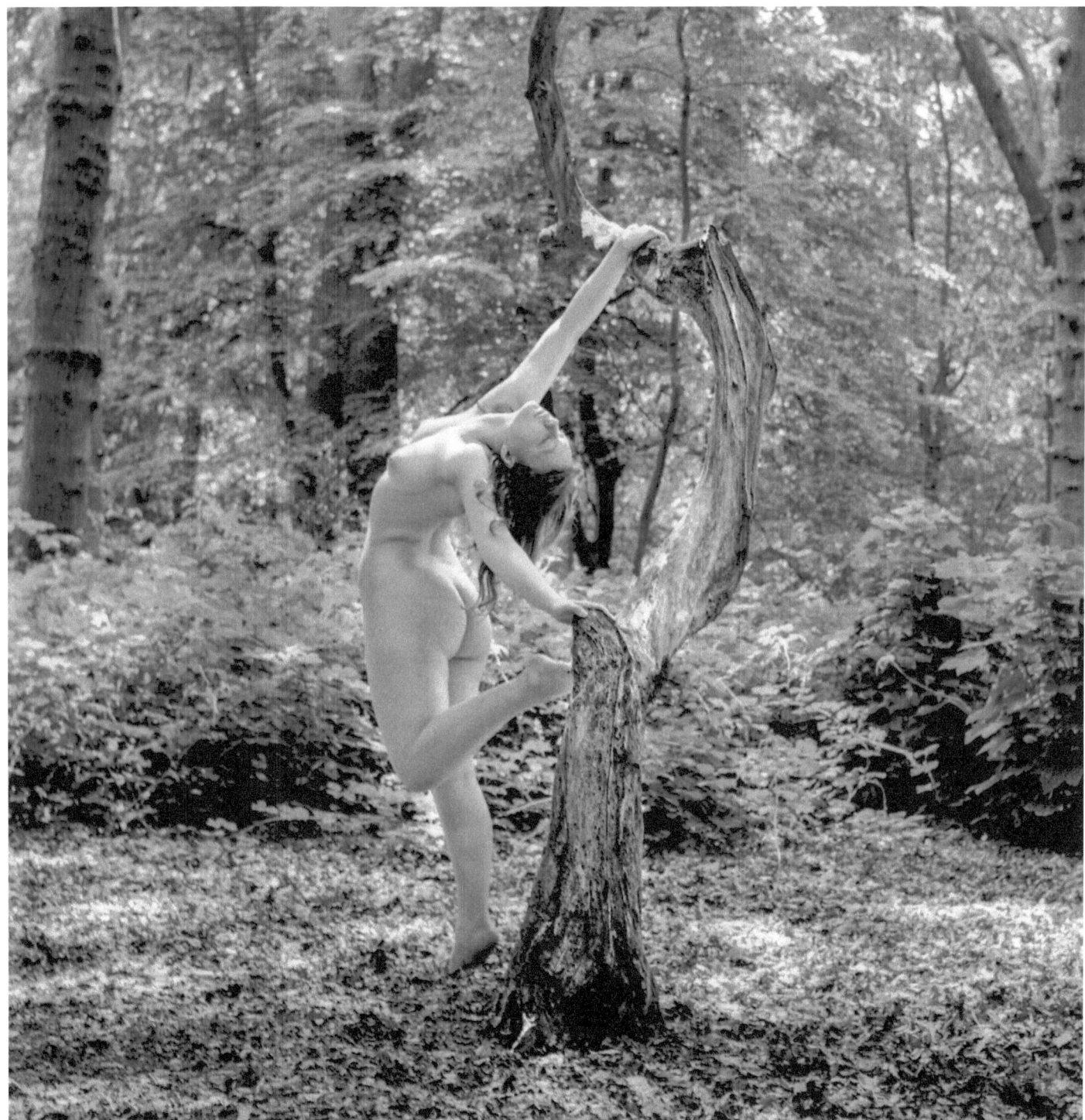

111

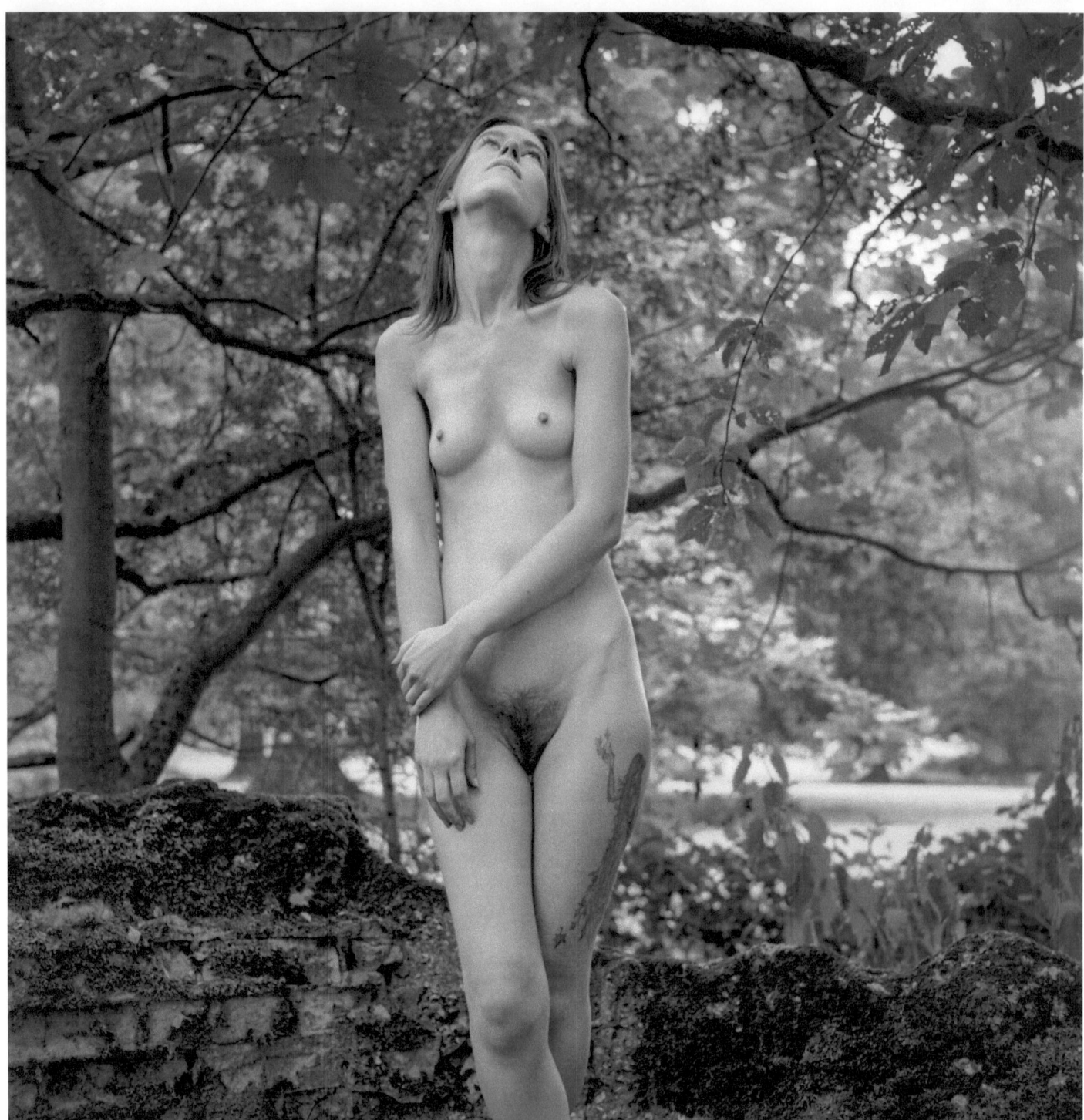

112

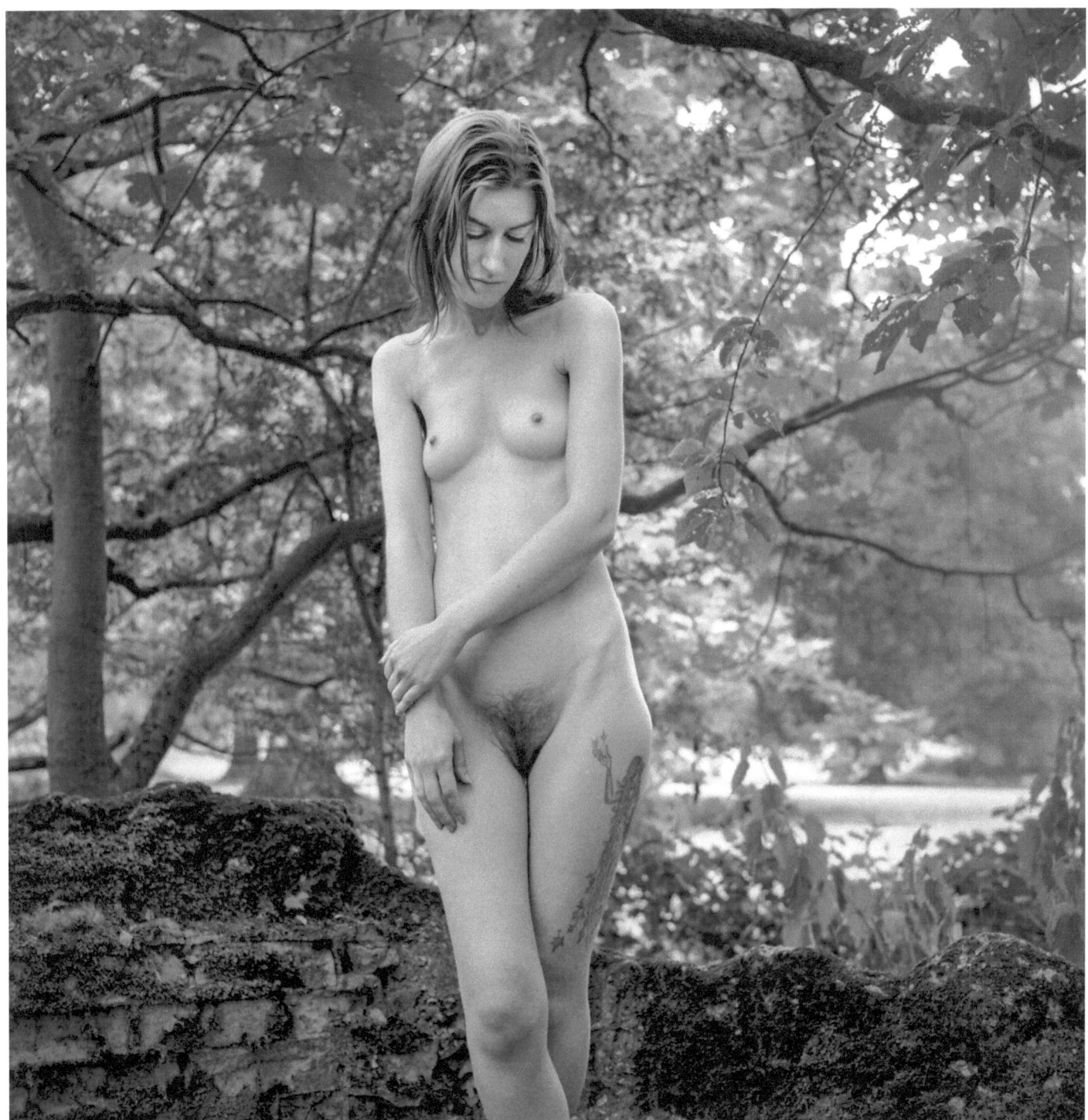

113

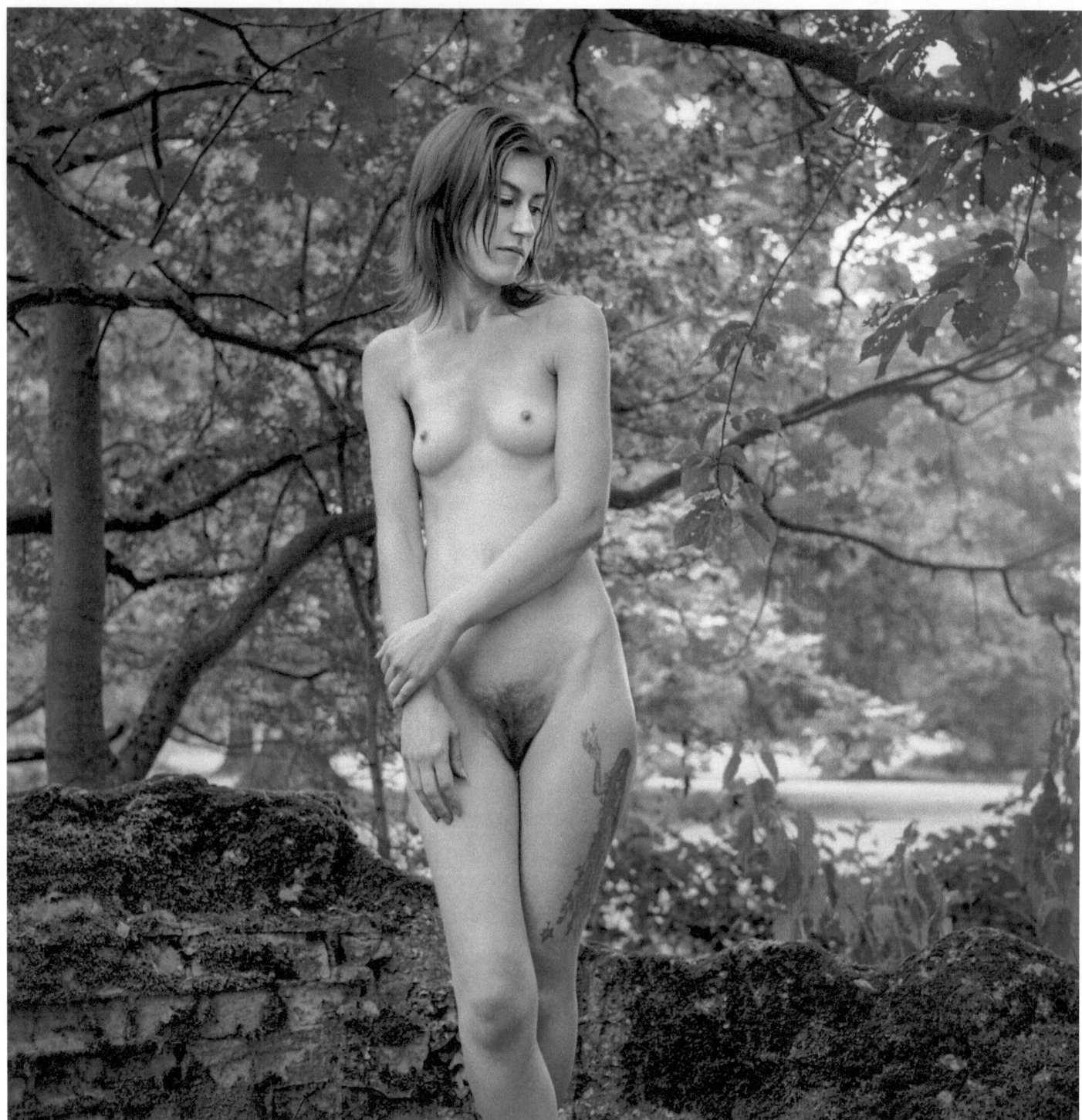

114

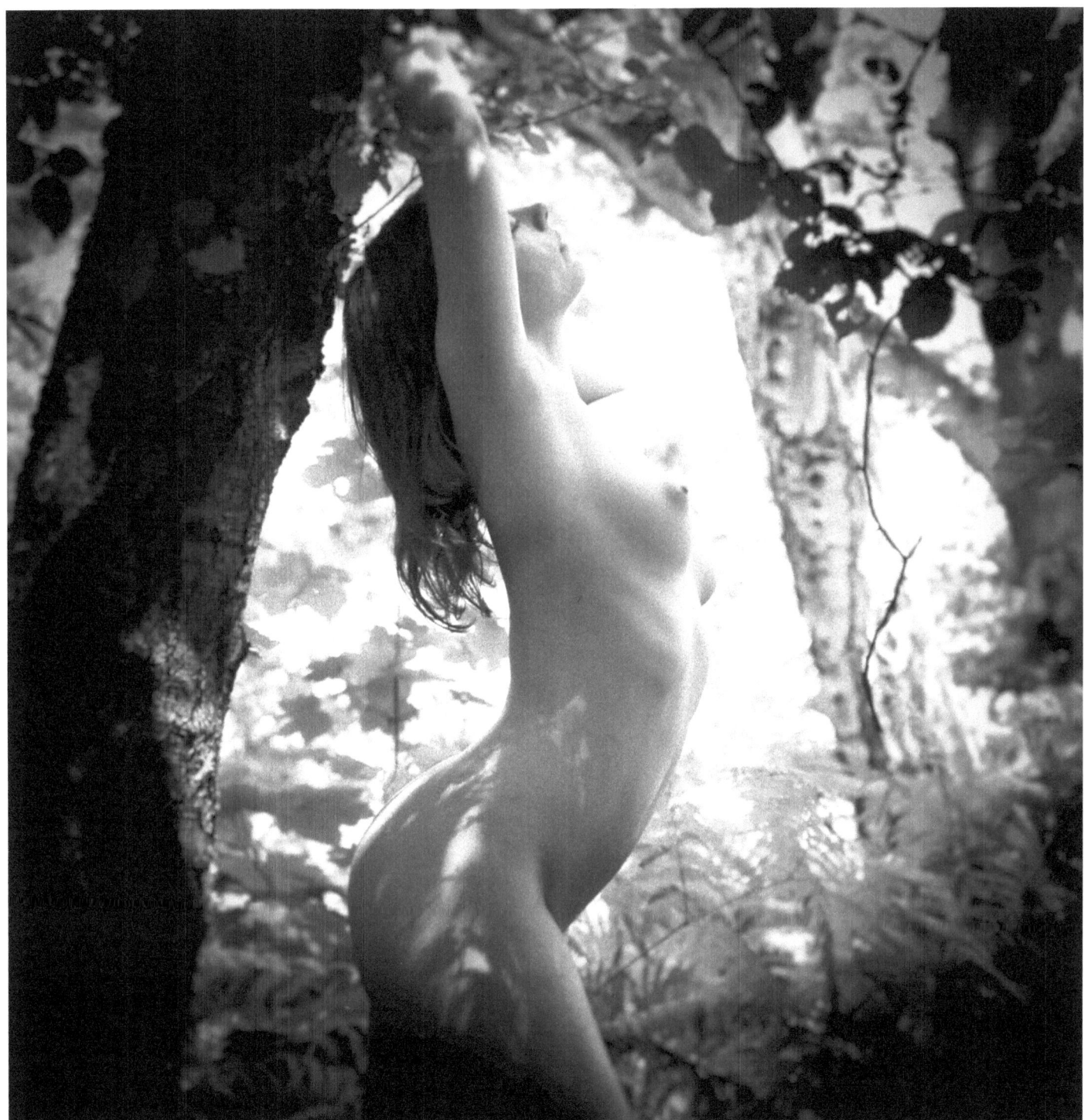

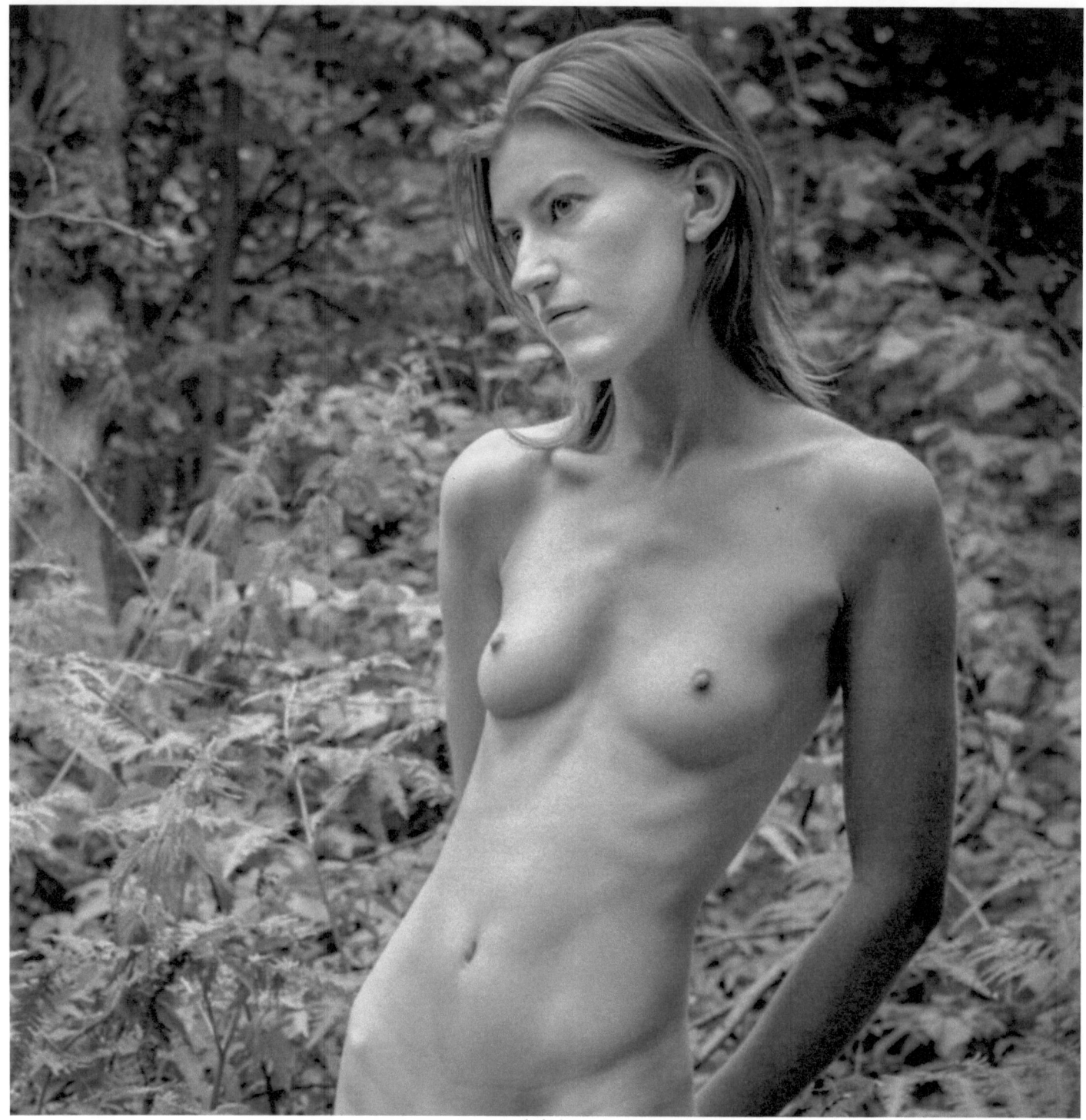

116

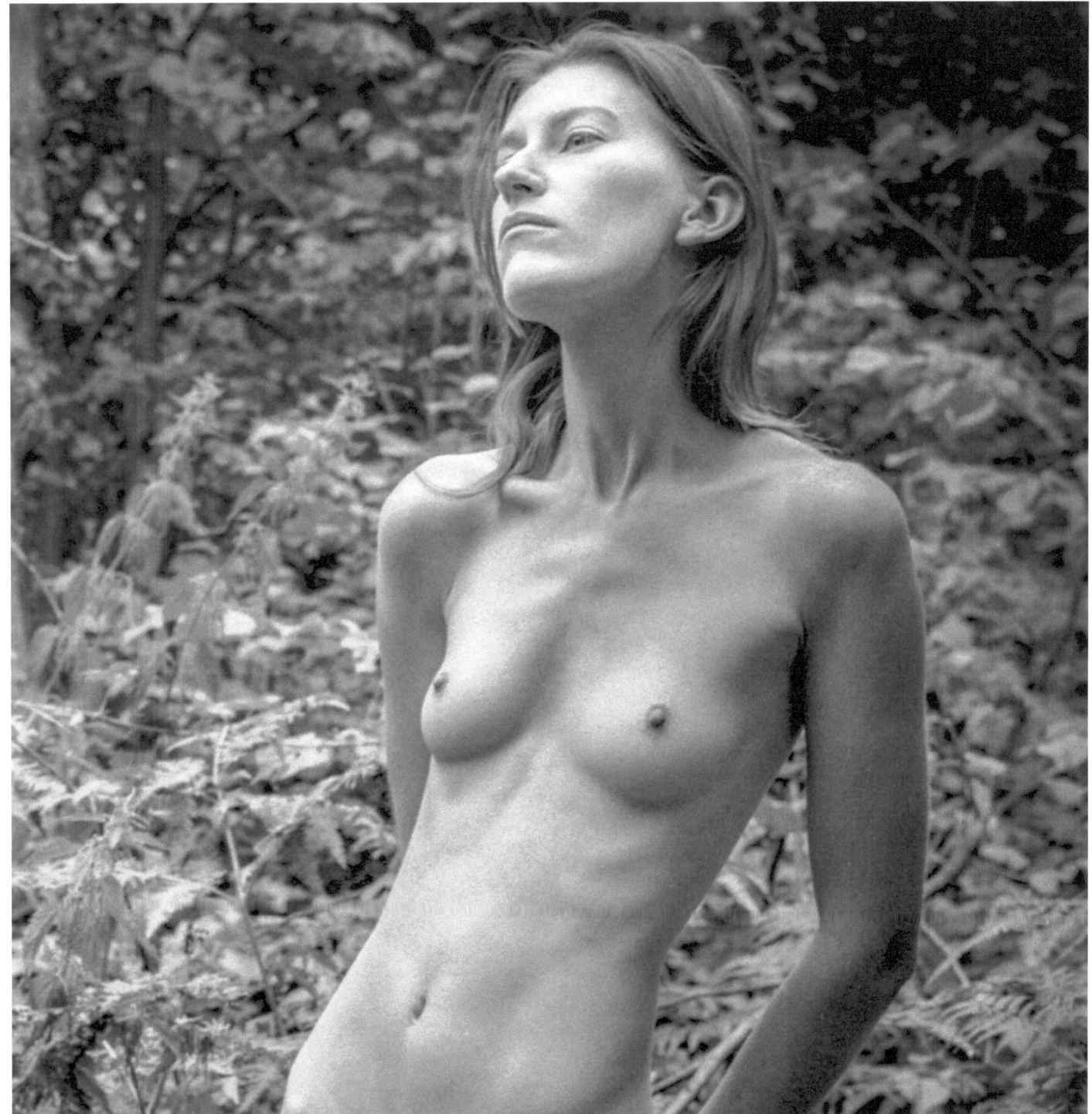

117

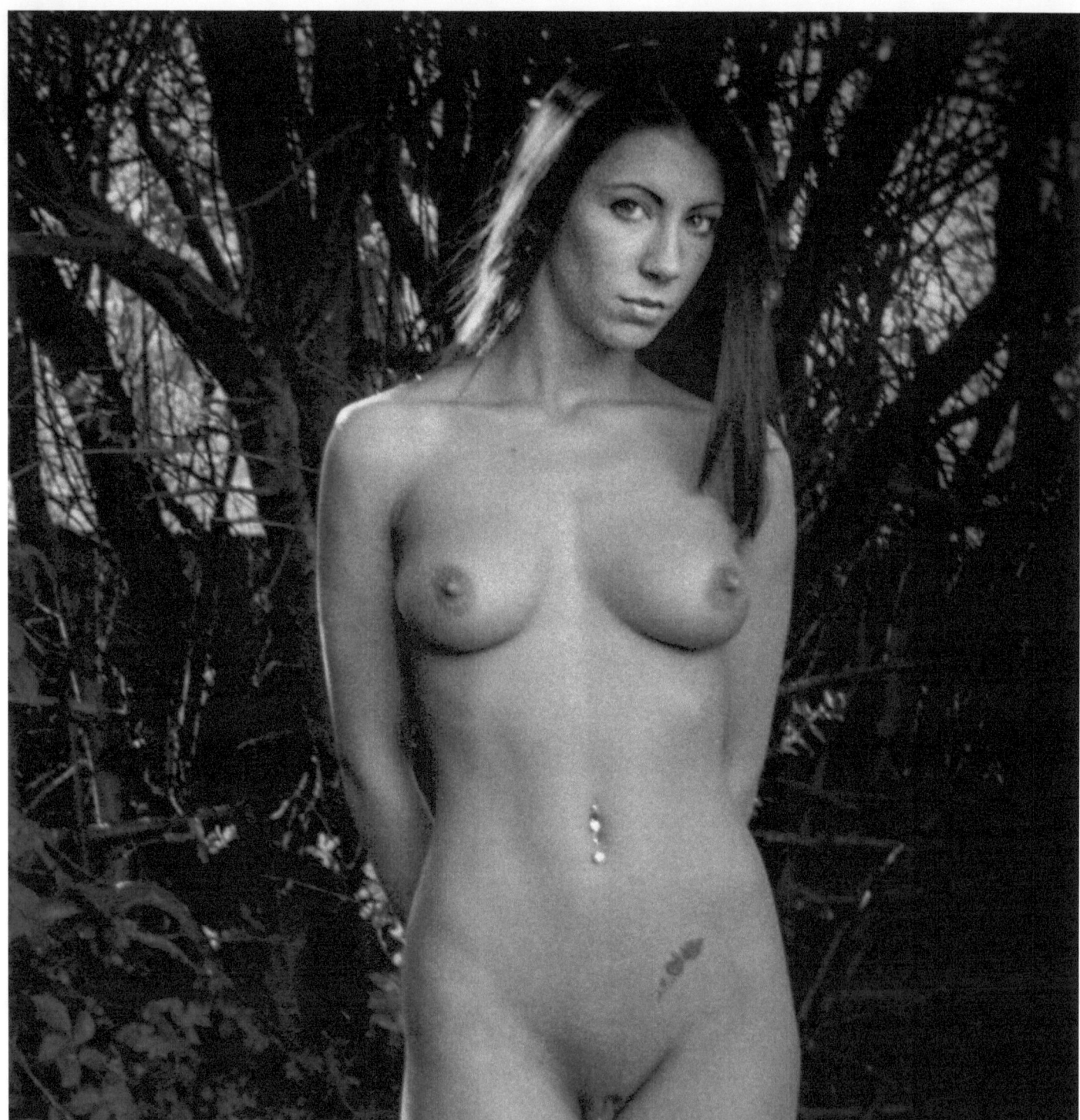

118

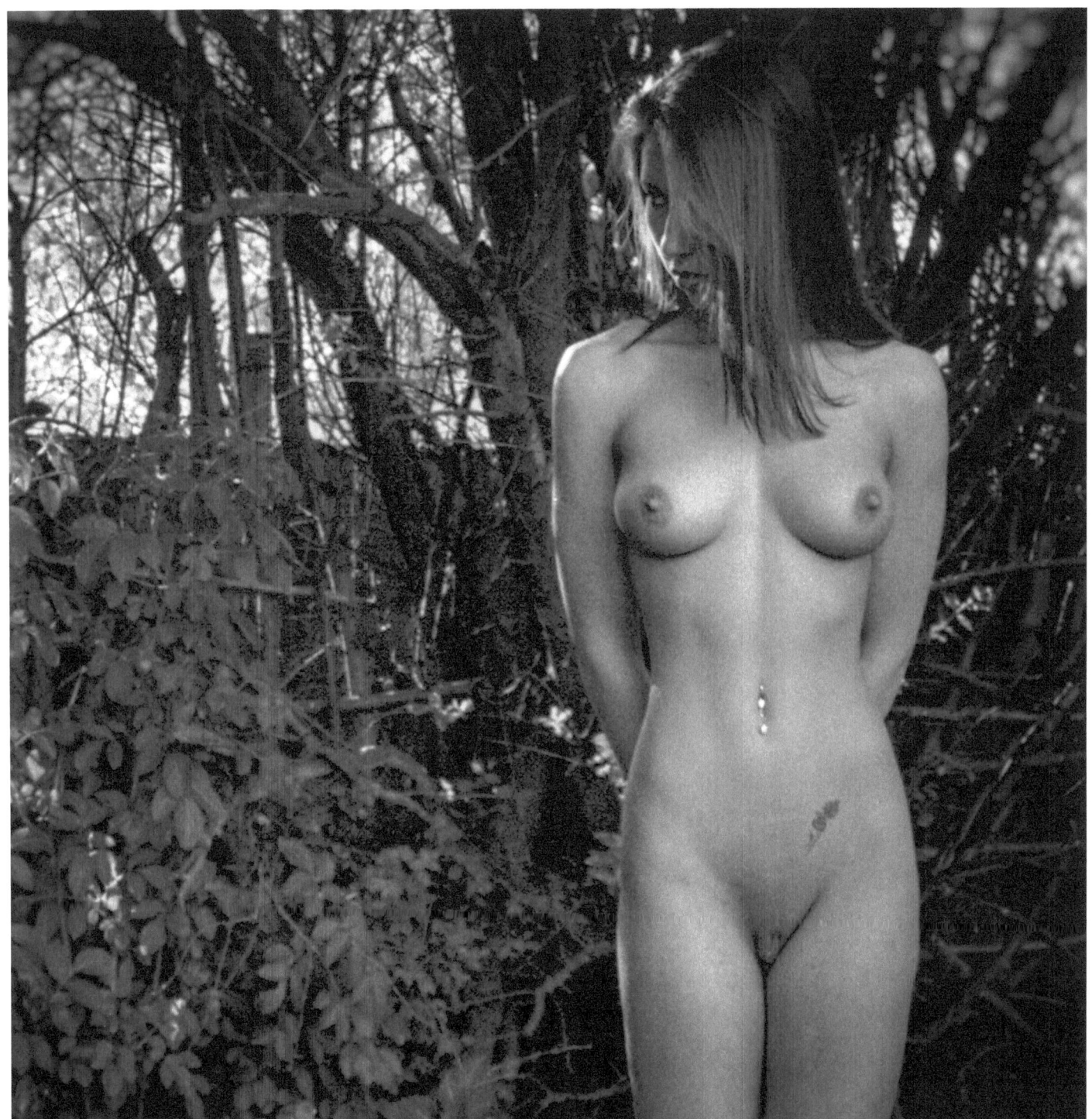

119

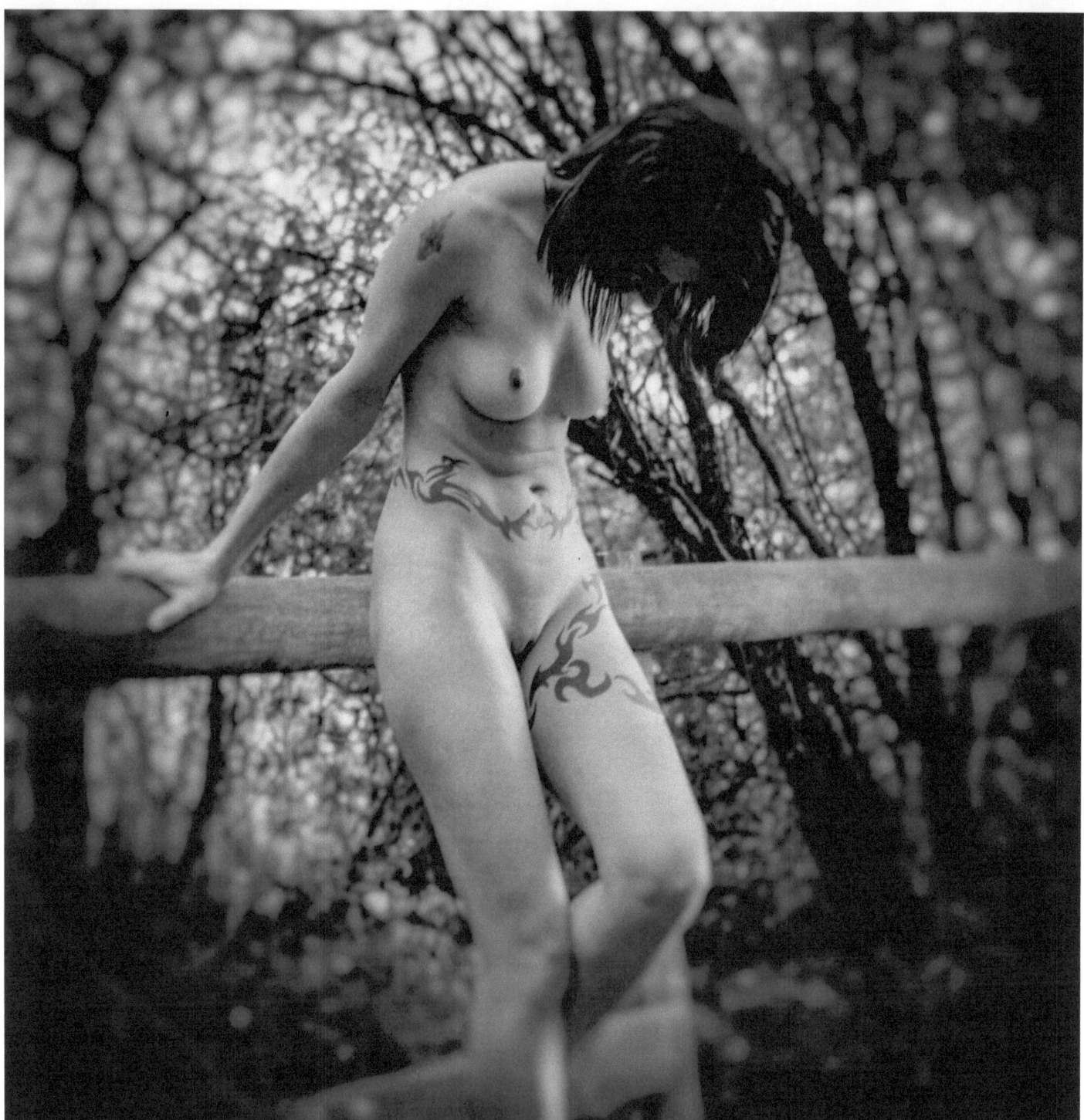

120

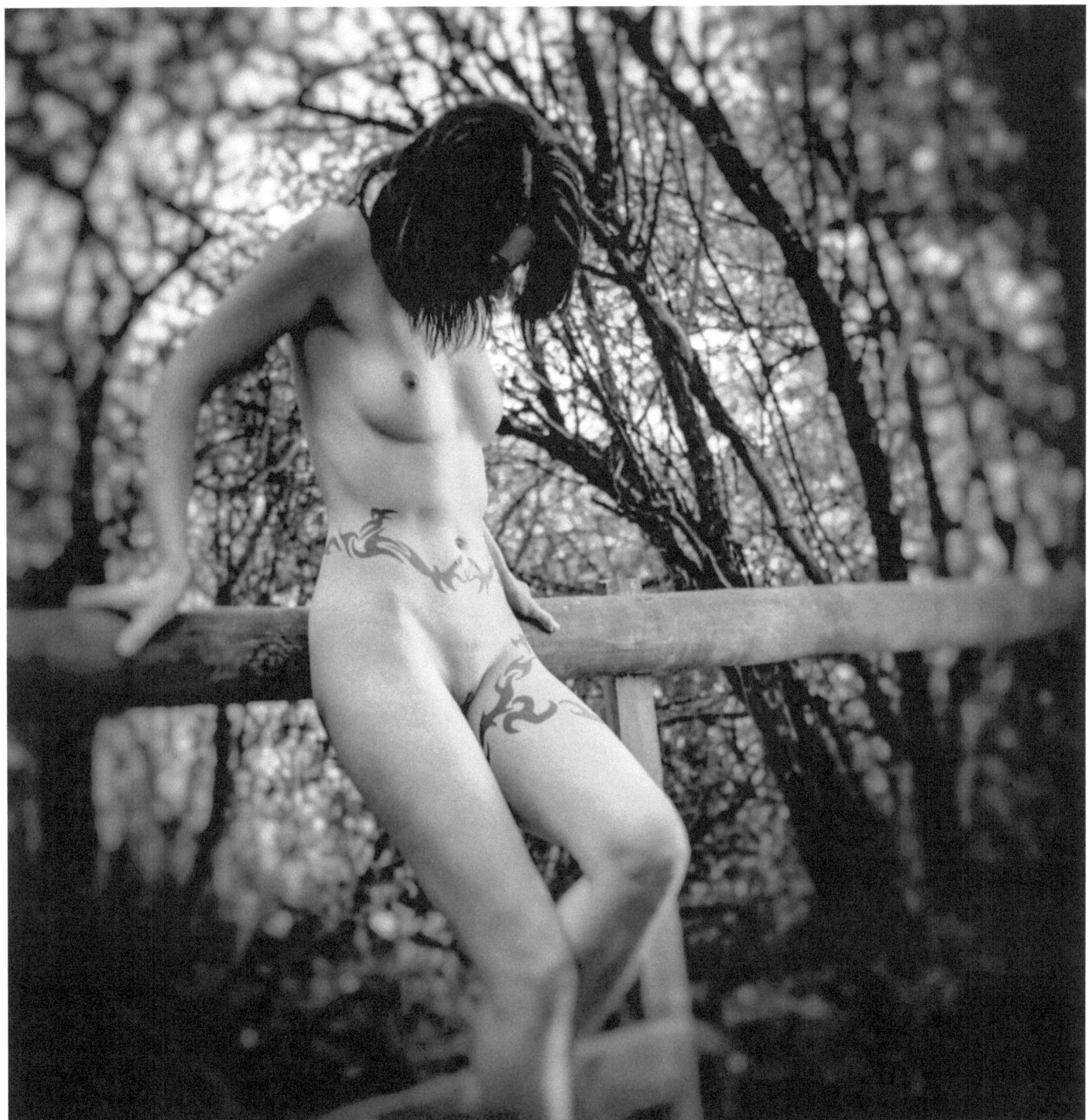

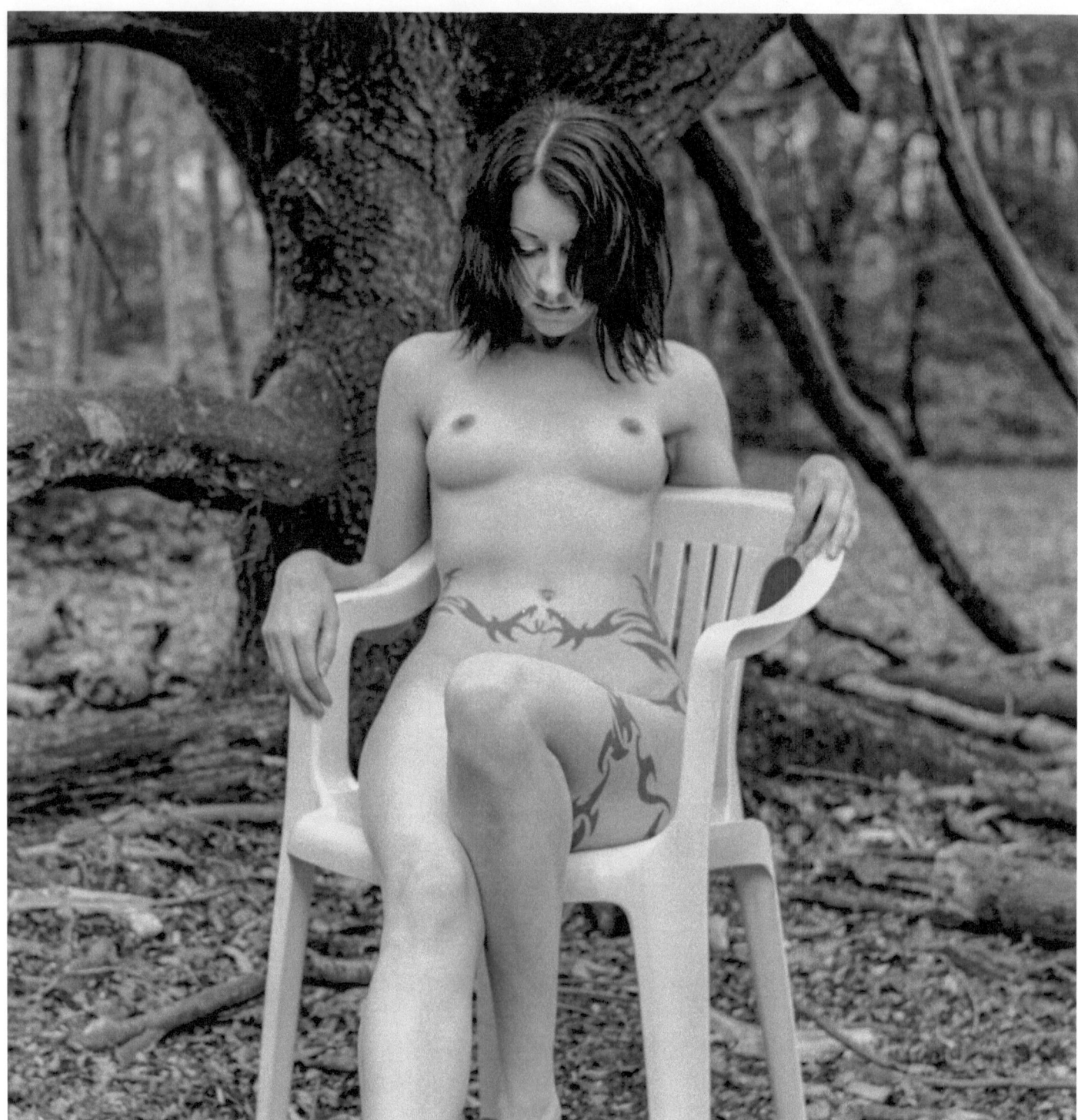

122

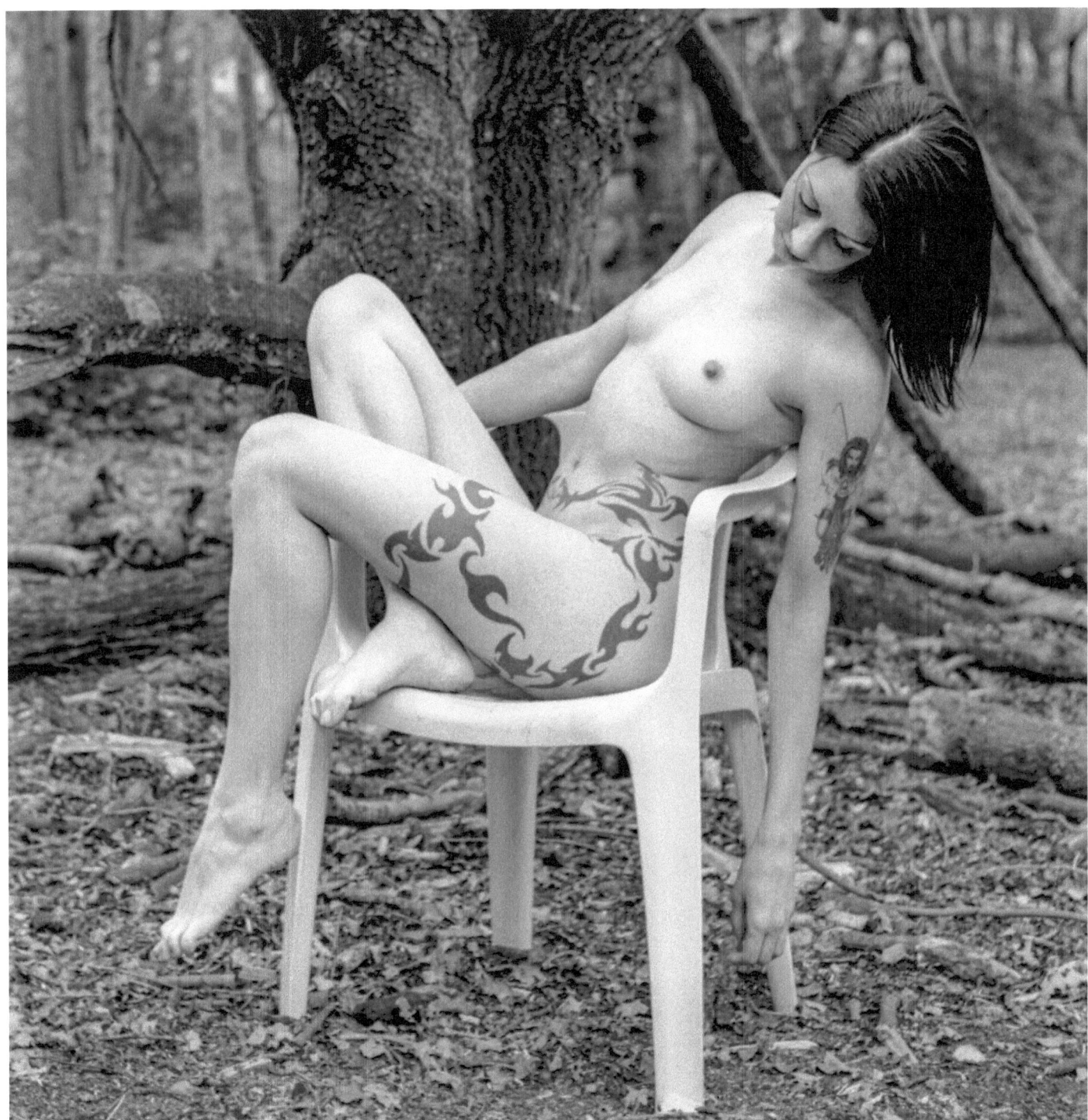

123

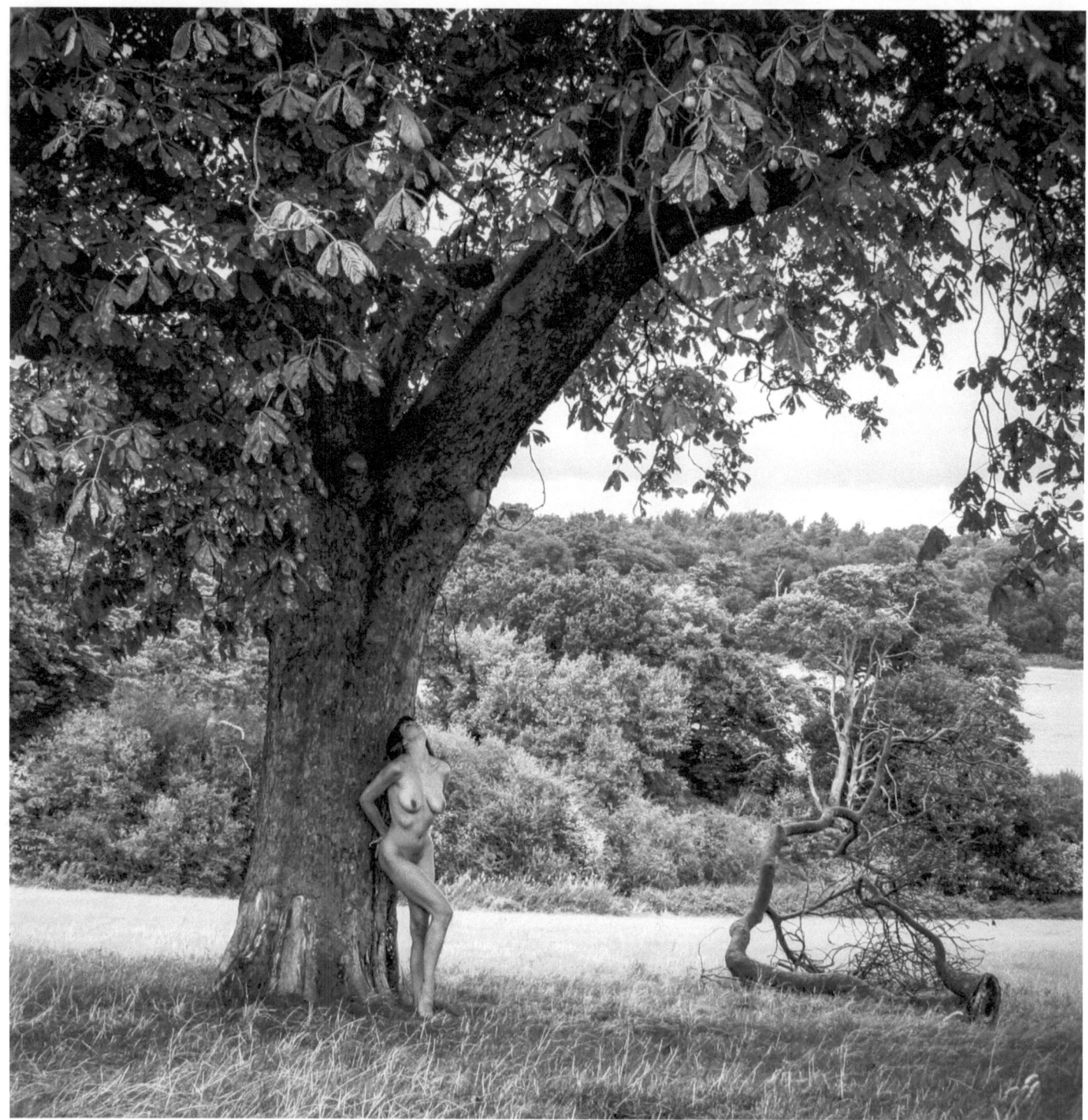

124

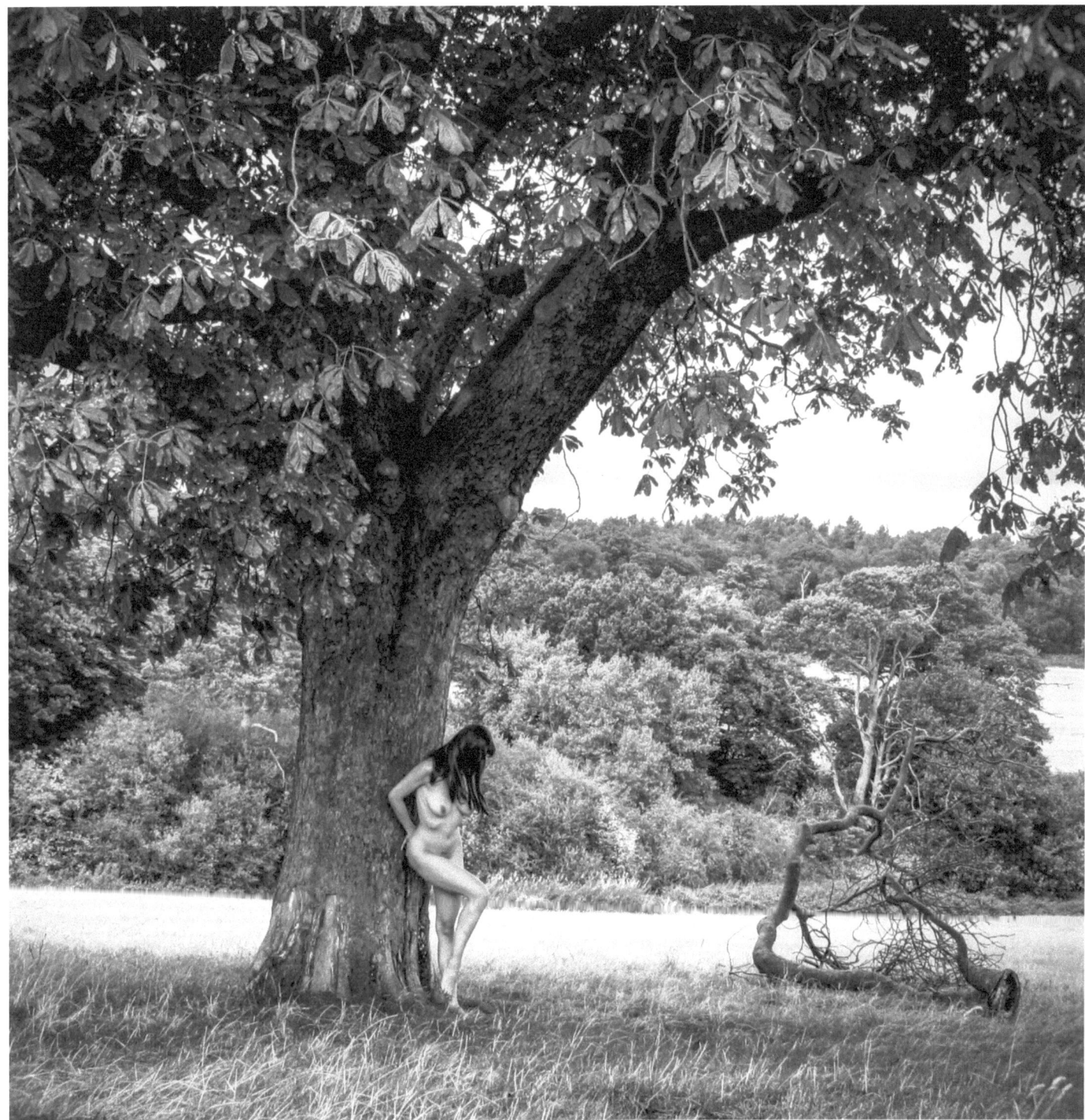

125

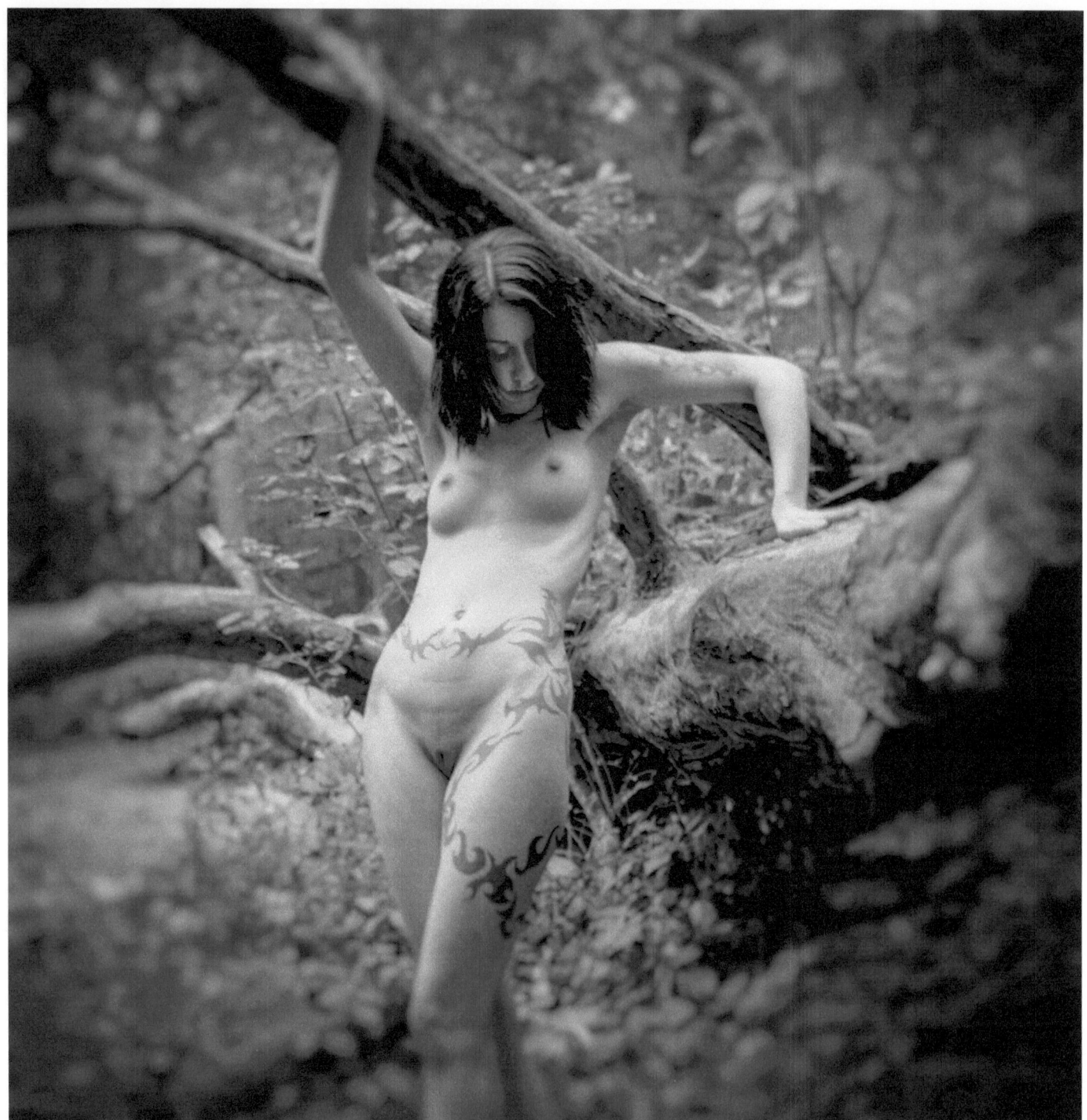

126

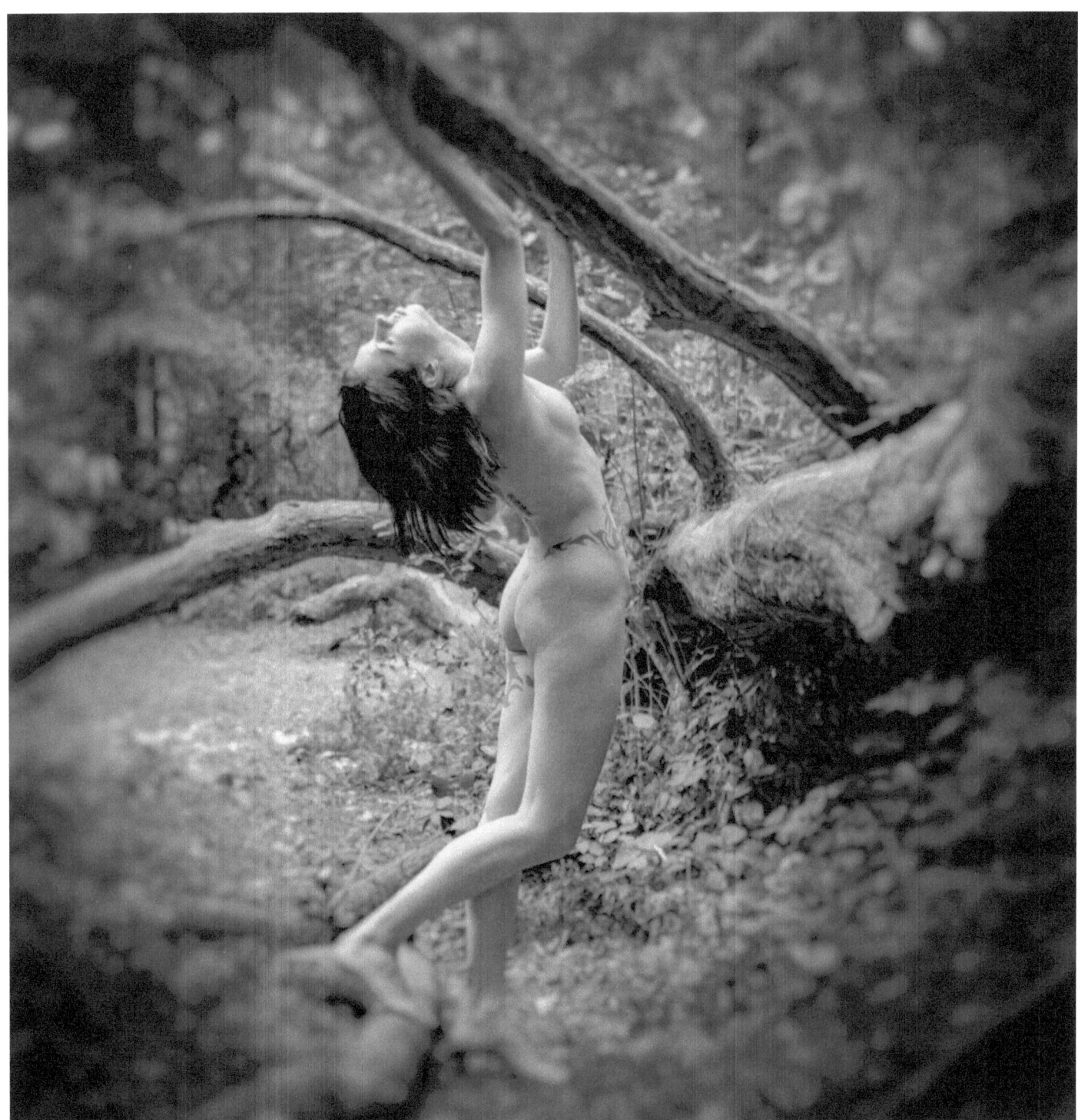

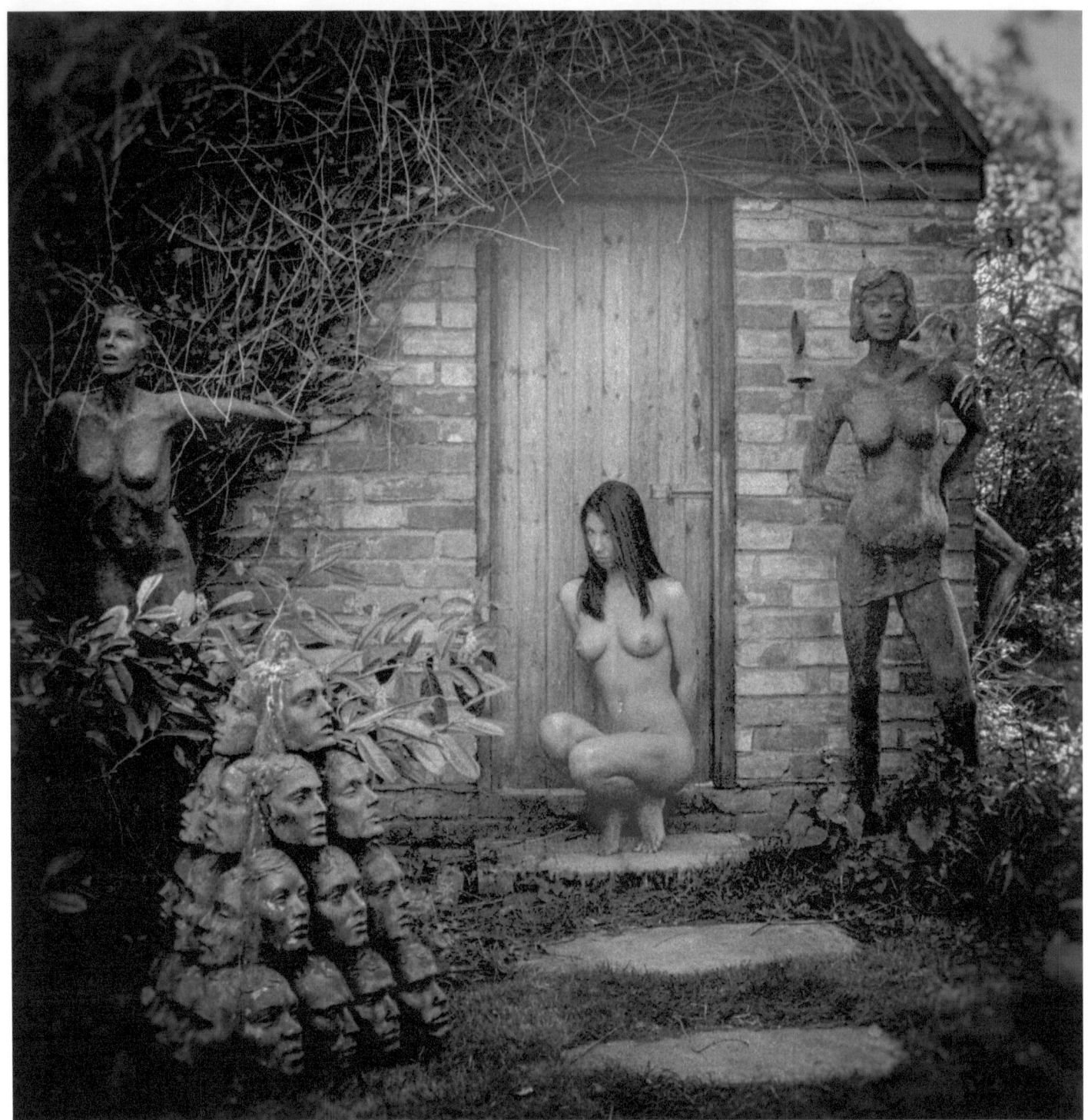

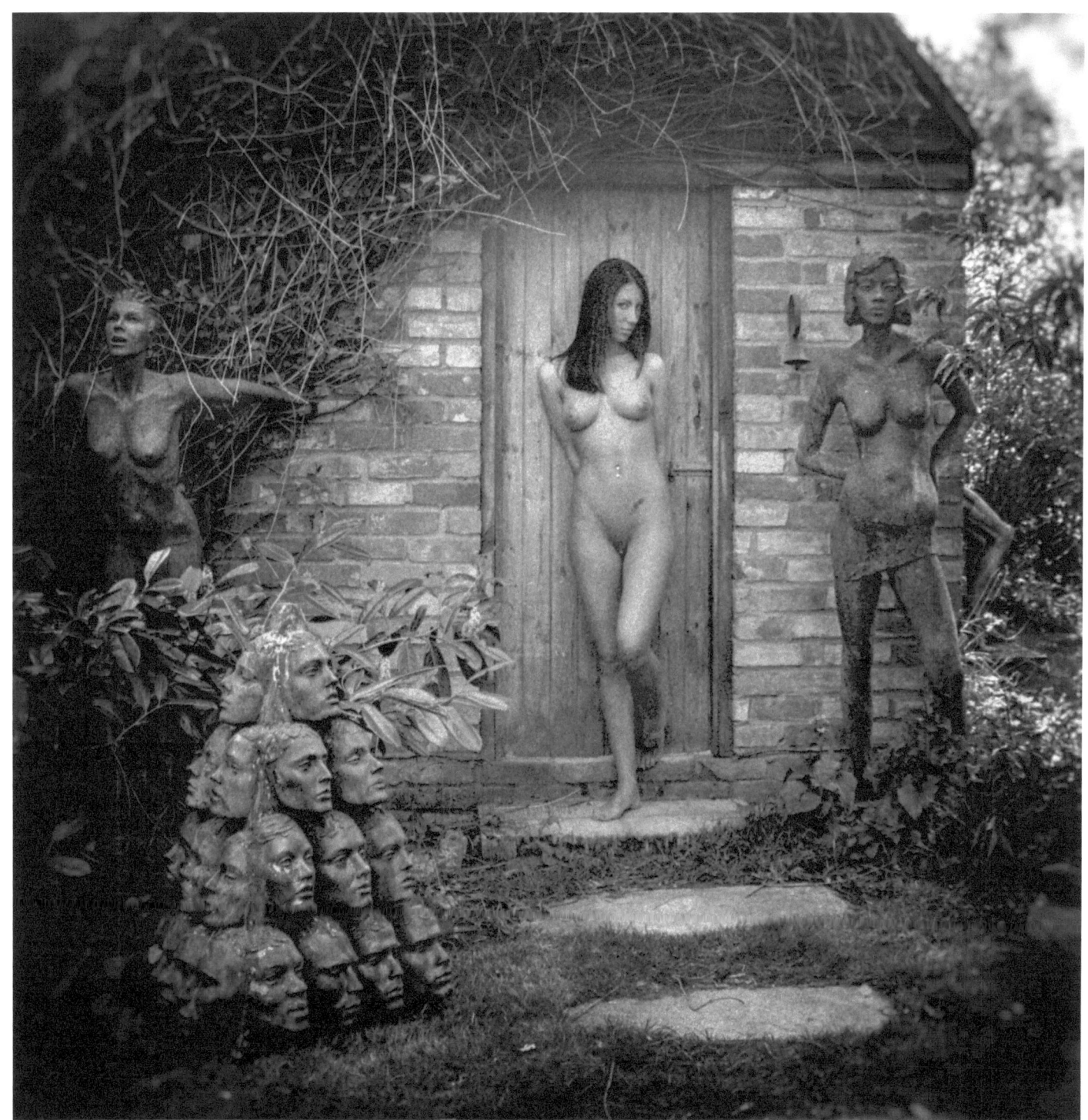

129

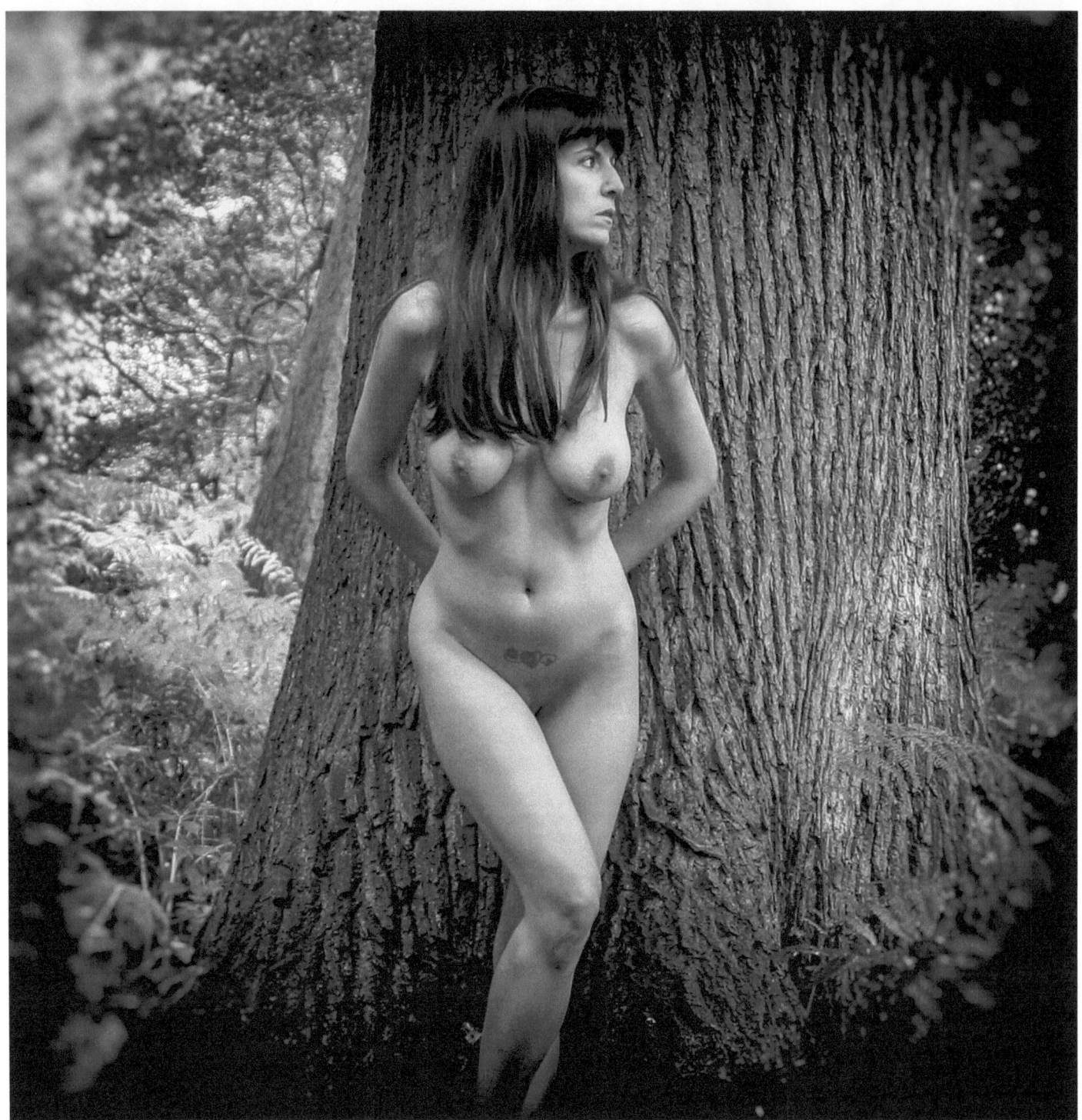

130

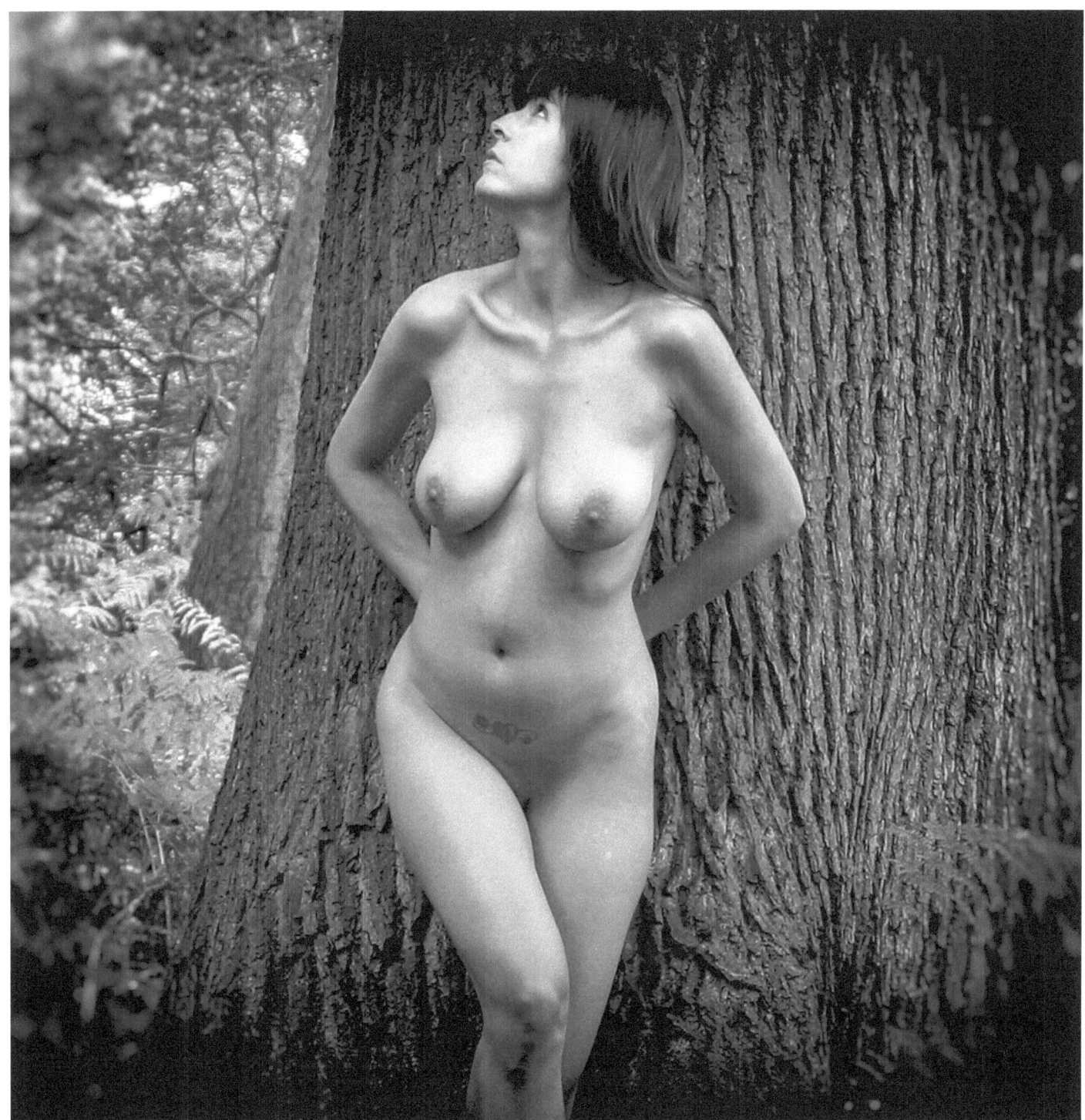

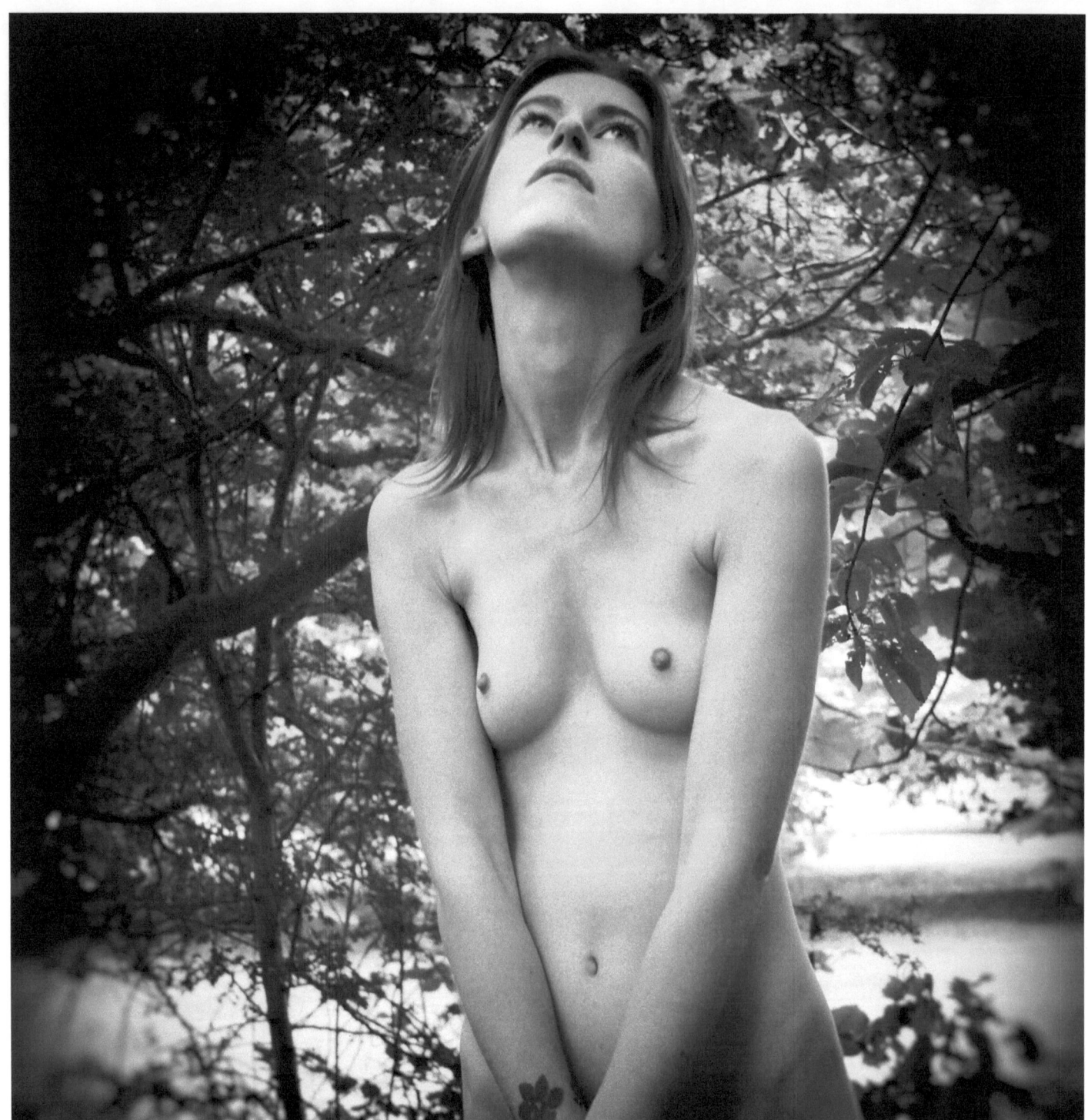

132

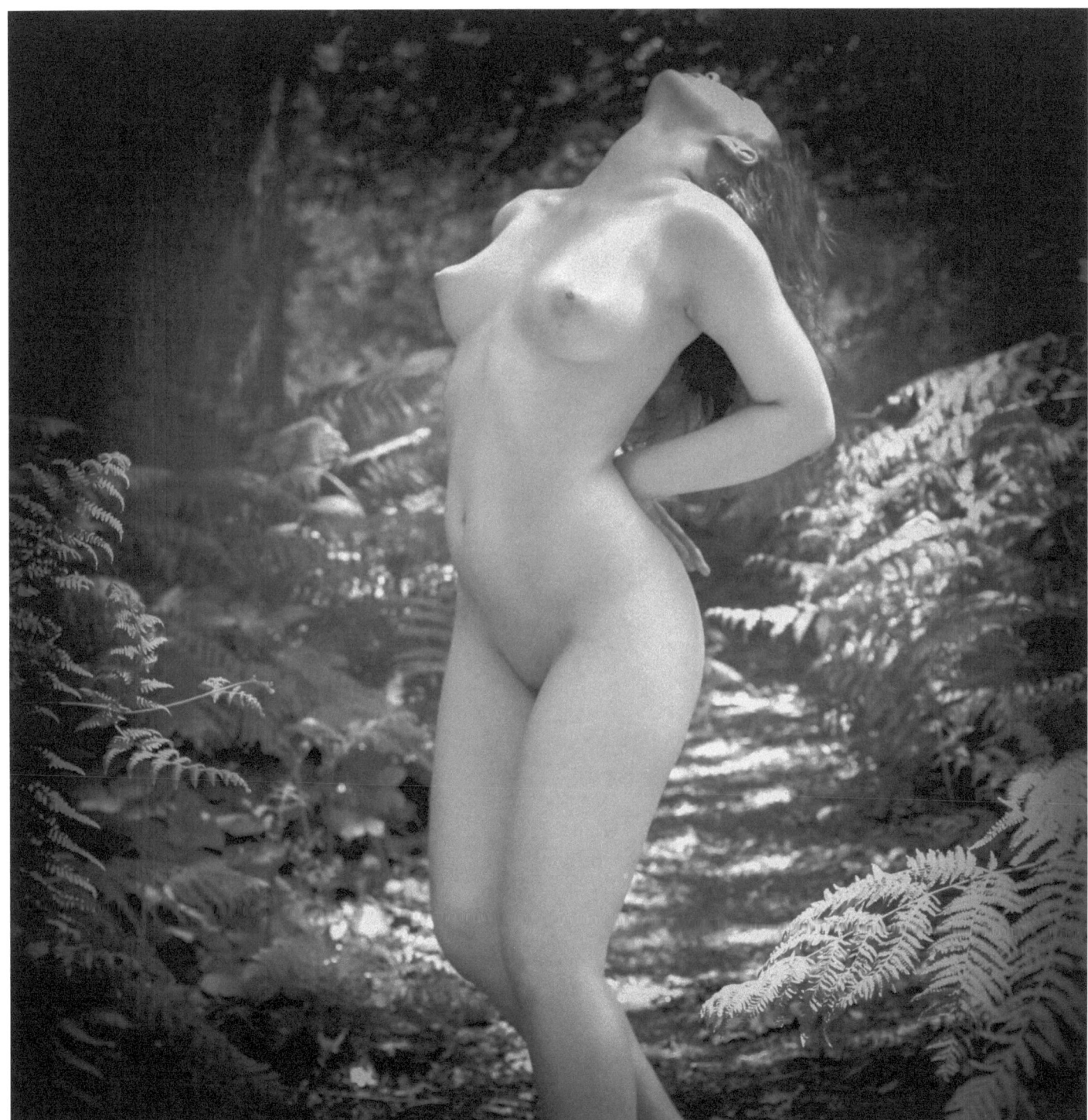

133

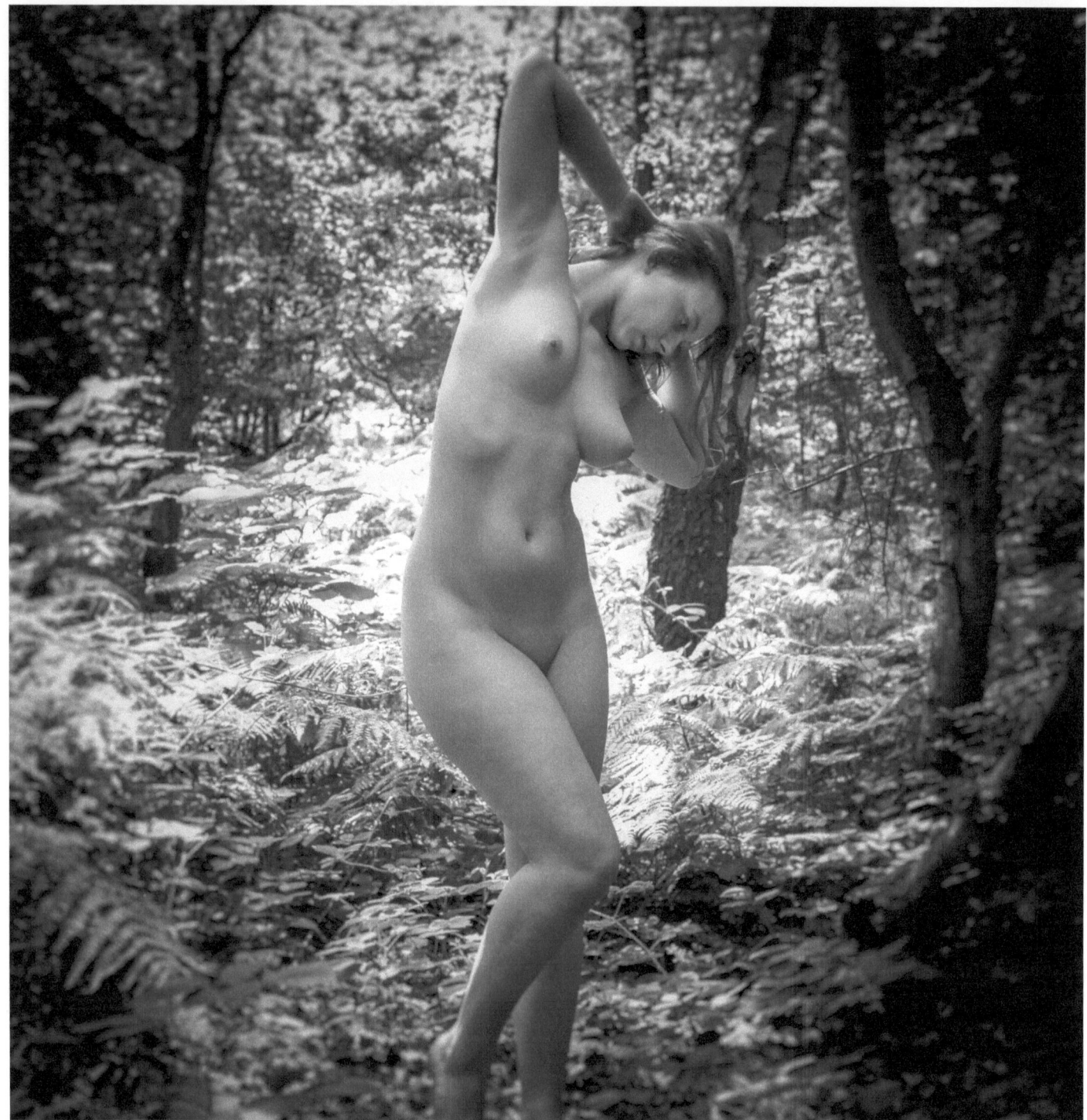

134

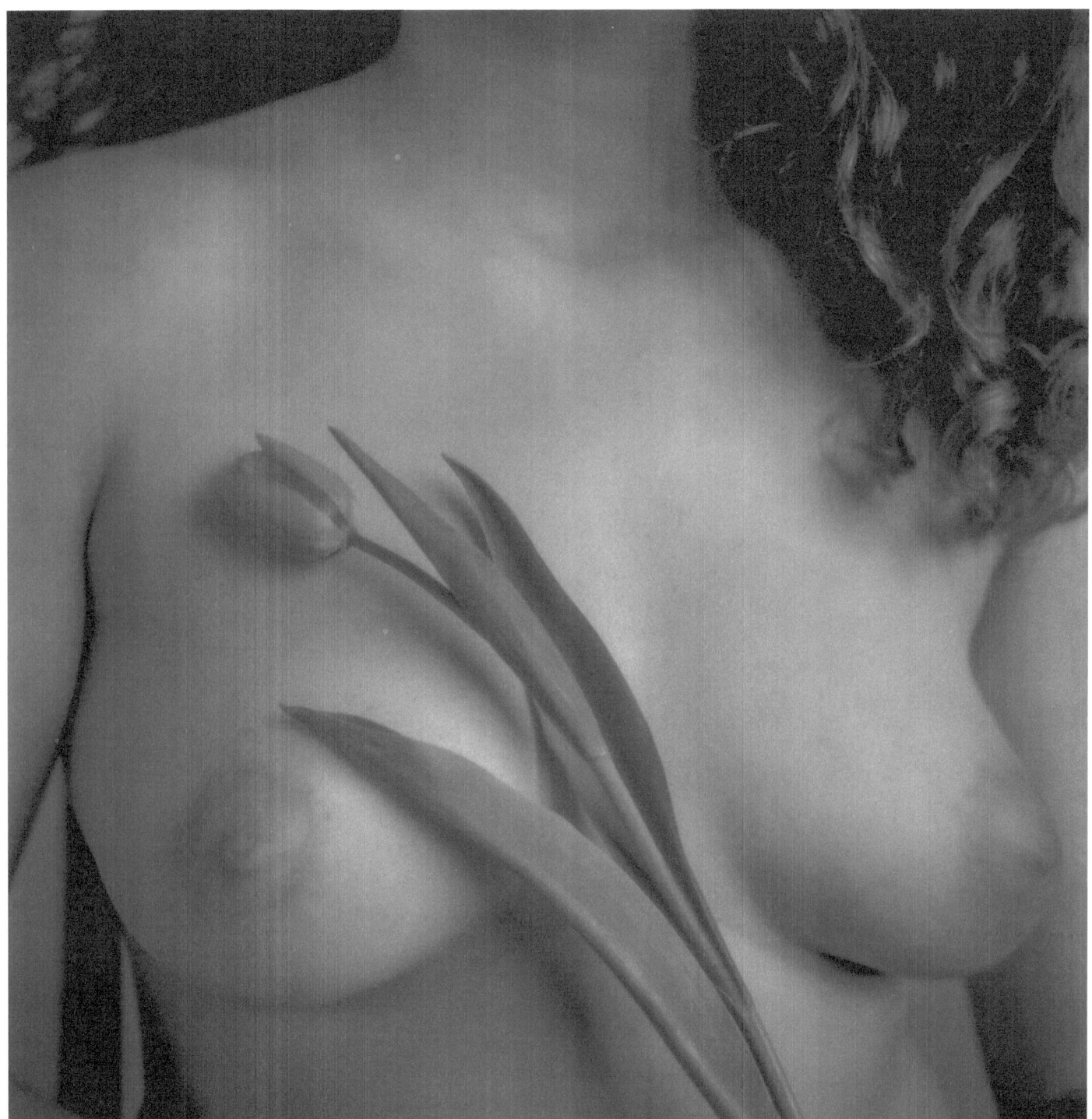

Biography.

Christopher John Ball BA (Hons) MA is a widely exhibited and published, award winning, London based, fine arts photographer, playwright, writer, campaigner, reviewer, publisher, curator, arts juror and lecturer. With over 45 years experience as an artist - his work is held within public and private collections worldwide and he was, together with artist Paul Woods, co-founder of The Association of Erotic Artists - an international academic and campaigning body that was committed to working towards a greater acceptance of the erotic arts whilst defending the genre from the dual threats of censorship and intolerance.

After several years within a commercial photographic background, including running his own studio, Chris became increasingly drawn to the use of photography as a fine arts medium and this, along with exploring the role of the arts within the community and education, has been the direction his work has taken him. In the 1980's Chris was a founder member of 'Action Factory' - a community arts group, based in Lancashire, created with the aim of democratising and expanding the role of the arts within the community - in particular amongst disadvantaged groups.

Given that he has been disabled since youth - Chris maintains an active role in the campaign to promote disability awareness and rights. He is particularly focused upon fighting the pernicious impact of the anti-disabled policies of the UK Conservative government. Said policies have been condemned by the UN, via the Convention on the Rights of Persons with Disabilities, as having created a 'human catastrophe.'

His art work, views and opinions are very much in demand and he has contributed articles on photography, the arts, politics, philosophy and other topics for various international publications and media outlets. His images have been showcased in Italian, German, Spanish, Hong Kong, British and mainland Chinese publications and displayed within the pages of several respected online galleries. He has also been interviewed on Radio and filmed at work for Television programmes that have been transmitted across Europe, the USA and Great Britain.

Christopher was selected as a juror for both the 2008/09 'Erotic Signature' annual international arts competition and the 'Erotic Review Photographer of the Year Prize 2009.' In 2011 Chris sat on the international Jury for the 2011 '12 inches of Sin' competition and juried exhibition sponsored by the Sin City Gallery, Las Vegas and organised by Dr Laura Henkel. The '12 inches of Sin' juried exhibitions/competitions were repeated each year, for 6 years, from 2012 through to 2017, again with Chris sitting on the selection committee.

Chris also works in film and theatre. "Throwing Stones: What's in your family album?" was co-written by Christopher John Ball and Dean Sipling. Performed in 2005, a revised version of 'Throwing Stones' was published in November 2013.

Acknowledgments

Special thanks to Wendy, Tansy, Cressida, Katie, Nikki, Farrah, Dawn, Cheryl, Alex, Arrabella, Eden, Faye, Iveta, Joanne, Manny, Kate, Mandy, Lou Lou and Stepanka!

Social Media

Visit www.christopherjohnball.co.uk for news of future publications, exhibitions, talks and details on how to purchase signed prints.

Regular photography videos can be found at www.youtube.com/cjballphotographer

Other Publications

'Throwing Stones' explores the decline of Adam Lazenby, a successful society and art photographer, when portraits of children he has made are found to have been distributed by an internet paedophile ring. He protests his innocence, claiming the images have been manipulated, but as the police, social workers and tabloid reporters delve into his life, even those closest to him start to have their doubts. His professional life falls apart, friends start to desert him and he risks losing his young daughter. 'Throwing Stones' is a challenging and thought-provoking modern drama that poses the question 'What's in your family album?'

"Mid-life male photographer meets young, nubile female student-cum-artistic muse - so far it's old hat. But photographer turned playwright Christopher John Ball and co-writer Dean Sipling, whose background is film and television, bring the pairing into a thoroughly contemporary world of intercepted emails, sinister insinuation and sharp retorts. Their 'guilty until proved innocent' plot ... is thoroughly watchable and believable - perhaps as a result of Ball's professional insights and DS Dom Lucas' services as police advisor to the production." Barbara Lewis – The Stage

Throwing Stones - 'What's in your family album' a play by Christopher John Ball and Dean Sipling. Published by Britannia Street Theatre and Arts Publishing. ISBN 978-0-9926899-0-2

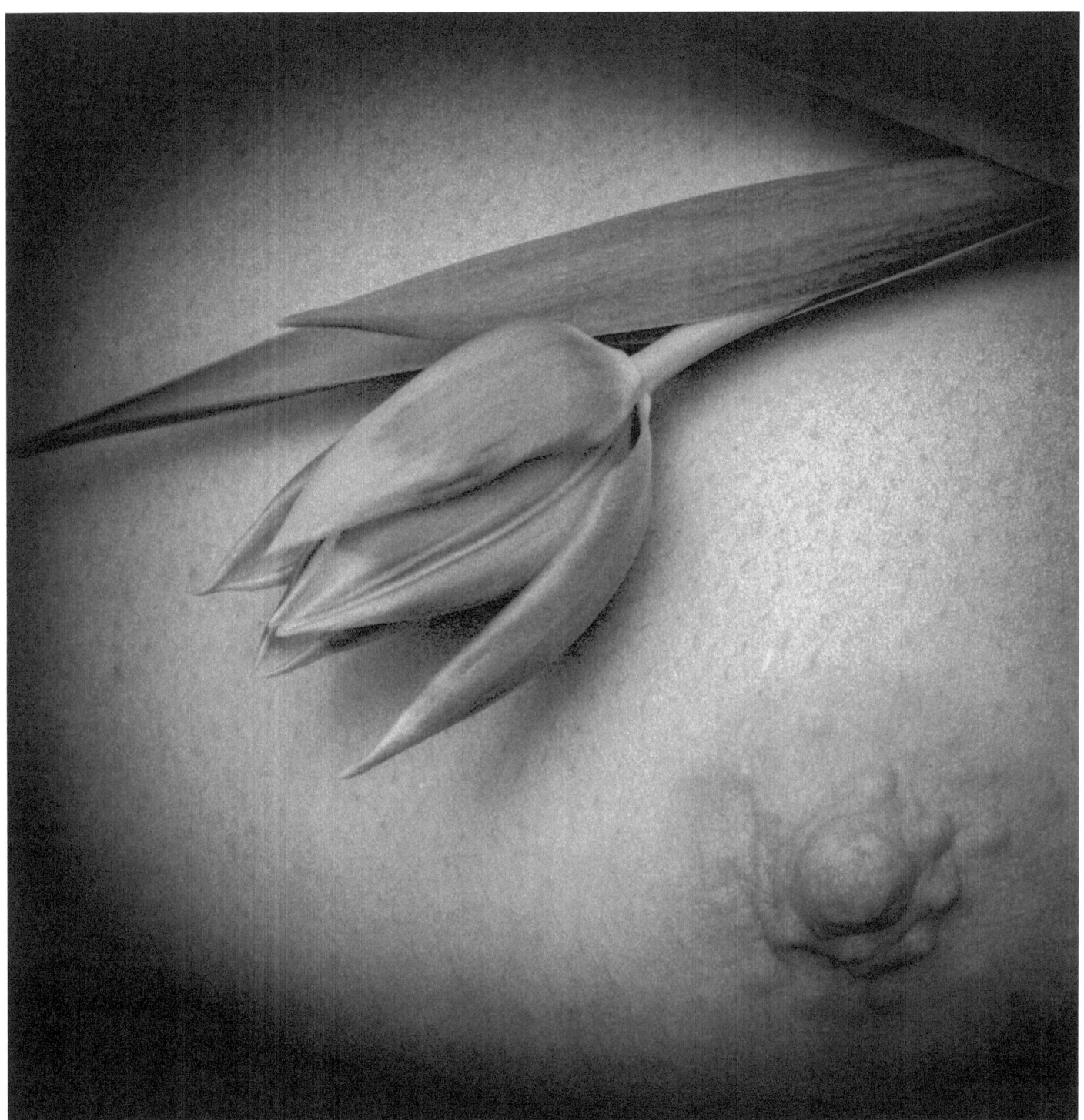